DIRECTORY OF
BRITISH
TRAMWAYS

VOLUME THREE

NORTHERN ENGLAND, SCOTLAND
AND THE ISLE OF MAN

DIRECTORY OF
BRITISH TRAMWAYS

VOLUME THREE

NORTHERN ENGLAND, SCOTLAND
AND THE ISLE OF MAN

KEITH TURNER

The
History
Press

For Margaret, without whose help, encouragement and forbearance this book would never have been completed.

First published 2010

The History Press
The Mill, Brimscombe Port
Stroud, Gloucestershire, GL5 2QG
www.thehistorypress.co.uk

British Library Cataloguing in Publication Data.
A catalogue record for this book is available from the British Library.

ISBN 978 0 7524 4239 6

Typesetting and origination by The History Press
Printed in Great Britain
Manufacturing managed by Jellyfish Print Solutions Ltd

Contents

Preface   6

Preface to the Second Edition   6

Acknowledgements   7

Introduction   8

Part 6   Tramways of Northern England   17

Part 7   Tramways of Scotland   155

Part 8   Tramways of the Isle of Man   197

Chronology   Major Landmarks in British Passenger Tramway History   209

Appendix 1   English Passenger Tramway Locations by Former County   210

Appendix 2   Welsh Passenger Tramway Locations by Former County   213

Appendix 3   Scottish Passenger Tramway Locations by Former County   214

Appendix 4   Irish Passenger Tramway Locations by County   215

Appendix 5   Horse-only Tramways   216

Appendix 6   Steam-only Tramways   216

Appendix 7   Cable Tramways   217

Appendix 8   Pier Tramways   217

Appendix 9   Railway-owned Tramways   218

Appendix 10   Tramway-owned Railways   218

Bibliography   219

Index   221

Preface

As a writer and transport historian I have felt for many years the need for a comprehensive one-volume reference work on the tramways of the British Isles. Not since 1962 in fact, when the fourth edition of Bett & Gilham's *Great British Tramway Networks* appeared, has the tramway enthusiast had easy access to a single, up-to-date basic 'where, what and when' of these lines. So, as much for my own reference purposes as for any other reason, I decided to compile such a work and now that it has been completed I hope it will prove of use to anyone else with an interest in this important aspect of our islands' transport history. Wherever possible I have endeavoured to check and double-check all listed facts and, if any errors have crept in, the responsibility for them is mine alone.

As regards the illustrations, these have been chosen to portray as many aspects of tramway history as possible, not just the tramcars themselves, with many being taken from postcards – whose heyday coincided neatly with that of the tramways – to reflect the integral part played by trams in the popular life of the period.

K. Turner
Kidderminster, 1996

Preface to the Second Edition

Since the first edition of this work appeared in 1996 – and went quickly out of print – much has changed in the world of British tramways. Four new systems have opened, serving the Birmingham to Wolverhampton corridor (Midland Metro, 1998), Croydon (Tramlink, 2000), Nottingham (Nottingham Express Transit, 2004) and Dublin (Luas, 2004). As regards the older generation of lines still operational, refurbishment programmes of the last decade have resulted in significant changes readily visible to passengers, whilst in the field of tramcar preservation the number of vehicles returned to exhibition – or even operational – condition continues to increase steadily.

As a consequence of the above events, it has been felt that in order to accommodate the resulting new entries, and to be able to expand many of the original entries in the light of subsequent events and additional information generated by on-going historical research, this new edition of the Directory should be published in three volumes. This decision also meant that many more illustrations could be included. The division of the Directory into three parts has been made on a topographical basis, the scope of each volume being as follows:

Volume 1: The counties of England south of the traditional Severn Estuary to The Wash's north-south boundary, plus the Channel Islands.
Volume 2: The broad central region of the British Isles, comprising the counties of the East and West Midlands, the whole of Wales and the whole of Ireland.
Volume 3: The northern counties of England, plus the whole of Scotland and the Isle of Man.

Finally, please note that the **Introduction**, **Chronology** and **Appendices** included here are repeated in each of the other two volumes.

K. Turner,
Kidderminster, 2010

Acknowledgements

I should like to thank all those archivists, librarians and their staff throughout the British Isles who have provided valued assistance over the years in helping to compile this Directory. Thanks must also go to those organisations and individuals who have kindly supplied material to help illustrate it; special thanks too to Jan and Lil for coming to the rescue in times of crisis, and to those readers of the first edition who have given freely of their own local knowledge to correct, clarify and add to the historical, technical and other details of many systems. Finally, and most importantly, grateful acknowledgement must be paid to all those writers, recorders and historians who have gone before; without their dedicated efforts my task would have been an impossible one.

The MER's only locomotive: No.23 of 1900, seen here at Laxey in 1993 after an extensive rebuild. It was named *Dr R. Preston Hendry*, in honour of the MER's noted historian, for the centenary celebrations. (*M. Donnison*)

Introduction

This Directory is intended to cover all the tramways that have operated within the British Isles: that is Great Britain, Ireland and all the off-shore islands, including the Isle of Man and the Channel Islands. It should be pointed out here, at the very beginning, that adjectives of locality are used in their geographical, not political or national, sense, so that 'British' hereafter refers to the whole of the British Isles, 'Irish' to the whole of Ireland and 'Welsh' to the Principality of Wales plus Monmouthshire. (Since virtually all British tramways were opened, operated and closed before the 1974 local government reorganisation in Great Britain, the names of the old counties have been used throughout for location purposes – indeed, several of them have since returned.)

The immediate problem facing a compiler of a directory of tramways is one of definition: what exactly is a tramway? In many cases, nomenclature is not a reliable guide – a tramway might well have been titled officially a 'light railway' (e.g. the Kinver Light Railway) while, conversely, a 'tramway' (e.g. the Rye & Camber Tramway) might actually have been a railway.

This confusion over identification arises from a number of historical causes. During the early years of the nineteenth century the terms 'tramway' and 'tramroad' were interchangeable, both denoting a horse-worked railed way (almost always for mineral or other goods traffic only, situated in a rural area and feeding a canal, river or port) crossing or occupying public highways without restriction or much inconvenience to other road users, few as they were. As the use of steam traction spread, however, locomotive-worked lines were separated physically from the roads for safety reasons, thus becoming, in the process, railways as we know them (though the older lines often retained their original names of tramway or tramroad); when tramways proper arrived on the scene in the latter half of the nineteenth century they could not command exclusive rights to the term. The confusion was further complicated by the fact that tramways in Britain were built under several different authorising mechanisms, one of which was the 1896 Light Railways Act.

How, then, have tramways been defined for the purposes of inclusion here? Three principal criteria have been employed for the main entries. Firstly, any line accorded a main entry (i.e. with key details listed at the start) must, at some time at least, have operated a regular public passenger service. Secondly, any such line must have had a significant part of its route along or beside a public highway without it being fenced off from other traffic and, consequently, it will have been subject to certain operating restrictions when using mechanical or electric traction in recognition of this fact. Finally, such tramways should be, or have been, discrete entities and worked as such with their own stock despite any physical connections with other systems or even – in some cases – the national railway network.

Obviously, the 'typical' British tramway found in many towns and cities between, say, 1890 and 1940 meets the above criteria without difficulty: a self-contained system operating a passenger service through the streets. Add an overhead power supply and the stock image of the British tramway is complete. There were, however, a great many lines that did not conform to this picture and yet still meet the same criteria. 'Public highway' for example might, in a wider context, include both open common and seaside pier decking, whilst for some tramways goods traffic was just as important as passengers, if not more so. Nor should it be assumed that being a tramway meant catering for the general public at large: some needed a prior qualification on the part of the passengers, such as their having paid the price of admission to a pier. Two criteria which have purposefully not been used are those of gauge and motive power; these are discussed more fully below.

Regardless of its official title (or indeed popular name), a line or system according with the above definition of a tramway has been given a main entry, whilst any line or system that meets only the last two criteria (i.e. it was a goods-only tramway), whether it be industrial, military, public or private, has been omitted. Any other line or system officially entitled 'tramway', but which was in practice a railway, light railway or tramroad, has been given a minor entry if it operated a passenger service and omitted entirely if it did not. In addition, railways with strong tramway connections or characteristics have been afforded minor entries, as have parent companies owning tramways operated through a number of subsidiaries.

Cross-references to main or minor entries have been made from place-name elements other than the first in a tramway's title (e.g. Upwell *see* Wisbech & Upwell) and to major places served where this might not be evident from the title (e.g. Great Orme Tramway *see* Llandudno: Great Orme Tramway). Cross-references in capital letters refer to entries in the same Volume and those in lower case to other Volumes.

There is one last category of working tramways to be considered, all afforded minor entries here. These, for want of a better name, may be called 'pleasure lines', since one reason for their existence has been to give pleasure rides in much the same way as seaside miniature railways do. Like the miniature railway, the pleasure tramway is a surprisingly ancient animal, the oldest traced being that opened in Shipley Glen in Yorkshire more than a hundred years ago. Although this venerable example was possibly unique for its time, the number of pleasure lines has grown in recent years: firstly, with the construction of several permanent working museum lines, secondly, with the opening of a number of semi-permanent miniature tramways and, thirdly, with their temporary use at recent Garden Festivals.

Tramcar preservation is as old as tramway modernisation, for when horse traction was displaced by (usually) electricity, several operators were heritage-minded enough to set aside the odd vehicle for museum display. The precedent for doing this had been set by the railway companies, but not until 1951, however, was there a standard for the preservation of a whole line – the narrow-gauge Talyllyn Railway in Wales – but even with this example to encourage enthusiasts, the prospect of running even part of an existing or restored tramway proved elusive at the very time the last great wave of system closures was taking place.

The main obstacle in the preservationists' path was the fact that, by and large, local authorities wanted rid of tramways completely, citing such reasons as that they impeded traffic flow (often true) or they were holding up road improvement schemes (where compromises could have been made). Whatever the pros and cons of the tramways *v.* the private motorcar or even tramways *v.* buses arguments, the fact remains that no local authority was willing to countenance a bunch of amateurs operating trams through its streets – and it was even less likely that national authorities, such as the Board of Trade, would have done so. Thus, by their very nature, most tramways were ruled out immediately as candidates for preservation; all that were left as possible projects were those lines – or portions of those lines – that occupied their own reserved rights of way (i.e. separated from any highway). Two such schemes, both consistently canvassed over many years now, have centred on the former Swansea & Mumbles and Llandudno & Colwyn Bay lines in Wales, but with no success for either as of yet.

Inevitably, the number of potential locations (never great to begin with) has decreased as formerly reserved stretches of tramway routes have been swallowed up by road widenings, whilst open-field sections have been built upon. Only one genuine length of tramway route has been restored to operational use – in Manchester's Heaton Park – and only then because of unique circumstances.

Until 1963 tramway preservation, then, meant tramcar or relic preservation (anything from shelters and standards down to tickets and uniform buttons); in that year though a new, purpose-built museum line was opened at Crich in Derbyshire in order that preserved cars could be operated in passenger service once more. Since then similar museum lines have opened elsewhere, whilst the overall total of preserved cars, working or static (and including imported foreign examples), is now well over the 300 mark. Details of where such cars can be seen have been included in the appropriate entries.

As with their railway counterparts, the difference between a miniature and a narrow-gauge tramway is not primarily one of size – or even gauge – but rather one of proportions. Thus, a very narrow-gauge (2ft) line, such as Fairbourne in Wales, could use cars still in proportion to its riders, whereas a miniature line, such as at Eastbourne, also of 2ft gauge, might employ scaled-down stock in the model engineering tradition that was not in harmony with its full-sized passengers.

Whilst miniature railways are thick on the ground in many parts of the British Isles, miniature tramways are not. There is a simple explanation for this: on a miniature railway usually only the locomotive is a scale model, with the passengers riding in, or on, non-scale carriages. With a tramway, a model tramcar has somehow to accommodate passengers as well. A secondary, but still important, reason

Above left: This comic postcard image, by the cartoonist 'Cynicus' (real name Martin Anderson), was sold up and down the country, usually overprinted with the name of a town or city (see p.195); this is a rarer variant for sale anywhere. *(Author's Collection)*

Above right: The one-time ubiquity of the tramway in Britain is reflected by its appearance on many other types of comic postcards – as on this 'perils of drink' example, posted in 1908. The sender has written: 'I expect that this is about your style now. Hope you are enjoying yourselves.' *(Author's Collection)*

is an economic one: a miniature train driven by one man might easily carry thirty or more fare-paying passengers, whereas a one-man tram is limited to half a dozen or so. For these two reasons miniature tramways have generally been short, portable exhibition lines operated by private individuals or model engineering societies and the like; because of their ephemeral nature, these are not included in this work, though the handful of more permanent ones have been.

The Garden Festivals held on various sites during the 1980s and early 1990s were the latest in a long line of shows, exhibitions and expositions dating back to the great-grandaddy of them all, the 1851 Great Exhibition held at the Crystal Palace in London. What set them apart from their predecessors, however, was that, in addition to providing an entertaining day out and a showcase for manufacturers and other exhibitors, their sites were areas of industrial dereliction, chosen deliberately so that the preparatory landscaping and other improvements would result in long-term benefits to their locality.

In all, five Garden Festivals were held: Liverpool (1984), Stoke-on-Trent (1986), Glasgow (1988), Gateshead (1990) and Ebbw Vale (1992). All provided forms of rail transport to move visitors around the site – miniature railways proving especially popular – but of relevance here is that both Glasgow and Gateshead laid full-size working tramways (albeit only temporary ones) for both pleasure and utility.

Although the Garden Festival movement has ended (in the sense that no further ones are planned), the principle of using semi-permanent tramways as crowd-movers (and pullers) has been demonstrated successfully, and there can be little doubt that the idea will be repeated someday, somewhere, in a different guise. Indeed, with the number of rescued, renovated, imported and operational tramcars growing yearly, and with a concomitant steady increase in the number of working museum and pleasure lines, either operational or planned – quite apart from the new generation of hi-tech metros – the outlook for the tramway enthusiast/lover/historian/supporter is brighter today than it has been for half a century or more.

In the interest of clarity, information common to main entries has been summarised at the beginning of each under the following headings:

Authority

The legal authority for the construction and operation of the tramway. On a general level, promoting a tramway was very much like promoting a railway: unless the line was to be built on land wholly owned by a consenting individual or body, some form of national or local governmental permission had to be obtained for its construction. The exact form of this authority varied according to the legislative framework in place at the time; to a lesser extent, it also varied according to where in the British Isles the line was to be built, and for this reason further details of the different authorities are given in the introduction to each Part within the different Volumes.

Gauge

For tramways laid with railway-type track (i.e. chaired bullhead or spiked flat-bottomed rails on sleepers), the gauge given is the distance between the inner edges of the rails as if it were a railway. For tramways laid with tramway-type (i.e. grooved) rails set flush with the road surface on street sections, the gauge given is the distance between the outer edges of the two grooves (i.e. between the inner edges of the running surfaces).

The range of gauges used by British tramways is a large one, as the (simplified) breakdown below shows:

12¼in. to 15in. – used for miniature tramways.
1ft 8in. to 2ft 6in. – generally regarded as the lower limit for narrow-gauge horse and steam tramways.
2ft 9in. – the lower limit for narrow-gauge electric tramways.
2ft 11½in. – a gauge which enabled 3ft gauge railway vehicles to run on their (deeper) flanges in the grooves of tramway rails, allowing through-running to take place.
3ft – Isle of Man 'standard gauge', the most common gauge for steam-worked light railways and tramways in Ireland.
3ft 6in. – the most common narrow gauge for electric tramways in Great Britain.
4ft – a common horse tramway gauge, less common for electric lines.
4ft 7¾in. – a gauge enabling standard-gauge railway vehicles to run in the grooves of tramway rails. Widespread in the Portsmouth area and on the Scottish systems alongside the River Clyde.
4ft 8½in. (or its nominal metric equivalent **1,435m**) – standard railway gauge in Great Britain, though if used with grooved rails through-working of railway vehicles could not take place (see above).
5ft 3in. – standard railway gauge in Ireland (and subject to the same restrictions as above).

Other gauges have been employed, usually as one-off examples, in line with this pattern of usage.

Traction

The type(s) of tractive power used on a regular basis to work the system. On British tramways the following have been employed (ignoring unsuccessful experiments with other movers):

Manual – hand-propelled stock, common on pier tramways.
Horse – narrower gauge lines tended to use a single horse pulling a single-deck car; wider gauge lines did likewise, even for light double-deckers on level routes. Where steep gradients and/or heavy double-deck vehicles were involved, two horses were normally used with a third (trace) horse being attached at the foot of the stiffest climbs.
Cable – passenger cars attached permanently to a cable in funicular railway fashion, or which could engage/disengage a continuously moving cable, in both cases the cable being housed in a conduit beneath the road surface. A variant was to have the passenger cars not attached to the cable but simply towed as trailers behind tractor vehicles.

Steam – either trailers hauled by special tramway locomotives or passenger vehicles fitted with their own steam power units.

Internal combustion – as above, but with diesel, petrol or similar fuel engines.

Battery electric – as above, but with electric motors powered by accumulators.

Gas – passenger stock fitted with gas-fuelled power units.

Petrol-electric – passenger stock fitted with a petrol engine driving a dynamo to power an electric motor.

Overhead electric – passenger stock fitted with electric motors supplied with current from an overhead wire (normally at 500V dc).

Surface-contact electric – as above, but with current supplied from roadway studs.

Conduit electric – as above, but with current supplied from a roadway conduit.

Where different methods of traction were in use at the same time they are listed in the main entry thus (for example): Horse, steam. Where one method of traction superseded another with no overlapping period of use, they are listed thus (for example): Horse/steam.

Details of other methods of traction used rarely, briefly or experimentally – including sails and clockwork! – are given in the main body of the entries themselves.

Opened/Took over

The date of the first public service. This was often, but not always, the same as that of the official opening ceremony (which occasionally preceded or followed it). Also, especially in the case of the larger systems, only part of the tramway might have been opened at this time. In the case of a significant takeover by another operator, the date given is when services commenced under the new ownership, the actual transfer normally being timed from the midnight of the final day under the previous ownership.

Closed/Taken over

In the case of a closure, the date of the tramway's final public service over the last section of the tramway to remain open is given (though stock movements often took place after the date of closure). In the case of large systems, usually only a fraction of the whole remained in use by this time. (It should be borne in mind that final journeys were often run late at night, finishing in the early hours of the day following that cited.)

In the case of a significant takeover, the date given is the day the new operator began working the system.

System

The physical layout of the tramway system's route(s), codified thus in a roughly ascending order of complexity (ignoring short spurs to depots, one-way loops in town centres and the like):

Single line – one route from A to B, usually town centre to an outlying district and/or railway station; occasionally from one town to another (an 'interurban').

Split single line – two routes from A to B.

Circle – a single line starting and finishing at the same point.

Branching – a single main line with one or more other lines branching from it.

Cross – two single lines crossing, but worked as separate routes.

Radial – a number of routes radiating from a central point (usually a natural focus such as a market square, town hall or railway station).

Radial network – a radial system with one or more linking lines between routes.

Network – a network of crossing and branching routes with no single focus, as found in many large towns and cities.

Combinations of the above are also to be found, e.g. branching circle. All systems should be taken to be predominantly urban in nature (though often extending beyond the original built-up area to serve isolated villages or districts) unless they are described in the notes as rural or interurban.

Length

As far as it can be ascertained, the route mileage of the tramway at its greatest extent, correct to the nearest one-hundredth of a mile (17.6 yards), based on official returns made by the operator. This may not be the total route mileage worked as, occasionally, a new line might be opened after an earlier section had been abandoned. Modern metro systems, constructed to metric specifications, have their lengths given to the nearest 100m, as recorded in official documentation.

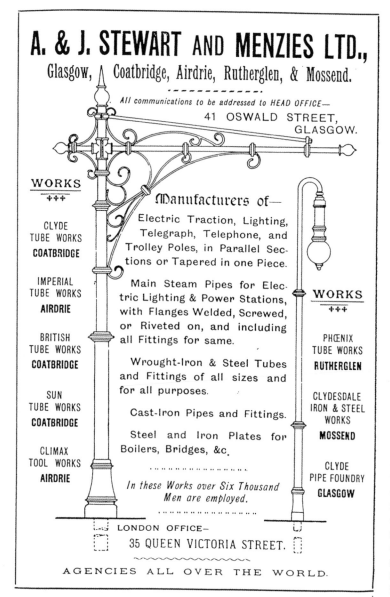

Overhead electric tramways employed two principal means of suspending the overhead wires above the tracks – either by hanging them from span wires attached to lineside buildings or, as shown here, by hanging them from pavement standards, such as this Scottish example depicted in a 1903 trade directory.

Stock

The total number of vehicles employed on passenger services by the tramway during its lifetime (though not necessarily all in use concurrently) and, where applicable, the number of locomotives used to haul them. Passenger cars are classified as single-deck vehicles (sd) or double-deck vehicles (dd), with numbers given for each traction system listed as being used. Unless noted otherwise, all vehicles can be taken to have four wheels and double-deck horse cars to have open tops (i.e. no roof to the upper deck). Also, all cars can be taken as being double-ended (i.e. with a driving position at each end); those horse cars described as 'reversible' had only one driving position, but with a body that could be rotated on its underframe at the end of the line so as then to face in the opposite direction. Cars are counted in their original state (e.g. before conversion from single to double-deck form).

Livery

Almost without exception, tramcars were painted in what would now be termed a 'two-tone' livery, usually a darker colour, such as green, red or blue, and a lighter colour, such as white, cream or yellow. There were several aesthetic reasons for the use of this scheme, tried and tested as it had been over the years, not only on tramcars but also on horse buses, railway carriages and stage-coaches: a dark colour around the 'waistline' gave the vehicle a visual sense of reassuring stability, whilst a lighter colour around the windows and above them emphasised the visibility afforded to its passengers and the lightness of the car – hence its swiftness – and its spaciousness. Lighter colour panels below the dark band were used to draw attention to the tramway's name, emblazoned on the side. Dark dashes at each end of the car protecting the driver were a legacy of horse-tram days when the colour served to hide the mud and splashing they inevitably suffered; the running gear would normally be red oxide or black for the same reason, whilst the roof would continue the lightening effect by being a very pale neutral colour, such as off-white or grey. Steam tram locomotives tended to be painted with a single dark shade to give an impression of solid dependability.

The two-tone livery also made the cars highly visible to potential passengers, as did the use of (usually) gold or cream for their often ornate lining, fleet numbers and name of the tramway or operator.

The difficulty in describing long-vanished liveries is that official records have not always survived, forcing the historian to rely on (sometimes contradictory) eye-witness memories. The problem is compounded by the fact that when a new colour was applied, it quickly weathered and, if judged unsuitable, was often replaced by a darker shade when the vehicle was repainted (or naturally darkened by the repeated application of varnish). For example, white was frequently used on new horse cars, but was quickly replaced by off-white (ivory) in the light of experience. Similarly, pale cream was normally darkened into primrose (or even a deeper yellow). For this reason the descriptions given are sometimes a compromise; e.g. red-brown or cream/yellow. Ignoring minor variations, the descriptions themselves are of the general livery used during a specific period; in the case of a change from one general scheme to another, this might well have taken months if not years to complete, depending on the number of cars involved.

Second-hand vehicles often ran for a while in their old liveries until a new paint job could be arranged. During the First World War, for reasons of wartime economy, cars needing a repaint would be given a uniformly grey livery, often retained for several years after the war ended.

Last Car/Train

The closure of a tramway was often a very emotional occasion, with the last public journey marked by speeches, wreaths and crowds trying to board the 'Last Car'. On many such occasions the identity of this tram was recorded for posterity; on others, the line was closed without fuss or ceremony and the identity of the vehicle that made the final trip is not generally known today (although the information may well be residing in private films or papers just waiting to be discovered). Sometimes an 'official' Last Car carrying local dignitaries was run behind the last service vehicle, or even on a later date.

Bibliography

In addition to the above list of details and the main body of the entry, wherever possible at least one comprehensive history of the line or system in question, which has appeared in book form, is cited in the **Bibliography** at the end of the book – though their accuracy in all matters is not guaranteed. (For minor lines, this history might well be part of a wider account.) Citations are given in the order: Title (Series and number), Author (Publisher, edition if not the first, date of publication), ISBN.

In order to save space and avoid tiresome repetitions, several frequently occurring names have been abbreviated in entries (e.g. those of companies and other organisations). Company titles are given in concise form, e.g. '& Co. Ltd' for 'and Company Limited'. Other abbreviations used, if not standard forms or cited in full earlier in the same entry, are:

Ashbury – Ashbury Railway Carriage & Iron Co. Ltd, Manchester (later Metropolitan)
Bagnall – W.G. Bagnall & Co. Ltd, Stafford
BB – Balfour, Beattie & Co. Ltd*
BEC – British Electric Car Co. Ltd, Trafford Park
BET – British Electric Traction Co. Ltd*
BH – Black, Hawthorn & Co. Ltd, Gateshead
Birmingham – Birmingham Railway Carriage & Wagon Co. Ltd, Smethwick
BM – Brown, Marshalls & Co. Ltd, Birmingham (later Metropolitan)
BNCR – Belfast & Northern Counties Railway
BoT – Board of Trade
BP – Beyer, Peacock & Co. Ltd, Manchester
BPs – Bruce Peebles & Co. Ltd, Edinburgh
BR – British Railways (in all its post-1948 guises)
Brill – J.G. Brill Co., Philadelphia
BTH – British Thomson-Houston Co. Ltd, Rugby*
Brush – Brush Electrical Engineering Co. Ltd, Loughborough
Burrell – Charles Burrell & Sons Ltd, Thetford
CIE – Coras Iompair Eireann
CLC – Cheshire Lines Committee
Cravens – Cravens Railway Carriage & Wagon Co. Ltd, Sheffield
DK – Dick, Kerr & Co. Ltd, Preston
EE – English Electric Co. Ltd, Preston (formerly UEC)
ERTCW – Electric Railway & Tramway Carriage Works Ltd, Preston (a DK subsidiary)
Falcon – Falcon Engine & Car Works, Loughborough (a Brush subsidiary)
Fowler – John Fowler & Co. Ltd, Leeds
GCR – Great Central Railway
GER – Great Eastern Railway
Gloucester – Gloucester Railway Carriage & Wagon Co. Ltd
GNR – Great Northern Railway
GNR (I) – Great Northern Railway (Ireland)
GNSR – Great North of Scotland Railway
Green – Thomas Green & Sons Ltd, Leeds
GSR – Great Southern Railways
GSWR – Glasgow & South Western Railway
GWR – Great Western Railway
Hardy – Hardy Rail Motors Ltd, Slough
Hawthorn – Robert W. Hawthorn & Co. Ltd, Gateshead
HC – Hudswell, Clarke & Co. Ltd, Leeds
Hibberd – F.C. Hibberd & Co. Ltd, London

HN – Hurst, Nelson & Co. Ltd, Motherwell

Hughes – Henry Hughes & Co. Ltd, Loughborough (later Falcon)

Kitson – Kitson & Co. Ltd, Leeds

Krauss – Locomotivfabrik Krauss & Cie, Munich

Lancaster – Lancaster Railway Carriage & Wagon Co. Ltd (later Metropolitan)

LBSCR – London, Brighton & South Coast Railway

LCDR – London, Chatham & Dover Railway

LMS – London, Midland & Scottish Railway

LNER – London & North Eastern Railway

LNWR – London & North Western Railway

LSWR – London & South Western Railway

LYR – Lancashire & Yorkshire Railway

Matthew – James Matthew, Bristol

Merryweather – Merryweather & Sons, London

Metro-Cammell – Metropolitan-Cammell Carriage & Wagon Co. Ltd, Birmingham

Metropolitan – Metropolitan Railway Carriage & Wagon Co. Ltd, Birmingham (later Metro-Cammell)

MGWR – Midland Great Western Railway

Midland – Midland Railway Carriage & Wagon Co. Ltd, Shrewsbury

Milnes – Geo F. Milnes & Co. Ltd, Birkenhead

MR – Midland Railway

MV – G.C. Milnes, Voss & Co. Ltd, Birkenhead

MW – Manning, Wardle & Co. Ltd, Leeds

NBR – North British Railway

NCC – Northern Counties Committee

NEC – National Electric Construction Co. Ltd*

NER – North Eastern Railway

Oldbury – Oldbury Railway Carriage & Wagon Co. Ltd (later Metropolitan)

Peckham – Peckham Truck & Engineering Co. Ltd

Pickering – R.Y. Pickering & Co. Ltd, Wishaw

Roberts – Charles Roberts & Co. Ltd, Wakefield

SECR – South Eastern & Chatham Railway

SER – South Eastern Railway

Starbuck – Starbuck Car & Wagon Co. Ltd, Birkenhead (later Milnes)

Stephenson – John Stephenson Co., New York

UEC – United Electric Car Co. Ltd, Preston (formerly ERTCW)

Wickham – D. Wickham & Co. Ltd, Ware

Wilkinson – William Wilkinson & Co. Ltd, Wigan

* see minor entry in all volumes

Other symbols used are:

[ ] – enclosing unofficial short title

? – preceding information uncertain or lacking

-- – not applicable

c. – about

* – see text/footnote below

Part 6

Tramways of Northern England

Ignoring, for the moment, anachronistic passenger-carrying tramroads, the history of the tramway in the British Isles is very much the history of the tramway in England. Certainly, it was here that the first street tramway was laid (Birkenhead) and the first regular use of steam (Wantage), cable (London) and safe electric traction (Blackpool) was made.

English tramway history is, in turn, a condensed parallel version of the development and growth of Britain's railways. The urban tramway arrived from the USA (where it was aptly known as a 'street railway') in the early 1860s and, just a quarter of a century later, had employed the same four main motive power systems that had been used on railways over a period four times as long: horse, steam, cable and electricity. Of these four, the first held sway during the 1860s and 1870s. It was familiar and acceptable to the travelling public, and a tramcar's journey was smoother than that of a horse bus. It was, however, not much quicker, hence the introduction (permitted by the 1879 Act for the Use of Mechanical Power on Tramways) of steam traction using specially designed tank locomotives with side-skirts to enclose the motion, safety guards to prevent anyone being run over and a driving cab at each end to allow the driver a clear view of the road ahead. In addition, the BoT required them to burn coke rather than coal to reduce smoke pollution, and to be equipped with condensing apparatus for their waste steam. Because of their power advantage over horses, these steam locomotives could pull much larger trailers – sometimes several – up steeper gradients, which meant that many existing horse systems went over to the new form of traction, notably in the major industrial towns and regions, and new, hilly routes opened. Self-contained tramcars fitted with seats and a steam power unit were also experimented with, generally unsuccessfully.

The adoption of steam traction gave birth to the fixed tram stop, because their greater momentum meant that, unlike horse cars, steam trams could not halt for prospective passengers wherever hailed in the street – a legacy later passed on to electric tramway and motor bus operators. However, steam trams were not very popular with the general public, being regarded as dirty and noisy and, when reliable electric traction was developed in the 1880s, the use of steam was quickly abandoned, with virtually all those lines employing it converted to electric by the early years of the twentieth century. (See **Appendix 6** for those special cases using no other form of traction.)

During the steam tram era cable traction was also employed – though on far fewer lines – to cope with gradients that locomotives could not manage. Its use met with mixed fortunes: those climbs that could be tackled by electric trams were soon converted to enable routes to become part of an integrated system (as in Birmingham and London), whilst those too steep for conversion (in England, only Matlock) kept faithful to it until closure. (See **Appendix 7** for a list of all British cable tramways.)

Undoubtedly, the most successful of the traction systems was electricity. First used (on any scale) in the British Isles in 1883 on Volk's Electric Railway in Brighton and the Giant's Causeway Tramway in Ireland, it was adopted two years later at Blackpool and from then on almost all new tramways employed it; existing ones that did not were almost all either closed or converted by the outbreak of the First World War. (See **Appendix 5** for a list of those horse lines never converted.)

Before 1870 tramway construction was normally authorised either by local authority permission or by a Private Act of Parliament. The former applied when the streets involved were under local authority control and the latter when compulsory purchase of land was required; in return for this power, an Act imposed certain conditions on the company formed to build and operate the tramway, notably the amount of capital that could be raised, time limits for the start and finish of construction, the gauge and type of traction to be used and so on. Obtaining a Private Act was an expensive business – and it was not guaranteed to succeed in the face of opposition from powerful landowners, railway companies, local authorities and the like – and in 1870 the Tramways Act was passed to make life easier for would-be promoters. Under its provisions an application could be made to the BoT for a Provisional Order which, if sanctioned after a local enquiry, was then confirmed along with any others outstanding in a Tramways Confirmation Act.

One important provision of the 1870 Act was to have profound consequences, affecting virtually all those lines built under such Orders: after twenty-one years (and at regular intervals thereafter) from the confirmation of an Order, any local authority with a tramway within its boundaries could normally purchase the whole undertaking at just its physical asset value. (Where a tramway crossed municipal boundaries, two or more authorities could act jointly in the matter.) Many authorities chose to do this – especially if the end of the twenty-one-year period coincided with the possibility of introducing electric traction – often to the intense annoyance of the operating companies, resulting in much legal squabbling and eventual independent arbitration to determine the price. (Originally local authorities were not allowed to operate tramways, although they could build and then lease them to private companies. This prohibition was later dropped.)

Another option was made available from 1896 onwards with the passing of the Light Railways Act in that year. Although intended to facilitate the construction of light railways – often as adjuncts to the national network – in much the same way as the Tramways Act had done for tramways, several private and municipal tramway promoters made use of its provisions, obtaining Light Railway Orders to authorise their undertakings. (One advantage of doing so for private companies was that no later municipal buy-out was threatened.)

The first great wave of tramway closures came in the 1920s and 1930s when many tracks and vehicles reached the end of their useful life – often hastened by lack of proper maintenance during the First World War – at a time when motor buses were claiming a rapidly increasing share of the public transport market. The situation was not helped by the fact that the bus operators, both private and municipal, were often the tramway operators themselves. Some respite was afforded by the transport demands of the Second World War, but after that the closures came thick and fast with Sheffield, in 1960, the last to go – the last, that is, except for Blackpool, which was England's sole tramway operator until 1970, when the Seaton line opened. The Devon line was a special case, however, and it was not until the opening of the Manchester Metrolink twenty-two years later that the resurgence of the tramway in the streets of England began. With a steady trickle of others following, the next decade or so will see the tramway's continuing fightback, with expanding hi-tech light rail systems designed to free our city streets from the slow and dirty motor cars threatening to choke them to death in exactly the same way as horse-drawn traffic once did.

Accrington Corporation Steam Tramways

Authority: Accrington Corporation Tramways Act 1882
Gauge: 4ft
Traction: Steam
Opened: 5 April 1886
Taken over: 20 September 1907
System: Radial
Length: 9.45 miles
Stock: 23 locos, 2 sd? 17+ dd
Livery: ?

The first tramway in the Lancashire town of Accrington was operated by the Accrington Corporation Steam Tramways Co., which leased the track for twenty-one years from Accrington Corporation from the date of the opening. Construction work began in 1884 with three mainly single-track routes being laid from the Market Place. The shortest one ran due east along the Blackburn Road, past the Town Hall, and then to the depot in Ellison Street, for 1 mile before terminating at the Commercial Hotel in Church, where a connection was later made with the BLACKBURN CORPORATION TRAMWAYS (though through-running never took place).

The second route ran north-west along Whalley Road for 1¾ miles to the Load of Mischief pub in the village of Clayton-le-Moors, whilst the third ran south-east for 2¼ miles down Abbey Street and the Manchester Road to terminate near the railway station in Baxenden.

Public services began over the Church–Market Place–Clayton portion of the system immediately after the BoT inspection on 5 April 1886 (with an official opening ceremony three days later). The Baxenden route followed on 12 June that year and was extended twice in 1887, firstly to the Commercial Hotel, Haslingden, on 27 August and on to Lockgate (the Haslingden/Rawtenstall boundary) in November, the track of the extension (2.9 miles) being owned by HASLINGDEN CORPORATION and leased to the company. Two years later, a connection was made here with the ROSSENDALE STEAM TRAMWAYS, but again through-running did not result.

The initial rolling-stock fleet comprised Green tram locomotives Nos 1–14 of 1886–87 hauling roofed double-deck bogie trailers 1–10 from Falcon. These were joined by similar Ashbury cars 11–14 in 1887 and Lancaster ones 15–17 in 1891, whilst the locomotive stud was increased by Green engines 15 and 16 in 1891, 17 in 1894, and 18 and 6 in 1898 – this last one replacing an older locomotive. Finally, in 1901, four more Green engines (Nos 19–22) were bought from Blackburn, whose system was then being electrified, plus an unknown number of trailers from there and the BURNLEY & DISTRICT TRAMWAYS.

In 1905, the Corporation obtained authority to take over and electrify the tramways on expiry of the lease, and preparatory work for the conversion began; the purchase price of £2,227 for eleven locos and eleven cars was paid on 20 September 1907, the Corporation thus becoming the system's operator (see below). Eight locos and seven cars were bought by Haslingden Corporation in order to work that authority's portion of the Lockgate route.

Accrington Corporation Tramways

Authority: Accrington Corporation Act 1905
Gauge: 4ft
Traction: Overhead electric, steam
Opened: 2 August 1907
Closed: 6 January 1932
System: Radial
Length: 7.02 miles
Stock: 13 sd, 25 dd electric; 11 locos, 11 dd steam
Livery: Bright red & cream
Last Car: No.6

Even before it had finalised its takeover of the town's steam tramways (see above), Accrington Corporation had opened its first double-tracked electric route along the former steam line from the Town Hall to Church, where it turned south, as a single track, down Union Road for another 1¼ miles to Oswaldtwistle. That same month through-running between Accrington and the BLACKBURN CORPORATION TRAMWAYS began. On 20 September the reconstructed Clayton route opened, the mainly single-track line now extended 200yd to the canal bridge there; this was followed on 26 October by a single-track north-eastern branch off Whalley Road, just north of the Market Place, along the Burnley Road to the Cemetery at Huncoat, with the line to Baxenden station (a mixture of double and single tracks) opening on 1 January 1908. It is not known precisely when the last steam tram ran.

The first electric cars were single-deckers 1–4 and top-covered double-deckers 5–18, joined in 1908 by two more single-deckers, Nos 5 and 6 (double-deckers 5 and 6 being renumbered 19 and 20). All were from Brush – as were all subsequent purchases – and housed in the rebuilt steam depot.

Through-running to the Commercial Hotel in HASLINGDEN (its portion of the former steam route having being taken over by that corporation from 1 January 1908) began on 28 September 1908, and on to Lockgate on 20 October to complete the system. On 1 April 1910 through-running began via RAWTENSTALL to Bacup. (Haslingden Corporation retained ownership of its portion of track throughout the tramway's life, though it never operated electric services of its own.)

In 1909 top-covered cars 21 and 22 and single-decker 23 were added to the fleet; these were followed in 1910 by top-covered 24 and 25; in 1912 by top-covered 26 and single-decker 27; and in 1915 by single-deckers 28–30 and enclosed double-deckers 38 and 39, these last five cars being bogie vehicles. Six cars were bought after the First World War: bogie single-deckers 31 and 32 and enclosed bogie double-deckers 40 and 41 in 1920, and enclosed low bridge double-deckers 42 and 43 six years later.

In Loving Memory

'Weep not for me, my life is past
Dearly you loved me to the last;
Grieve not dear friends but continue kind
On the Electric Cars I leave behind'

STEAM TRAMCAR, (Bank Fleet.) ACCRINGTON.

A number of tramways were the subject of *In memoriam* postcards – comic or sentimental – issued to mark the closing of a tramway or the passing of an era. This example commemorates the end of Accrington Corporation's steam trams in 1907 or 1908. Their 'Baltic Fleet' nickname derived from their supposed resemblance to ships of the Russian Baltic Fleet, evident in the North Sea in the 1900s. *(Author's Collection)*

By the late 1920s the future of the tramway was looking bleak, for in 1928 the Corporation began bus operations and on 30 April 1930 the line to Rawtenstall was jointly closed, followed on 26 August by the Clayton and Oswaldtwistle routes. This left just the Burnley Road line to survive into the next year.

Several of the cars were disposed of to other systems before and after the closure. Nos 42 and 43 were sold in 1931 to SUNDERLAND CORPORATION, Nos 28–32 in 1932 to the Llandudno & Colwyn Bay Electric Railway, No.39 in 1933 to LYTHAM-ST-ANNES and Nos 38, 40 and 41 in 1934 to Southend-on-Sea Corporation.

Ashton-Under-Lyne Corporation Tramways

Authority: Ashton-under-Lyne Corporation Tramways Order 1900; Hurst Urban District Council Tramway Order 1900
Gauge: 4ft 8½in.
Traction: Overhead electric
Opened: 16 August 1902
Closed: 1 March 1938
System: Radial network
Length: 6.92 miles
Stock: 14 sd, 25 dd
Livery: Dark blue & cream (plus maroon pre-1905)
Last Car: No.32*

Prior to the opening of the Corporation's own system, trams had been operating in Ashton since 1881 (MANCHESTER TRAMWAYS horse) and 1899 (OLDHAM, ASHTON & HYDE electric). Then, in 1900, the adjoining local authorities of Ashton and Hyde obtained Orders authorising their own lines, with construction beginning the following year.

The first lines opened formed a circular, single-track route running north-east from the Market Place in Ashton (where there was a connection with the OAH's track) to Hurst Cross, out via Union Road and King Street and back via either Whitacre Road or – further to the south – Queen Street and Mossley Road, past the depot. Services began with two open-top double-deckers from ERTCW (probably Nos 1 and 2) followed a week later by another pair (probably 3 and 4); these were joined over the next nine months by open-toppers 11 and 12 and single-deck combination cars 5–10, again from ERTCW. Route length was some 3½ miles, of which Hurst UDC owned 1.35 miles.

The Manchester Carriage & Tramways Co.'s last horse tram to Ashton and on to Stalybridge ran on 31 March 1903, when the lease expired on the line, but services recommenced on 17 April and lasted until 14 October. A through electric service commenced the next day from the Audenshaw boundary,

Commemorative postcards were also issued locally to mark the opening of tramways, this example being published on such an occasion – though whether Accrington No.11 of 1907 was simply going to the Haslingden boundary, or working right through, is unclear. *(Author's Collection)*

eastwards along the horse tramway route via the Manchester Road and Stamford Street (across the OAH line), through Ashton and out to Stalybridge Town Hall, over STALYBRIDGE, HYDE, MOSSLEY & DUKINFIELD metals. On 22 February 1904 MANCHESTER CORPORATION electric cars began through-running beyond the Snipe at the Audenshaw boundary into Ashton to replace the Corporation's own cars on this section, whilst in March that year a short branch (less than ½ mile) was opened south from Stamford Street down Cavendish Street to the Dukinfield boundary at Alma Bridge; this was followed twelve months later by a second, to the east, down Scotland Street to meet the SHMD's tracks. (In April 1906 the SHMD took over the service in Scotland Street into the centre of Ashton.)

In 1905 ERTCW supplied single-deckers 13–18, and in 1908 UEC supplied top-covered cars 20–22, followed by similar vehicles 23 and 24 in 1912, and 25 and 26 two years later. The final purchases were made in 1921 when top-covered cars 27–38 were bought from EE and twenty-four OAH vehicles were acquired with the Corporation's purchase of part of the system. Only two single-deck combination cars from this batch – Nos 39 and 40 – were ever put into service, though, such was their generally abysmal condition.

Following the OAH purchase, the track layout in the town centre was rationalised slightly to enable that system's two routes to be integrated into the Corporation's network, and the Stanford Road part of the southern section doubled. In March 1923 the Corporation began motor bus services and two years later introduced trolleybuses under the Ashton-under-Lyne Corporation Act 1924; on 26 August 1926 these latter vehicles took over the former OAH northern route to Hathershaw. Also in 1926, Hurst was absorbed by Ashton and, with it, its nominally separate tramways; the following year the first car scrappings took place.

On 10 January 1928 the southern section from Denton to Hyde was closed, after which the remaining services were cut back gradually. The Hurst lines closed in June 1932 and the Ashton–Denton route in October 1936, leaving just the original horse tramway east–west route through the town to survive another two years. The last Corporation car in service was No.32, on the afternoon of 1 March 1938, though further passengers were carried by a Manchester car leaving the town later that day.

Balfour, Beatty & Co. Ltd

This firm was established in 1909 by A.H. Beatty of the tramway contractors J.G. White & Co. Ltd and George Balfour, a director of several tramway companies. It eventually owned, operated or had a substantial interest in, a number of tramway and/or electricity supply companies, including the systems of CARLISLE, Cheltenham, Dartford, Ilkeston, Leamington & Warwick, Luton, Mansfield and Nottinghamshire & Derbyshire in England, Llandudno & Colwyn Bay and Llanelly in Wales and DUNFERMLINE, FALKIRK and WEMYSS in Scotland.

Barnsley & District Electric Tramway

Authority: Barnsley and District Light Railway Order 1900
Gauge: 4ft 8½in.
Traction: Overhead electric
Opened: 31 October 1902
Closed: 3 September 1930
System: Branching
Length: 3.06 miles
Stock: 1 sd, 13 dd
Livery: BET green & white
Last Car: ?

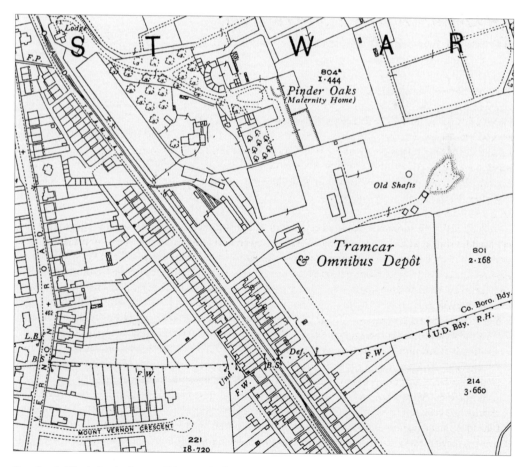

Barnsley & District's sole depot, off Upper Sheffield Road – also used as a bus garage from 1913 onwards – from the 1931 Ordnance Survey 25in. to 1 mile map.

Although of the same gauge as the neighbouring SHEFFIELD–ROTHERHAM–MEXBOROUGH & SWINDON–DEARNE DISTRICT network and, at one point, only a matter of yards from a possible connection with it, this south Yorkshire system always remained physically isolated from its neighbour.

At the close of the 1890s two rival proposals were made for an electric tramway in the town, by Barnsley Corporation and the BET, and it was the latter's scheme that won out. The tramway was owned and operated by a BET subsidiary, the Barnsley & District Electric Traction Co. Ltd (registered 3 February 1902) and consisted of a mainly single-track main line running south from the Smithies terminus in Monk Breton, just over the borough boundary, along Mill Lane and Eldon Street to the MR and GCR/LYR stations. (This 1 mile was always worked by a shuttle service.) From here it continued on south through the town centre and out along the Sheffield Road and past the depot to a terminus in Park Road, Worsborough Bridge. The system's one branch was a ½-mile line at the southern end, running south-east along Worsborough Dale High Street, making the whole track plan look like an inverted Y.

The first year's services were worked by Brush open-toppers 1–10, joined in 1903 by two more (Nos 11 and 12); all were later fitted with top covers. In 1905 BEC demi-car 59 was loaned by YORKSHIRE (WOOLLEN DISTRICT) ELECTRIC TRAMWAYS for trials and purchased that same year (renumbered 13); the passenger car fleet was completed in 1912 when No.14, a Brush balcony car, was bought.

The little system settled down to an uneventful life, though in 1919 a pointer to the future came when the Company, by now running motor buses, dropped the word 'electric' from its name. In 1924 the Dearne District finally reached Barnsley, but the Company refused to allow a physical connection to be made or through-running to take place in order to protect its bus services which, six years later, killed off its own tramway.

Barrow-In-Furness Tramways

Authority: Barrow-in-Furness Corporation Act 1881
Gauge: 4ft
Traction: Steam/overhead electric
Opened: 11 July 1885
Closed: 5 April 1932
System: Radial
Length: 6.39 miles
Stock: 14 locos, 10 dd steam?; 33 sd, 15 dd electric
Livery: Maroon & white steam?; maroon & cream BET, olive green & cream Corporation electric
Last Car: No.45

In 1881 Barrow-in-Furness Corporation secured an Act to authorise the construction of tramways, which it then leased to a private concern, the Barrow-in-Furness Tramways Co. Ltd. The system was formed of three lines radiating from Ramsden Square to the steelworks (north-west), past the Furness Railway's Barrow Central station to Abbey (north-east), and to Roose by the FR's station there (east); a fourth route, opened on 28 July 1886, branched off the last line, by the Town Hall, and ran south through Tea House to the FR's station at Ramsden Dock. Total route length of the single-track system was 5½ miles.

Eight Kitson tram locomotives (Nos 1–8) were supplied during 1885–92 and a similar number of Falcon top-covered bogie trailers (also Nos 1–8) were bought in 1885, all stock being based on a depot in Salthouse Road on the Roose route.

In 1898 the BFT Co. Ltd went into liquidation and was taken over on 23 December the following year by the BET, the Corporation having declined to purchase the concern. The BET's intention was to electrify the system in accordance with its usual policy but, whilst awaiting the appropriate authorisation, they improved the service somewhat by the addition, in 1900, of (possibly) BP Wilkinson patent locos and (possibly) two more trailers from the North Staffordshire Tramways in the Potteries. The next notable event in the tramway's life occurred on the night of 27 June 1902 when a fire at the depot destroyed ten locos and four trailers; these were never replaced (but probably some were repaired) and by the time of the system's closure on 13 July 1903 the surviving items of rolling-stock – three locos and three trailers – were in very poor shape.

Barrow-in-Furness single-decker No.22 of 1913 photographed during the First World War (note the conductress). The job of the boy was to jump off and change the points as needed. *(Author's Collection)*

The electrified system – authorised by the Barrow-in-Furness Tramways Order 1903 – opened to the public on 6 February 1904 with the Roose and Abbey routes in service; the Ramsden Dock line followed in June. (The short line to the steelworks was lifted in 1903, having been abandoned early in the steam days.)

In October 1904 a new route opened: a short branch, midway off the Ramsden Dock line, to Walney Ferry. The intention was to extend this line over a new bascule bridge to Walney Island and on to Biggar Bank on its western coast, and on 4 August 1911 the whole route was in operation (with the line across the island built by the Corporation).

The routes were mainly single-track and a new depot was constructed on the site of the old one. Services were worked, initially, by a fleet of seven Brush open-top cars (Nos 1–7) and five Brush bogie single-deckers (Nos 8–12); these were joined in 1905 by two more Brush open-toppers (Nos 15 and 16) and two BEC demi-cars (Nos 13 and 14). Later additions to the fleet were four large Brush bogie open-toppers in 1911 (Nos 17–20), four Brush bogie single-deckers in 1913–14 (Nos 21–24) and two Midland bogie single-deckers (Nos 25 and 26) bought c.1915 from the Potteries Electric Tramways.

After suffering the customary neglect during the First World War, the tramway was purchased on 1 January 1920 for the sum of £96,250 by the Corporation, who added a further twenty-two single-deck cars to the fleet over the next two years, numbering them 1–4 (ex-SOUTHPORT), 29–34 (ex-SHEFFIELD) and 35–46 (new from Brush). Several of the expired BET cars were scrapped, and by 1931 a total of thirty-one were left in stock. A year later the system closed, replaced by bus services, in the face of the cost of modernisation.

Batley Corporation Tramways

Authority: Batley Corporation Tramways Order 1900
Gauge: 4ft 8½in.
Traction: Overhead electric
Opened: 26 October 1903
Closed: 4 March 1934
System: Radial
Length: 6.65 miles
Stock: 8 dd
Livery: Green & cream to 1914, then maroon & primrose
Last Car: ?

Although a tramway (and tramcar) owner, Batley Corporation was never a tramway operator in its own right. It had obtained the necessary authorisation to construct tramways in 1900, but a dispute with the BET over using part of the former DEWSBURY, BATLEY & BIRSTAL line prevented the immediate and complete implementation of its plans. Construction, however, went ahead and eight cars were ordered from BEC.

The dispute with the BET was settled eventually: under the provisions of the BET-promoted Dewsbury, Batley and Birstal Tramways Act of 1903, the Corporation was to reconstruct and electrify the relevant portion of the old DBB, then lease the whole system to the BET for a period of twenty-eight years. Trials and inspection were carried out in the summer of 1903 using cars on loan from the BET's YORKSHIRE (WOOLLEN DISTRICT) system – of which the Batley lines were to become a part, although the opening was delayed as the Corporation-owned cars did not arrive until October.

As built, the system was roughly in the shape of an H, leaning to the right, with the two lines either side of the town centre linked to the Bradford Road (in the north) and Halifax Road (in the south) routes of the YWD; the central bar of the H was a short linking line along Clerk Green. A stub branch from the uppermost arm of the H led to the Market Place; all lines were single-track with passing places and short double-track sections. From the opening, the system was worked as an integral part of the YWD and the eight Corporation cars were absorbed into the larger fleet as Nos 49–56 (whilst retaining their own livery until the closure).

Beamish: North of England Open Air Museum

Occupying a huge, 300-acre rural site in County Durham, this museum recreates the flavour of early twentieth-century town and country life in the North of England. A 4ft 8½in. gauge overhead electric tramway opened in May 1973 to carry visitors to various parts of the site. It has been extended in stages over the years and now provides a circular ride of nearly 2 miles in length around the perimeter of the site, operating on a year-round basis with a variety of preserved northern tramcars on long-term loan from elsewhere. Currently operational, or on display, are BLACKPOOL 31 of 1901, GATESHEAD 10 of 1925, NEWCASTLE & GOSFORTH horse car 49 of 1873, NEWCASTLE CORPORATION 114 of 1901, SHEFFIELD 264 of 1907 and SUNDERLAND CORPORATION 16 of 1900, plus a 1935 Oporto bogie single-decker rebuilt as Beamish 196.

Birkdale & Southport Tramways *see* Southport Tramways

Cityscape at Beamish, with restored Gateshead & District No.10 of 1901 in operation. *(North of England Open Air Museum)*

STREET RAILWAY-CARRIAGE, PATENTED BY G. F. TRAIN, RUNNING AT BIRKENHEAD.—SEE PAGE 243.

A car on G.F. Train's historic Birkenhead line, as depicted in the *Illustrated London News* of 15 September 1860, published two weeks after the tramway opened.

Birkenhead Tramways

Authority: Local authority permission
Gauge: 5ft 2in./4ft 8½in.*
Traction: Horse
Opened: 30 August 1860
Closed: 24 January 1901?
System: Network
Length: 10.64 miles
Stock: 6 sd, 31 dd
Livery: Mahogany, red & cream? (Street Railway light green & cream)
Last Car: ?

Although by the middle of the nineteenth century passenger-carrying rural roadside tramroads had been familiar in Britain for several decades (notably the Oystermouth Tramroad in South Wales and the Stratford & Moreton Tramroad in Warwickshire – see Volume 2), Birkenhead's first street tramway was of immense historic importance, being the first of its kind in the whole of the British Isles. It was the brainchild of George Francis Train, an American entrepreneur of great drive and enthusiasm who, in 1860, convinced the Birkenhead dock and municipal authorities that a new-fangled American-style 'street railway' would be just the thing for their town.

Despite considerable opposition from certain interests (notably horse bus operators), the scheme went ahead with a 1½-mile line from the Woodside Ferry approach, up Shore Road, Argyle Street and Conway Street to terminate at the entrance to Birkenhead Park. The operator was the Birkenhead Street Railway Co. Ltd (registered 7 May 1860). Two open-top double-deck cars (Nos 1 and 2) and two closed single-deck saloons cars (Nos 3 and 4) were supplied by an American builder and assembled by Robert Main, a Woodside coachbuilder.

Some confusion exists as to the original gauge of the tramway. Train laid the mainly single-track line using step rails: 6in.-wide flat wrought-iron rails with a ¾in. lip or flange along the outer edge (as opposed to a traditional British plateway, where the flanges were on the inner edges). It would appear that, as the gauge used on the American lines upon which Train modelled his was commonly given as 5ft 2in. (sometimes 5ft 2½in.), Train specified the same dimension. Unfortunately, the American measurement was that taken between the *outsides* of the flanges and was actually railway standard gauge as measured between the *insides* (i.e. normal British practice), so when the British track-layers positioned the rails to the specified gauge, they were wider apart than Train intended! The track was laid by the kerbside (both kerbsides in the case of Conway Street) and soon gave rise to complaints from other road users on account of its profile; the line was popular with its passengers though, and in late April 1861 a 1-mile extension round Birkenhead Park along Park Street East and Park Road South, then down Palm Grove to Oxton (and the depot) was opened. That year the stretch in Shore Road was abandoned, replaced by a new line in Chester Street and Bridge Street.

The horse bus opposition reached its peak in 1862 when Thomas Evans, a local operator and dignitary of some weight, began running what were, in effect, private tramcars along the tracks. The problem was of Train's own making, for when seeking permission to lay his tramway he had attempted to mollify any opposition by promising to allow other road users to run vehicles on the tracks. Beaten, in early 1862 he leased the line to Evans, only to see it closed down that August – but then reopen that same month, to be leased to Charles Castle of Liverpool.

Improvements to the layout were made in the summer and autumn of 1864, when the Conway Street line was singled and another line laid in Price Street and Hamilton Street to provide a one-way loop, plus a short extension to the new ferry terminal at Woodside. At the same time the entire line, now just less than 2½ miles of mainly single track, was relaid to 4ft 8½in. gauge with grooved rails (thought to have been the invention of a Laird's shipyard engineer). Thereafter, the tramway was alternately leased out and operated by the Company until 1876, when it was put up for sale. A new concern, the Birkenhead Tramways Co., was then formed to buy it, and in 1877, empowered by the Birkenhead Tramways Act of that year, did so (the BSR Co. Ltd being dissolved at the same time). On 1 August 1878 a 1½-mile route south from Argyle Street along Borough Road past Clifton Park and Higher Tranmere to North Road, Prenton was opened.

In 1879 the Company purchased its close neighbour, the HOYLAKE & BIRKENHEAD TRAMWAY (see below), thus beginning the long process of unifying the town's tramways. On 1 June 1881 a ½-mile extension from North Road south to Prenton Lane was opened (double tracks like the rest of the Prenton route), and at the end of that year the relatively new Price Street line was closed with cars in both directions now using Conway Street once more (doubled again since October 1878).

The Street Railway's original four cars were followed by four American single-deckers (Nos 5–8) in 1861, of which at least two were named, in American fashion, *Young England* and *Young America*. It is thought that most, if not all, of the eight were converted to 4ft 8½in. gauge in 1864 and were withdrawn over a number of years, in effect being replaced by eight Starbuck cars of 1876, all open-toppers, bought by the BT Co. and numbered 1–8 also. These were joined two years later by eight more, slightly smaller, Starbuck cars (probably Nos 9–16) and, in 1879, by eight H&B double-deckers, which took the numbers 17–24. These ran until 1887, when they were withdrawn around the same time as the 1876 Starbuck cars. (No.7 was sold to BIRKDALE & SOUTHPORT, but has managed to survive – see BIRKENHEAD: WIRRAL TRAMWAY (2) below – along with No.20 of 1901) Finally, in 1887–88, five small Milnes double-deckers were bought to replace some of the ex-H&B cars, taking their numbers.

By the end of the 1880s the Company was in financial trouble – mainly because of the spread of railways in the area – and in September 1888 it went into liquidation. On 8 August 1889 the Birkenhead United Tramway, Omnibus & Carriage Co. Ltd was formed to purchase it (and also the Birkenhead & District Omnibus & Carriage Co. Ltd), the takeover being completed on 15 August 1890 with the purchase price of £37,500 buying, amongst other things, twenty-seven cars (of which only seventeen were serviceable). The track was bought by the Birkenhead Corporation for £5,000 (to lease back to the Company until 31 December 1900), who soon found themselves spending large sums of money repairing or relaying it and, consequently, by the late 1890s, had decided to purchase and electrify all the town's horse lines, including the WIRRAL TRAMWAY. The only new cars purchased during this period were two small Milnes double-deckers (which again appear to have taken vacated fleet numbers). All surviving cars were sold at auction after the system's closure, which occurred quietly during early 1901 when the last services, based on the New Ferry Depot, were terminated.

Birkenhead: Hoylake & Birkenhead Tramway

Authority: Hoylake and Birkenhead Railway and Tramways Act 1872
Gauge: 4ft 8½in.
Traction: Horse
Opened: 6 September 1873
Taken over: 12 October 1879
System: Single line
Length: 2.29 miles
Stock: 8 dd
Livery: Maroon & cream?

This short line was promoted in 1872 by the Hoylake & Birkenhead Rail & Tramway Co. in order to link Woodside Ferry in Birkenhead with the Docks station of the financially troubled Hoylake Railway in the district of its title to the north-west. (The HBRT Co. took over the railway company at the same time.) Opened the following year, the tramway ran from the ferry approach along Canning Street, Bridge Street, Cleveland Street and Beaufort Road, to the station where a covered interchange was provided – something rarely found on British tramways and which probably originally housed the tramway's fleet of eight open-top Starbuck cars. The legend carried by the cars read: 'THE HOYLAKE RAILWAY'.

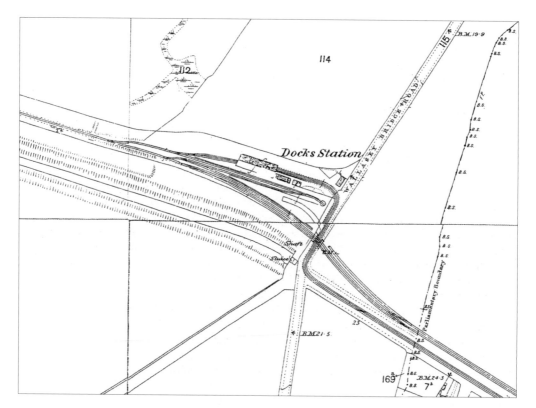

The early, isolated rural nature of the 1873 Hoylake & Birkenhead Tramway's Docks station depot is clearly apparent on this extract from the 1875 Ordnance Survey 25in. to 1 mile map. Closed in 1888, the site was later used for Birkenhead North engine shed – the only known instance of such a reuse.

From 2 May 1876 the line was worked by W.W. Townson, a local vet, and it is thought that purpose-built stables and depot by the Docks station were rented by him from the Company. This whole arrangement ended three years later when, on 12 October 1879, the BIRKENHEAD TRAMWAYS Co. purchased the line for £27,000 (including the cars, but not the depot buildings, which the railway company leased to the BT Co.).

Birkenhead: Wirral Tramway (1)

Authority: Wirral Tramways Order 1874
Gauge: 4ft 8½in.
Traction: Horse
Opened: 23 July 1877?*
Closed: 22 January 1901
System: Single line
Length: 2.99 miles
Stock: 16 sd, 4 dd
Livery: ?
Last Car: ?

Birkenhead's third independent horse system was owned by the Wirral Tramways Co. Ltd, who operated a single-track line south from Woodside Ferry along Chester Street and New Chester Road as far as the depot in New Ferry by New Ferry Road, running close to the Mersey shore and the Tranmere and Rock ferries.

The line was inspected by the BoT on 23 July 1877, but not passed for traffic. Nevertheless, public services commenced and ran for some days before the BoT put a stop to them. It was not until after another inspection on 1 November 1877 that the line was passed fit to open. A short extension (built and owned by the Birkenhead Commissioners but rented to the Company) opened 19 January of the following year and took the tramway onto the Woodside Ferry approach.

Three Birkenhead Corporation cars awaiting passengers at the Woodside Ferry Terminal, with No.30 of 1901 – fitted with a top-cover in the early 1920s – nearest the camera. *(Author's Collection)*

The line was an obvious success, for heavier rails were substituted for the originals in 1879 whilst, at the same time, the original seven small Starbuck single-deckers were replaced by seven longer cars. (A low railway bridge over Chester Street by Tranmere Pool precluded the use of double-deckers.) The 1877 cars are thought to have been sold to WALLASEY TRAMWAYS and their numbers 1–7 allocated to the new cars. Two more (Nos 8 and 9) were bought in 1880, followed by open-top double-deckers Nos 10 and 11 (1894), 12 (1895) and 13 (1896), all probably from Milnes. It is presumed the double-deckers worked on the long stretch of line from New Ferry to the Mersey Railway's Green Lane station just south of the low bridge (and close to the Tranmere Ferry pier and Laird's shipyard).

By now Birkenhead Corporation was planning to purchase and electrify the three horse systems in the town; in 1900 a figure of £22,666 was arbitrated for the price and on 8 May 1900 the last WT trams ran to make way for reconstruction work. Eight days later the stock was auctioned off. This was not quite the end of the story, though, for some of the single-deck cars (including Nos 4, 8 and 9) were purchased by the Birkenhead United concern (see BIRKENHEAD TRAMWAYS earlier) and put back into makeshift service around the affected track sections until 22 January 1901, after which they were auctioned once again.

Birkenhead Corporation Tramways
Authority: Birkenhead Corporation Act 1897
Gauge: 4ft 8½in.
Traction: Overhead electric
Opened: 4 February 1901
Closed: 17 July 1937
System: Network
Length: 79.08 miles
Stock: 13 sd, 52 dd
Livery: Maroon & cream
Last Car: Nos 31 (service) and 22 (official)

The Corporation's 1897 Act gave it the power to work tramways and the Birkenhead Corporation Act of 1899 authorised its purchase of the town's existing horse tramways. Reconstruction work took place during 1900–01 and the first route reopened was the old WIRRAL TRAMWAY's New Ferry line (see above), followed slowly by the bulk of the old horse system, plus new routes to Claughton Village in the west and Tranmere to the south, the whole network being mainly double-track. The principal depot (opened 28 July 1903) was at Laird Street on the Claughton Village route, whilst a second at New Ferry served the south-eastern side of the system.

The initial car fleet was made up of thirteen single-deckers (Nos 1–13) and thirty-one open-top double-deckers (Nos 14–44), all from Milnes; during 1908–10 the single-deckers were rebuilt as top-covered double-deckers low enough to pass under the Chester Street railway bridge. In 1902 Milnes supplied a further fifteen open-top cars (Nos 45–59), this time bogie vehicles. (Except for No.46, all the double-deckers were fitted later with a variety of top covers.) The last cars bought were Nos 63–68, six HN low top-covered cars of 1913 for the New Ferry route. (Nos 60–62 were works cars.)

In 1919 the Corporation began running motor buses, at first as tramway feeders, but from 30 August 1925, when they took over from the trams on the Claughton Road route to Claughton, as their replacements. By 1931 the buses were operating a route network in their own right, and from 28 December that year they took over from the New Ferry trams. The Tranmere line closed on 20 September 1934 and the Prenton route the very next day, whilst the Docks route (the old HOYLAKE & BIRKENHEAD line – see earlier) closed on 1 April 1935, leaving only the long, circular route out through Claughton Village round Oxton and back. The last public service tram to run was No.31, followed by No.22 (converted into an illuminated car for King George VI's Coronation) carrying the official party.

A long-term project by the Merseyside Tramway Preservation Trust to restore open-topper No.20 of 1901 to operational condition was completed in 1999 and the car can be seen at the Pacific Road Transport Museum when it is not running on the new WIRRAL TRAMWAY (see below).

One of the Hong Kong-built cars on
the second Wirral Tramway (opened
1995), Birkenhead. *(Courtesy Wirral
Leisure Services & Tourism Department)*

Birkenhead: Wirral Tramway (2)

Authority: Wirral Tramway Light Railway Order 1994
Gauge: 4ft 8½in.
Traction: Overhead electric
Opened: 14 April 1995
System: Single line
Length: *c.*0.75 miles
Stock: 2 dd
Livery: Maroon

One of Britain's youngest tramways adds yet another chapter to Birkenhead's long history of such lines with its opening nearly sixty years after the last trams ran in the town. Again starting from Woodside Ferry terminal (and bus station), it ran originally north-west as a single track on a roadside reservation for some 400yd along the ferry approach and Shore Road, past the depot, to its terminus by the corner of Pacific Road. The track was laid using rails from reclaimed LIVERPOOL tramway track. In May 1995 the tramway was extended another ¼ mile to Egerton Bridge as part of the docklands redevelopment project, and in 2000 another ¼ mile was added, taking it to the Old Colonial public house, with a new depot built there in Taylor Street. Whilst built as a pleasure line, it was hoped that the tramway would meet a real public transport need in serving the variety of different-use sites planned for the area, though a ruling by the Railway Inspectorate has confined the trams to a tourism role.

The tramway's two enclosed double-deck cars were constructed by Hong Kong Tramways Ltd in 1992 and are numbered 69 and 70 so as to continue the BIRKENHEAD CORPORATION number series (see above). They were painted a shade of dark red similar to that system's former livery, though in 2007 No.69 was painted in the Birkenhead bus livery of blue and cream that would have been applied to the Corporation's trams had they lasted into the 1950s. Both cars ran in BLACKPOOL from mid-1993 until the opening of the line, which was operated by Blackpool Transport Services on behalf of the owner, Wirral Metropolitan Borough Council, until 2005 when the Council took it over. The tramway is operated in conjunction with the Pacific Road Transport Museum, incorporating workshops where long-term tramcar restorations are carried out. Newly-restored DUNDEE & DISTRICT steam trailer No.2 serves as a waiting room in the depot, whilst restored BIRKENHEAD 20, LIVERPOOL CORPORATION 762, WALLASEY CORPORATION 78 and LISBON 730 are operated on the line on occasion.

Birstall *see* Dewsbury, Batley & Birstal

Blackburn & Over Darwen Tramways

Authority: Blackburn and Over Darwen Tramways Act 1879
Gauge: 4ft
Traction: Steam
Opened: 16 April 1881
Closed: 16 October 1900
System: Single line
Length: 4.93 miles
Stock: 17 locos, 23 dd?
Livery: Red & cream
Last Car: ?

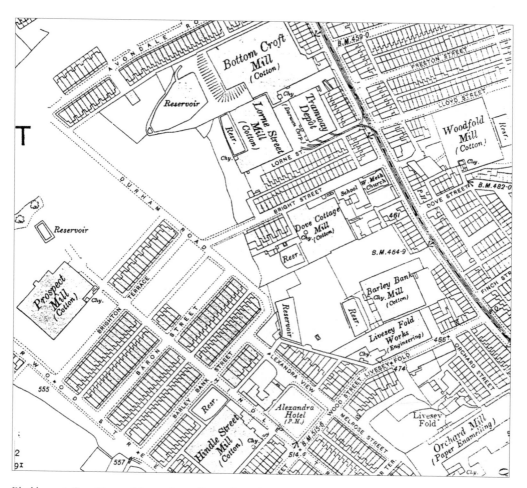

Blackburn & Over Darwen's Lorne Street Depot, from the 1911 Ordnance Survey 25in. to 1 mile map. Opened in 1900 (and surrounded on all sides by mills in this intensely industrial area of Lancashire), it first housed steam locos and trailers, then later the tramway's electric cars.

Blackburn's first tramway was a single-track steam line, owned and operated by the Blackburn & Over Darwen Tramways Co., which ran south from the centre of Blackburn along Darwen Street (with a second terminal spur off this in St Peter Street) and the Bolton Road through Ewood, Earcroft, Hawkshaw (past the depot in Lorne Street) and Darwen to terminate at Whitehall. It was the first British tramway authorised to use steam traction only and had its official opening two days before public services began.

The first stock fleet was made up of Kitson tram locomotives Nos 1–7 of 1881–82 hauling Ashbury open-top double-deck trailers Nos 1–8 of the same period, the cars being mounted on Eades patent reversible trucks. These were joined in 1884 by bogie enclosed double-deckers 9–12, also by Ashbury. During the years 1885–96 another seven locos (Nos 8–14) were bought, this time from Greens, plus bogie enclosed double-deck trailers 13–19 from Lancaster. In 1897–98 three further Kitsons were added (Nos 15, 1 and 2) to complete the locomotive stud. No other trailers were purchased, though it is thought that four open-top workmen's cars were used in 1883 for a short while (source unknown).

As from the first day of 1899, the line was purchased jointly by the corporations of BLACKBURN (see below) and DARWEN for £22,337 and £26,400 respectively as a prelude to electrification, with closure taking place the following year. Of the thirteen engines and thirteen cars taken over (the others presumably having been scrapped or cannibalised), Blackburn acquired ten of each and Darwen the remainder.

Blackburn Corporation Tramways

Authority: Blackburn Improvement Act 1882
Gauge: 4ft
Traction: Steam, horse, overhead electric
Opened: 28 May 1887
Closed: 3 September 1949
System: Network
Length: 14.73 miles
Stock: 22 locos, 19 dd steam; 8 dd horse; 13 sd, 48 dd electric
Livery: Holly green & cream
Last Car: No.74

Blackburn's second tramway was a horse and steam radial system promoted by the Corporation and operated by the Blackburn Corporation Tramways Co. Ltd. Focussed on the Church Street/Railway Street junction in the town centre, two horse routes ran west along Whalley Banks Street to Witton Stocks and along Preston New Road, past the horse tram depot in Simmons Street, to Billinge End, while two steam routes ran (firstly) east along Accrington Road, past the steam depot in Intack and the Blackburn Road to Church, and (secondly) north-east up Whalley New Road to the Cemetery. All four routes were single-track and totalled 8.76 miles.

The interior of the rebuilt Blackburn Corporation Tramways' Intack Depot, with a range of open-topped and fully enclosed double-deckers on show. (Author's Collection)

The original steam rolling-stock comprised Green tram locomotives Nos 1–15 of 1887–88 and closed Ashbury bogie double-deckers 1–12 of 1887. These were joined in 1888 by similar trailers 13–15 from Falcon and (probably) in 1889 Nos 16–19 from Milnes. The eight open-top horse cars, Nos 20–27, were also from Milnes. The only addition made to this fleet was the purchase, in 1899, of seven BP locos (Nos 16–22) from the North Staffordshire Tramways in the Potteries; these were bought by Blackburn Corporation who, on 24 August 1898, had taken over the system in order to electrify it (at a cost of £87,000 agreed the previous year).

The first line to be converted was the 1½-mile Billinge End route which, mainly double-tracked, reopened on 20 March 1899. Eight Milnes open-top bogie double-deckers, Nos 28–35, were bought to work it and housed in the rebuilt horse car depot. This was followed by the electrification of the other horse and steam routes (including an extension of the Witton Stocks line on 31 March 1899 along the Preston Old Road to Witton, extended in 1903 to the Cherry Tree) and the conversion of the 2½ miles of the BLACKBURN & OVER DARWEN line in Blackburn (see above), which reopened on 1 December 1900. The Cemetery route reopened in 1901 (extended to Wilpshire in 1902) and a new 1½-mile south-east route to Audley was opened in 1903, so completing the mainly double-track network based on a long one-way system in the town centre.

To help work the growing electric tramway, forty more Milnes bogie open-toppers (Nos 36–75) were added to the car fleet in 1901 (many of which were later top-covered), followed by UEC bogie single-deckers Nos 76–87 in 1907–08 for the Audley route and a single-deck bogie cross-bench car (No.88) a year later, built by the Corporation.

In August 1907 through-running to ACCRINGTON, via Church, began. Thereafter, the system remained little changed for more than two decades (apart from the results of the car rebuilding programme) until the 1930s, when many of the tramway's neighbours began to close. It was not long before similar economic and political pressures produced the first Blackburn abandonments: on 13 February 1935 the Audley route was closed and on 31 March 1939 so was the Cherry Tree route, both being replaced by bus services.

The tramway survived the Second World War without further cuts, but on 5 January 1946 the Preston New Road line closed, followed on 21 December 1947 by the Wilpshire route. On 16 January 1949 the Church route was cut back to the depot and on 2 July that year the line to the Darwen boundary was abandoned, leaving just the Blackburn-Intack Depot section to last out the summer.

Blackpool Corporation Tramways
Authority: Blackpool Corporation Tramways Order 1884
Gauge: 4ft 8½in.
Traction: Horse, conduit electric, overhead electric
Opened: 12 September 1885
System: Network
Length: 20.97 miles
Stock: 4 sd, 14 dd horse*; 176 sd, 179 dd electric
Livery: Green & teak to c.1905, red, white & teak to 1933, then green & cream

The Blackpool Tramway (as it is now generally known, being reduced to virtually a single line) will always have its place in history – and in the heart of tramway lovers. Not only was it the first electric tramway in England, it somehow managed to survive whilst all its counterparts were abandoned. The purpose of its construction was to assist the growth and development of the town as the premier seaside resort of the region and, in its first form, was a single line conduit tramway running from Cocker Street on the north side of Talbot Square, by the North Pier and close to Blackpool's first railway station (now Blackpool North), along the Promenade to Dean Street by the South Pier – a distance of some 1¾ miles.

Services began with Starbuck open-top double-deck electric cars Nos 1 and 2, similar Lancaster cars 3–6 and open toastracks Nos 7 and 8 (Starbuck again) and 9 and 10 (Lancaster) – though all were horse-drawn, without motors, until 29 September 1885 when electric working began. Nos 9 and 10 – which had been used as trailers to the other cars during the period of horse haulage – were replaced in 1891 by new cars 9 and 10, two Milnes open-toppers. In the following year, on 10 September 1892, the Blackpool Electric Tramway Co. Ltd's lease expired and the line's owner, Blackpool Corporation, took over its working. In 1895 the first branch was opened from midway along the Promenade up Lytham Road to meet the LYTHAM ST ANNES line, for which large Lancaster bogie open-toppers 11–14 were bought. In 1897 a link between the two Blackpool routes was laid down Station Road (near what is now Blackpool South station) and the following year two large Midland bogie open-toppers, numbered 15 and 16 and nicknamed 'Dreadnoughts' on account of their size, were purchased.

Although of historic significance in showing that electric street tramways could be operated safely, the Blackpool Conduit Tramway (as it was known) was not a success in regard to its method of current supply. The system was prone to all sorts of disruptions caused by sand and water getting into the conduit – a seaside promenade being just about the worst place possible for such a line – and temporary horse traction often had to be resorted to. So, in the summer and autumn of 1899, the three lines and sixteen cars were converted to overhead working, and in 1900 they were linked to the recently opened BLACKPOOL & FLEETWOOD line at Gynn Square.

After this the system grew steadily, both in terms of route and stock. By 1 January 1920, when the Corporation took over the B&F line, it operated some 12 miles of tramway along the seafront and through the town's streets (mainly as loop lines). Meanwhile, the fleet was built up with many of the trams constructed by the Corporation under a car-building programme that has continued to this day, based on its main depot and workshops in Blundell Street off the Lytham Road route (although other builders' products are still bought). This is the only non-seafront portion of the system left in Blackpool, as ten years after the last extension opened – in 1926 – along the South Promenade to Clifton Drive (Starr Gate), cutbacks were begun of the non-seafront lines. Their passing was missed by many for, as with some other seaside resorts, 'circular tours' were run over them for the benefit of holidaymakers, and so well-loved were they that it is recorded that in 1913, at the height of their popularity, some 700,000 passengers were carried, with up to thirty-six cars employed on this service alone on any one day!

Cars added to the fleet, following on from those mentioned above, were:

Nos 17–26: Midland 'Dreadnoughts' of 1900
Nos 27–41: Midland open-toppers of 1901
Nos 42–53: HN bogie open-toppers of 1902
Nos 54–61: Midland 'Dreadnoughts' of 1902
Nos 62–68: UEC bogie balcony cars of 1911–12
Nos 69–92: UEC bogie toastracks of 1911–14
Nos 93–98: Milnes bogie open-toppers bought 1919 ex-London United Tramways

Above left: Two Blackpool Corporation 'Dreadnoughts' passing in Talbot Square, near the Hotel Metropole on the (mis-captioned) Princes Parade. The tracks off to the right lead into the town. *(Author's Collection)*

Above right: Blackpool Corporation toastrack No.74 of 1912 on a sight-seeing 'circular tour' through the town – a type of excursion once a feature of several seaside tramways. *(Author's Collection)*

The Blackpool circular tour was undoubtedly popular with holidaymakers – especially when it was not raining! – as this crowded toastrack clearly proves. *(Author's Collection)*

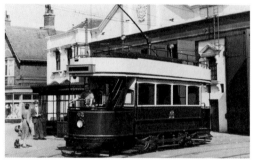

Above left: A unique feature of Blackpool's tramways has long been the running of specially transfigured cars to complement the town's famous illuminations. The first of these was the Lifeboat, rebuilt in 1926 from Midland open-topper No.40 of 1901, which saw annual service until it was withdrawn at the end of the 1961 season. *(Author's Collection)*

Above right: Blackpool Corporation No.45, an HN open-topper of 1902, outside Marton Depot in Watergate Drive at the back of the town. Opened in 1901, the depot was closed in 1962, used for cutting-up withdrawn trams, then demolished to make way for a filling station. *(Author's Collection)*

Nos 28, 33–42, 45, 47–51, 53, 99, 100, 142–145, 153–160: Corporation bogie balcony cars of 1923–29 ('Standards')

Nos 146–152: HN bogie balcony cars of 1924–25

Nos 161–166: Corporation bogie toastracks of 1927

Nos 167–176: EE bogie single-deckers of 1928

Nos 200–224: EE bogie streamlined single-deckers of 1933–34 ('Railcoaches')

Nos 225–236: EE bogie open single-deckers of 1934–35 ('Boats')

Nos 237–249: EE bogie open-toppers of 1934

Nos 250–263: EE bogie enclosed double-deckers of 1934–35 ('Balloons')

Nos 264–283: EE 'Railcoaches' of 1935

Nos 284–303: Brush 'Railcoaches' of 1937

Nos 10–21: EE semi-open 'Railcoaches' of 1939 ('Sun Saloons')

Nos 304–328: Roberts bogie streamlined single-deckers of 1952–53 ('Coronations')

Nos T1–T10: Metro-Cammell bogie single-deck 'Railcoach' trailers of 1960–61

No.641: East Lancashire Coachbuilders bogie single-decker of 1984 ('Centenary Car')

Nos 642–648: East Lancashire Coachbuilders bogie single-deckers of 1986–88

(Nos 100–141 were allocated to the ex-B&F cars)

Many of the above vehicles have been extensively modified over the years (including the fitting of top covers, conversion to one-man operation and complete rebuilds). In addition, in 1968 the surviving cars were renumbered in a new series so that the 'Boats' became Nos 600–607, the single-unit 'Railcoaches' 610–638, the last 'Coronation' 660, the two-car unit 'Railcoaches' 671–680 and their trailers 681–690, and the EE double-deckers 700–726 (all now totally enclosed).

One other feature of the fleet must be mentioned. Whilst many British tramways have run illuminated cars – usually on special occasions such as coronations – Blackpool has, since 1912, made a grand annual show of doing so, later converting passenger vehicles into semi-permanent replicas of railway trains, space rockets, hovercraft and the like to complement the town's famous illuminations.

Because of the sheer number of cars built for the tramway, and the fact that a lot of the withdrawals have been comparatively recent, many of them survive as preserved vehicles on museum lines up and down the country – and even abroad. In return, Blackpool plays host to operational preserved cars from elsewhere, affording visitors the unique sight of vintage double-deckers at work in their natural urban setting – though the cost of maintaining the large fleet of ageing stock and infrastructure is an ever-present threat to the tramway's survival in its current form. However, in 2009 sixteen Bombardier 'Flexity 2' 32m-long low-floor trams, due for delivery from May 2011, were ordered, the intention being that they take over the bulk of the services. At the same time, plans were unveiled for a futuristic £20 million depot on Council-owned land at Starr Gate to house the new cars (leaving Rigby Road for the 'heritage fleet'), to be completed by May 2011; possibly a tramway museum will be incorporated into the structure. The whole, long overdue upgrade of the system – including new trackwork and relocated stops – will cost some £100 million, the money coming from local, national and European Union sources.

Details of operational preserved cars are given in the appropriate entries elsewhere in these volumes.

Blackpool North Pier Tramway

Authority: -
Gauge: 3ft
Traction: Internal combustion
Opened: 2 September 1991
Closed: Autumn 1994
System: Single line
Length: 0.15 miles
Stock: 3 sd
Livery: Burgundy & cream
Last Car: All cars

The three-car train on Blackpool's newest but now sadly defunct tramway, the 1991 North Pier line. (Author)

Blackpool's newest tramway was constructed as part of a £6 million, 4-year refurbishment of the North Pier by its owner, the First Leisure Corporation. The ½-mile pier first opened in 1863, but has been added to and damaged by ships, fire and storms – the last such incident occurred on 24 December 1997 when the landing jetty at the pier head was badly damaged by gales.

The single-track line (with no passing loops or sidings), designed by the London firm of Beresford Sherman, was laid with flat-bottomed rails laid flush with the decking on the northern side of the mid-section of the pier, partially railed-off from the rest of the promenade area.

The tramway was worked by three similar enclosed single-deck bogie cars coupled as a train, custom-built by Harry Steer Engineering of Breaston, Derbyshire, fairground equipment specialists. Total passenger seating was fifty-six. The centre car housed a Perkins diesel engine which, via a hydraulic pump, drove wheel motors in the cars. (The centre car had four of its eight wheels powered, and the driving trailers had two each of theirs powered.) Another unconventional feature of the cars was that they had doors on their north sides only.

Although short in length – just 270yd – the tramway was not simply a pleasure line, but served a useful purpose in ferrying passengers between the landward and seaward structures on the pier in inclement weather – which the cars were specially built to withstand as there were no shed facilities for them.

Sadly, this account is couched in the past tense as the line was closed at the end of the 1994 summer season – presumably it was thought not to be financially viable – and the cars reportedly scrapped.

Blackpool & Fleetwood Tramroad

Authority: Blackpool and Fleetwood Tramroad Act 1896
Gauge: 4ft 8½in.
Traction: Overhead electric
Opened: 14 July 1898
Taken over: 1 January 1920
System: Single line
Length: 8.21 miles
Stock: 41 sd
Livery: Nut-brown & cream

Following the pioneering success of the BLACKPOOL electric line, a continuation northwards along the Lancashire coast to the fishing port of Fleetwood on the Wyre estuary was promoted by the Blackpool & Fleetwood Tramroad Syndicate (later Company). Construction began from the Fleetwood end in July 1897 and within four months the line had reached Uncle Tom's Cabin on the northern edge of Blackpool as a mainly reserved, sleepered single track (hence the Tramroad rather than Tramway title). The desired route into Blackpool from Gynn Square, just south of this point, was opposed by Blackpool Corporation, so the tramway had to forsake the shoreline and traverse the back streets to the joint Furness Railway and LNWR Blackpool Talbot Road (later Blackpool North) station, though this last mile of the line did not open until 29 September because of the road-widening works necessitated here. Within Blackpool itself, the tramway was constructed by the Corporation and leased to the Company for twenty-one years.

Initial services were worked by ten open cross-bench cars (Nos 1–10) and three open cross-bench trailers (Nos 11–13) – these latter vehicles being lengthened and motorised c.1905 – joined in the autumn of 1898 by six saloon cars (Nos 14–19). In 1899 the fleet was enlarged further by the purchase of five more saloons (20–24), three more cross-bench cars (25–27) and seven composite cars (Nos 28–34). All the cars were single-deck bogie vehicles from Milnes, apart from the last seven, which were supplied by ERTCW. The fleet remained this size until 1910, when three more bogie toastracks were bought, this time from UEC (Nos 35–37), followed four years later by Nos 38–41, four UEC bogie saloons.

The first depots were in Copse Road, Fleetwood and at Bispham near Blackpool; these were joined in 1899 by a small depot built over the terminal road across Bold Street in Fleetwood to house the first and last trams of the day.

The tramway was popular, profitable and undoubtedly led to the growth and development of Fleetwood (and all points south), but as the Company's lease of the Blackpool section expired at the end of 1919, its long-term future looked uncertain. In the event, the Company sold the whole tramway to Blackpool Corporation that year for £284,000 (having first failed to interest the LYR), the bulk of the line subsequently becoming the major surviving portion of the municipal system.

Car No.2 is preserved and operated at the National Tramway Museum, Crich, whilst No.40 is preserved at Blackpool, also in operational condition.

Bolton Corporation Tramways

Authority: Bolton and Suburban Tramways Order 1878
Gauge: 4ft 8½in.
Traction: Horse, overhead electric
Opened: 1 September 1880
Closed: 29 March 1947
System: Radial
Length: 32.36 miles
Stock: 48 sd & dd horse?; 3 sd, 162 dd electric
Livery: Maroon & cream
Last Car: No.406 (service) and No.440 (official)

Bolton's horse tramways were promoted jointly by Bolton Corporation and the Astley Bridge, Farnworth and Kearsley local boards and, when constructed, were leased to Edmund Holden, a local horse bus operator. The first three routes ran from the centre of the town south-east along the Manchester Road to Moses Gate on the boundary with Farnworth, north up the Blackburn Road to Dunscar and north-west along Halliwell Road to the district of that name. By 1882, two further radial routes had been opened: south-west along Derby Street and Ens Road to Daubhill station, and west along Chorley New Road to Lostock Junction Lane – making for a grand total of just over 14½ miles for the system. The depot was in Shiffnal Street off Bradshaw Gate on the east side of the town centre.

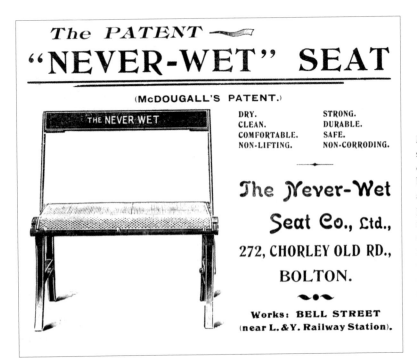

Many tramcars had seats with backs that could be flipped over by the conductor at a terminus so passengers always faced the direction of travel. This Bolton firm's Edwardian trade advertisement extols the virtues of its patented model, particularly suited to open-top cars in the wetter northern climes.

Above left: Bolton Corporation open-topper No.32 of 1899 on an Oxford Street postcard. *(Author's Collection)*

Above right: An unidentified Bolton Corporation single-decker on a special working, the occasion as yet unknown – possibly a civic outing, or even a funeral. *(Author's Collection)*

By 1899 another 16½ miles of track had been laid on new routes and extensions, and that year the tramway was offered to Bolton Corporation, the price paid that June being £58,000 for the business and forty-eight cars (some of which were fitted with reversible bodies). The Corporation was ready to electrify the system – it had opened its own generating station in 1894 – and on 9 December 1899 they began electric tram services over three new routes: south from the town centre for a mile down Fletcher Street, Grecian Street and Rishton Lane to Lever Edge Lane in Great Lever, east for 1½ miles along the Bury Road as far as Toothill Bridge, and north-east for 2 miles up Folds Road and Tonge Moor Road to the district of that name, terminating at the corner of Turton Road.

The last horse trams ran on 2 January 1900 on the old system, that same day seeing the opening of seven new or converted radial routes to help form the basis of its electric successor which, when the last extension opened on 19 December 1924 (as 3 miles of single track along the Wigan road to Westhoughton), consisted of thirteen lines focussed on a complex one-way arrangement in the town centre. Originally the lines were mainly single-track and, where possible, utilised the old horse tramway rails, though these had to be replaced in the 1900s when a road-widening programme enabled many sections to be double-tracked. The former horse tramway route from Moses Gate to the Black Horse, Farnworth, was electrified by Bolton Corporation and worked by it from 13 April 1900, with an extension opening around January 1902 to Kearsley; from 1 June 1902, however, it was worked by FARNWORTH CORPORATION as an independent system.

The first electric cars were ERTCW open-toppers 1–40, which were followed by similar cars 41–49 in 1900 (the last of these being a bogie vehicle). In 1901 came Brush bogie open-toppers 50–59, followed during 1901–02 by Nos 60–81, similar vehicles from ERTCW and, in 1903, by top-covered cars 82–86, again from ERTCW. (The open-toppers were later fitted with top covers.) In 1906 ten more of the same, Nos 87–96, were added to the fleet, this time from Brush. The pre-First World War purchases were completed by Nos 97–103 (top-covered bogie cars), Nos 104–106 (bogie single-deck combination cars) and Nos 107–112 (more top-covered bogie cars), all bought from UEC. A depot was built on the site of the former stables, with a second added in 1909 in Bridgeman Street as the car fleet grew, with three smaller depots built near the Horwich terminus, on St Helens Road, and at Tonge Moor.

In 1921 EE supplied top-covered cars 113–120, followed by ten more, Nos 121–130, in 1923. That year also saw the Corporation commence serious motor-bus operations (having experimented with them before the war) and over the next quarter of a century the bus fleet grew steadily to eventually displace the trams. That was far in the future though, and in 1924 eight second-hand Brush top-covered cars (Nos 131–138) were bought from SUNDERLAND CORPORATION. In 1927 enclosed cars 139–150 were purchased new from EE, followed by similar cars 104–106 a year later (which took the running numbers of the tramway's only single-deckers).

No further new cars were purchased, though twelve more second-hand ones were bought. The first eight, top-covered cars Nos 33–40, were acquired in 1933 from the SOUTH LANCASHIRE TRAMWAYS (where they had been numbered 44, 45, 47, 48, 50, 54, 55 and 58) whilst the last four were enclosed cars 331 and 451–453 bought from BURY CORPORATION (Bury 21, 55, 56 and 58) ten years later. (The high numbers resulted from the addition in 1940 of 300 to the existing car numbers.)

On 29 December 1923 the Corporation began a bus service over the route of the short branch to Darcy Lever, south-east of the town centre, and five years later the trams were withdrawn; further closures followed during the 1930s until the Second World War offered a brief respite. In 1945 only four routes remained: north-east to Tonge Moor, south-west to Westhoughton, north-west to Horwich and north to Halliwell. Of these, the Halliwell route went on 5 August that year, the Horwich route on 6 October 1946, the last portion of the Westhoughton route on 8 December 1946 and the Tonge Moor line the following year.

One car from the fleet survives: No.66, which has been in regular public service at BLACKPOOL since 1981, following its 1964 rescue from its new life as a static caravan and subsequent restoration by a group of enthusiasts.

Bradford City Tramways

Authority: Bradford Corporation Tramways Order 1880
Gauge: 4ft
Traction: Horse, steam, overhead electric
Opened: 1 February 1882
Closed: 6 May 1950
System: Radial network
Length: 63.52 miles
Stock: 6 sd, 10 dd horse; 44 locos, 39 dd steam*; 2 sd, 410 dd electric
Livery: Locos maroon, horse and steam cars nut-brown & cream; Prussian blue & white to 1937, ultramarine & white to 1942 then light blue & primrose electric
Last Car: No.104

In classic fashion Bradford's tramways progressed through the horse, steam and electric traction phases, beginning with a single horse-operated route running north-west from Rawson Square in the city centre along North Parade, Manningham Lane, Oak Lane, St Mary's Road and North Park Road to Lister Park Gates, worked by six Ashbury double-deckers (Nos 1–6). Although built and owned by Bradford Corporation, the line was leased to the Bradford Tramways Co. Ltd (later the Bradford Tramways & Omnibus Co. Ltd) for operating purposes.

In 1890 two single-deck cars (Nos 36 and 37) were built locally for the line and another two (Nos 29 and 40) were added in 1892 – possibly second-hand vehicles from SHIPLEY TRAMWAYS. In 1894 the Company constructed two roofed toastracks (Nos 16 and 17), which could not have proved very popular in this part of the country, and later that year four more Ashbury double-deckers, Nos 16–19, were bought (the toastracks being renumbered 46 and 47). It is thought that all the cars were mounted on Eades reversible trucks.

The horse line closed on 31 January 1902 in order for it to become part of the Corporation's electric system, but by then other routes had been opened – again worked by the Company, bringing the route mileage to 17 – using steam traction on account of the steep hills surrounding the city centre. The first, opened 8 August 1882, ran east along the Leeds Road to Stanningley and was followed by other radial lines to Tong Cemetery (south-east), Allerton via Four Lane Ends (west) and from Manningtree to Undercliffe as an extension of the horse line. One further steam route, south-west to Odsal and Shelf, was worked by the BRADFORD & SHELF TRAMWAY Co. Ltd.

The first steam locomotives were Nos 1–6 from Kitsons (1882), No.7 from Wilkinsons (1883) and No.8 from Kitsons again (1884); a replacement No.7 was bought in 1885, along with Nos 9–11, all from Greens. Green locos 12 (1887), 13–22 (1888) and 23–36 (1896) followed, with second-hand engines 37–40 being purchased from the North Staffordshire Tramways in the Potteries c.1896, and 41–43 from the Bradford & Shelf line in 1887 (B&S Nos 1, 2 and 4, No.3 being broken up for spares).

The steam passenger fleet was made up of ten former double-deck horse cars fitted with top covers and numbered 7–16, which were joined by Milnes purpose-built double-deckers 18 and 19 in 1885; the same firm supplied similar cars 20–35 over the next four years. In 1892 the Corporation rebuilt horse cars 16 and 17 as top-covered bogie steam trailer No.38, and 18 and 19 as similar vehicle No.41; the last additions were Nos 21, 49 and 50 bought from North Staffs in 1899 and Nos 51 and 52 bought new in 1901 – again all Milnes cars.

By the last years of the nineteenth century, the Corporation had decided to construct and operate an electric tramway system itself, and in 1898 it opened lines to Bolton Junction (30 July) and Great Horton (27 August). Further new routes and extensions were opened, and on 1 February 1902 Company services were terminated to make way for the electric cars. In 1904 the MID-YORKSHIRE TRAMWAYS in SHIPLEY was bought and incorporated into the northern part of the system, which was completed on 13 October 1914 when the last extension (Bingley to Crossflats) was opened north-west of the city. The short distance from here to KEIGHLEY was never bridged (despite pressure from that Corporation) and the only through-running agreement made with a neighbour – from 1907 to 1918 – was with LEEDS via Stanningley using ten cars fitted with ingenious sliding axles to negotiate the change of gauge involved.

The first route to close was the section between Undercliffe and Greengates on 11 November 1928, replaced by a motor bus service. A year later, on 29 November 1929, the Allerton trams went, replaced by trolleybuses (which the Corporation had been operating since 1911). After that the remaining routes were closed one by one throughout the 1930s and 1940s, the last to go being the former B&S line from the centre to Odsal and Horsfall playing fields.

The system's first electric tramcars were open-top double-deck powered cars 1–24 and similar configuration trailers 25–28, all 1898–99 vehicles from Brush. The trailers were motorised c.1900; between then and 1902 the same firm supplied Nos 29–128, a hundred more open-toppers. (Unless otherwise stated, all Bradford's electric cars were double-deckers.) These were joined in 1902–03 by a hundred similar cars (Nos 129–228) from Milnes, all of which were later top-covered, rebuilt and/or renumbered. Car No.229 was a short-lived 1903 bogie single-decker constructed from two ex-B&S trailers, whilst Nos 230–239 were HN open-toppers absorbed into the fleet after the Mid-Yorks takeover.

From 1912 onwards the Corporation began its own car construction programme, and between then and 1931 built a total of 140 top-covered cars, the only ones purchased from outside manufacturers being UEC Nos 247–258 of 1920 and 213–232 of 1921, again all top-covered vehicles. (Bradford's cars were numbered and later renumbered in an erratic manner up to 258 with numbers of withdrawn vehicles being allocated to new cars as and when they became vacant.) The Corporation built one other single-decker at its main Thornbury Works: No.1 of 1926, an experimental bogie car with coupled wheels. Put into service in 1927, it proved too long (at nearly 40ft) and too fast for the tracks, and in 1930 it was sold to become a holiday home at Filey.

Apart from the Mid-Yorks vehicles, no second-hand cars were bought – presumably because of the value placed on the Corporation's own construction policy – and only ten of its own trams were ever disposed of to another operator. Significantly, these were not Bradford-built vehicles, being UEC Nos 237, 242, 243, 251 and 257 of 1920 and 214–217 and 219 of 1921, which were all sold in 1942 to SHEFFIELD CORPORATION. Later converted to works car 330 there, No.251 is preserved at the National Tramway Museum, Crich, whilst Last Car No.104 of 1925 vintage, which until 1953 served as a scoreboard at Odsal Stadium, is now on show fully restored in the BRADFORD INDUSTRIAL MUSEUM along with operational horse car No.40 of 1892.

One other aspect of the Bradford system deserves mention. From 1916 until the end of the First World War, a specially laid tramway, comparable to the Mousehold Light Railway in Norwich (see Volume 1), was in operation linking Thornbury Works (turned over to munitions production), the nearby Phoenix Works, where aircraft parts were made, and the railway exchange sidings in Laisterdyke goods yard. In all, just over a mile of 4ft gauge track was put down with materials and products being moved around the Phoenix Tramway (as it was known) using a combination of goods wagons, Corporation-built electric locos (on tramcar trucks) and cut-down passenger cars.

Bradford Industrial Museum

As mentioned above, Bradford Industrial Museum (opened 1974 in the former Moorside Mills buildings) is home to BRADFORD electric car 104 of 1925 and horse car 40 of 1892, the latter vehicle being operated occasionally on a short stretch of track in the museum grounds.

Bradford: Transperience

This museum, also known as the West Yorkshire Transport Discovery Centre, was opened on 1 July 1995 by the West Yorkshire Metropolitan Council on the site of the former Low Moor locomotive depot. On 21 September that year, a ½-mile standard-gauge overhead-electric tramway was opened on the site with rides given by Budapest single-deckers 2576 and 2577. The whole project cost some £11.5 million, but visitor numbers were lower than expected and the museum closed at the end of the 1997 summer season.

Bradford & Shelf Tramway

Authority: Bradford Corporation Tramways Order 1880
Gauge: 4ft
Traction: Steam
Opened: 8 September 1884
Taken over: 2 September 1903
System: Branching
Length: 7.54 miles
Stock: 21 locos, 7 sd, 12 dd
Livery: Prussian blue & cream to 1892, then chocolate & cream

Although the rest of the Bradford system was operated originally by the Bradford Tramways Co. Ltd (see above), one line was not. Instead, it was run by the Bradford & Shelf Tramway Co. Ltd on behalf of the Corporation. The first portion opened ran south from the Town Hall down Manchester Road to Bankfoot, where the depot was situated in Rathwell Road.

On 11 June 1886 this single-track line was extended further south, under the Bradford and Shelf Tramway Order 1885, through Odsal to Wyke, with a branch south-west from Odsal to Shelf, via the Halifax Road, to complete the tramway. Steam traction was employed from the outset, beginning with Green locomotives 1–5, hauling similarly numbered Starbuck bogie double-deck trailers. In 1885 loco No.5 met with an accident and was replaced by another No.5, a second-hand purchase ex-North Staffordshire Tramways in the Potteries. This was joined that year by No.6, a Burrell loco, and between then and 1887 by Nos 7–9, three more from Greens, following which Nos 1–4 were sold to the Bradford Tramways Co. Ltd. Between 1887 and 1894 Greens supplied another eleven locos numbered 10–14 and 1–6, the latter batch replacing withdrawn engines.

In 1885–86 the car fleet grew with the purchase of Starbuck bogie double-decker No.6, locally-built single-deck trailers 7–11, Ashbury bogie double-decker 12 and single-deckers 13 and 14 (again constructed locally). Evidently, the single-deck cars did not prove satisfactory, for in 1887 six of them were converted into three bogie double-deckers numbered 8, 9 and 13 (renumbered 10 in 1891), whilst another bogie double-decker, No.7, was bought from Ashbury. The last additions to the car fleet were Nos 7, 11, 13 and 14 from Milnes in 1893–94, all double-deck bogie vehicles.

The first cutback to the system came in 1902 when, on 31 January, steam services ceased between the Town Hall and Bankfoot, replaced the next day by the Corporation's new electric trams (the Corporation having paid £12,000 the same day to buy out the Company's lease). On 29 May 1903 the electric cars began running through to Buttershaw on the Halifax Road, and on 1 September the rump steam service stopped altogether, replaced the following day by electric workings.

British Electric Traction Co. Ltd

The BET was by far and away the biggest of the private owners of tramways in the British Isles. It was formed in 1895 by Emile Garcke and set about, at that timely juncture in tramway history, buying up existing horse and steam lines with a view to extending and electrifying them (usually successfully), thereby creating a number of linked networks in the process (notably in the London area and in the Black Country). The Company also had extensive business interests other than tramways, particularly electricity supply and, later, bus operation.

In the tramway field the Company controlled, at one time or another, the Metropolitan Electric and South Metropolitan systems in and around London as well as the BARNSLEY, BARROW-IN-FURNESS, Birmingham, Birmingham & Midland, Devonport & District, Dudley & Stourbridge, GATESHEAD, Gravesend, HARTLEPOOLS, JARROW, Kidderminster & Stourport, Leamington & Warwick, MIDDLETON, OLDHAM, ASHTON & HYDE, Peterborough, Poole, Potteries, Sheerness, South Staffordshire, SOUTHPORT, Taunton, TYNEMOUTH, Weston-Super-Mare, Wolverhampton District, Worcester and YORKSHIRE (WOOLLEN DISTRICT) electric tramways elsewhere in England, plus those of Merthyr Tydfil, Swansea, Swansea & Mumbles and Wrexham in Wales, AIRDRIE, GREENOCK & PORT GLASGOW and ROTHESAY in Scotland, and Cavehill & Whitewell in Ireland.

Lines at one time controlled but never electrified by the Company were those of Brighton & Shoreham, Cambridge, ROSSENDALE VALLEY, SOUTH SHIELDS and Yarmouth.

British Thomson-Houston Co. Ltd

The BTH, as well as being a major supplier of tramway equipment and the parent company of the British Tramways & General Construction Co. Ltd, owned or controlled the electric tramways systems at Chatham and the Isle of Thanet in England, PAISLEY and LANARKSHIRE in Scotland, and Cork in Ireland.

Burnley & District Tramways

Authority: Burnley and District Tramways Order 1879
Gauge: 4ft 8½in.
Traction: Steam/horse/steam
Opened: 17 September 1881
Closed: 17 November 1901
System: Single line
Length: 7.15 miles
Stock: 17 locos, 18 dd steam & horse
Livery: ?
Last Car: ?

Burnley Corporation No.41 of 1903, one of the single-deckers employed on the Towneley service. *(Author's Collection)*

Owned and operated by the Burnley & District Tramways Co. Ltd, this otherwise unremarkable steam tramway was later taken over by no less than five local authorities – surely some sort of record. It was built to link Burnley with tramway systems to its west and north and ran from Padiham, 3 miles west of Burnley, along the Padiham Road to the town centre, where it swung north past the depot and out along the Colne Road and Manchester Road through Reedley and Brierfield to Nelson, where it terminated at Nelson Centre.

Services began with Kitson tram locomotives Nos 1–5 and Starbuck top-covered trailers 1–7; these were joined in 1883 by Falcon locos 6–9, the first in a series of replacements for the Kitsons, which had begun to be withdrawn from 1 May 1882 as unsatisfactory. Until the new engines arrived in the March of the following year, horses were used as motive power, hauling the steam trailers (which had had their top covers removed, presumably to lessen their weight). More Falcons came later: No.10 in 1884, Nos 11–13 in 1885, No.14 in 1889, No.15 in 1896 and Nos 16 and 17 another year later. Further trailers were also added, all open-top bogie double-deckers: Starbuck cars Nos 8–10 in 1884 and 3, 6, 11 and 12 in 1885, Falcon No.13 in 1888, Nos 14 and 15 in 1897 and, finally, Metropolitan No.16 in 1900 ex-ST HELENS.

On 1 March 1900 the line was purchased jointly by Burnley and Nelson corporations, Padiham and Brierfield UDCs and Reedley Parish Council (which, with 0.4 miles of track, was the only tramway-owning parish council in Great Britain). The purchase was the prelude to electrification and extension with the BURNLEY CORPORATION system opening just a month after the tramway's closure. (See below.)

Burnley Corporation Tramways

Authority: Burnley Corporation Tramways (etc.) Act 1898
Gauge: 4ft
Traction: Overhead electric
Opened: 16 December 1901
Closed: 7 May 1935
System: Radial
Length: 13.05 miles
Stock: 19 sd, 53 dd
Livery: Chocolate & cream
Last Car: No.63

Burnley's municipal tramway system eventually comprised four principal routes running north, east, south and west from the town centre (Burnley Centre), with all but the southern route having branches off them. Following the 1901 closure of the BURNLEY & DISTRICT TRAMWAYS (see above) the line from Padiham east to Burnley, then north to Nelson Centre, was reopened for electric working four weeks later. The track either side of the town in Padiham, Reedley Hallows, Brierfield and Nelson was leased by Burnley Corporation (it paid £53,000 for its own portion of the B&D).

The first services were worked by Milnes open-toppers 1–24, built 1901–02, and based on the reconstructed B&D depot in Queen's Gate. These were joined in 1903 by similar cars 25–38 and ERTCW bogie single-deckers 39–46, bought to work the three new routes opened that year: south-west to Rose Grove via the Accrington Road leaving the Padiham line in Westgate; south down the Manchester Road to Summit; and east along Brunshaw Road then south down Todmorden Road to Towneley.

In 1910 another branch was opened, north-east off the Colne Road up Briercliffe Road to Burnley Lane Head (extended two years later to Harle Syke). By then the car fleet had grown with the addition of UEC single-decker 47 (of 1907), HN bogie balcony cars 48–52 (1909) and UEC bogie single-deckers 53 and 54 (1910), followed by similar cars 55–57 in 1911 and UEC bogie balcony cars 58–67 two years later. The last purchases were Nos 68–72, EE single-deckers of 1921 (by which time all the open cars had been top-covered). The system was completed in 1927 by the construction of a short branch east off the Towneley line, continuing along the Brunshaw Road, past the Turf Moor football ground, to Brunshaw (and worked, like the Summit and Towneley routes, by single-deck cars). The previous year, car 68 was renumbered 73 when No.10 was rebuilt and renumbered 68 after a crash at Lane Head. (The same car had been involved in an identical accident in 1925!) Another victim was car No.9, which crashed in 1933 and had to be withdrawn.

Bury Corporation No.20 of 1902, shortly before receiving its top cover, having its trolley pole reversed at the Radcliffe terminus. (Author's Collection)

The first tramway abandonment came in 1932 when the Rose Grove–Harle Syke service was replaced by buses, thus leading to the closure of two of the branches. On 1 April 1933, following the setting-up of the Burnley, Colne & Nelson Joint Transport Committee, Burnley cars began working right through to Nelson and Higherford (their fleet numbers suffixed with a B). Remaining routes closed in 1934 (except for the original Padiham–Nelson line, which lasted another year), after which the surviving cars – all double-deckers – were scrapped.

Bury Corporation Tramways

Authority: Bury Corporation Act 1899
Gauge: 4ft 8½in.
Traction: Overhead electric*
Opened: 3 June 1903
Closed: 13 February 1949
System: Radial network
Length: 13.67 miles
Stock: 60 dd*
Livery: Red & cream
Last Car: No.13

By the 1890s Bury Corporation was eager to take over those lines of the steam-worked MANCHESTER, BURY, ROCHDALE & OLDHAM tramways within its boundaries and use them as the basis of an electric system. In 1899 it obtained parliamentary authority to construct its own tramways, and in March 1903 work started on converting the MBRO lines with the first routes to Farfield opening three months later. This was followed on 19 April 1904 by the line to Heap Bridge and on 20 May by the Walmersley Road line. (Steam services continued to be operated by the steam tramway company on behalf of the Corporation until the changeover.)

The first electric cars, Nos 1–14, were Milnes open-top bogie vehicles (enclosed 1925–26) housed in a new depot on Rochdale Road. They were joined in 1903 by Milnes open-toppers 15–28, in 1904 by balcony cars 29–34 from BEC and the following year by a similar vehicle, No.35, from the local joinery firm of Wilson & Stockall (incorporating Westinghouse electrical gear). In 1906 Brush supplied balcony cars 36–41 and between 1907 and 1913 UEC supplied similar cars 42–54. The last additions to the fleet were Nos 55–60, fully enclosed EE vehicles of 1925 construction.

Other new routes followed. On 20 May 1907 through services began to BOLTON over a south-western route via Breightmet, this being part of the western portion of Bury's system operated on behalf of Radcliffe UDC. Through-running arrangements were also made with ROCHDALE via HEYWOOD to the east, SALFORD and MANCHESTER to the south (commencing 4 January 1926) and, south from Heywood, to MIDDLETON (19 May 1928).

The system's decline began in the early 1930s when, on 3 July 1932, the through service to Rochdale ceased; on 18 February 1933 the service to Middleton was likewise abandoned, as were the services to Salford and Manchester on 15 October and Bolton on 22 January 1934. By the outbreak of the Second World War only the northern lines to Tottington and Walmersley – both former steam routes – were left; though in 1939 a wartime service down the Manchester Road to Gigg Lane (another former steam route) was re-introduced. This lasted until 6 July 1946, with the Tottington service going on 15 February 1948 and the Walmersley one a year later, after which all surviving cars were scrapped. Nos 21, 55, 56 and 58 had, however, escaped that fate by being sold to Bolton in 1943, with No.30 going to SUNDERLAND CORPORATION four years later.

City of Carlisle Electric Tramways

Authority: Carlisle Tramways Order 1898
Gauge: 3ft 6in.
Traction: Overhead electric
Opened: 30 June 1900
Closed: 21 November 1931
System: Radial
Length: 5.73 miles
Stock: 7 sd, 23 dd*
Livery: Chocolate & cream to 1912, then dark green & cream
Last Car: No.8

Although a low-mileage system, the Carlisle tramways somehow managed to cover the city more than adequately with no less than six lines radiating out from the LNWR's Carlisle Citadel station. All opened together, they ran north to Stanwix, east along the Warwick Road, south along the London Road, south along Blackwell Road to Boundary Road, south along Denton Street to Denton Holme, and west along Newton Road to the district of that name. Despite this extensive coverage – or perhaps because of it as most of its branches were well under a mile in length – the tramway was not a financial success and in 1910 the owner, the City of Carlisle Electric Tramways Co. Ltd, agreed to sell out to BB. The new owner took control in November 1911 and promptly set about renewing the already failing track and overhead and, in the following year, replaced the entire fleet of fifteen ERTCW cars (single-deckers 1–3 and open-top double-deckers 4–15, all of 1900) with twelve new UEC vehicles (double-deckers 1–8 and single-deckers 9–12). The rebuilt system was inaugurated on 9 December 1912, over £18,000 having been spent on the improvements.

After the First World War the refusal of the Company to extend the old routes or to lay new ones meant that, as the city expanded, so motor bus services from the suburbs effectively stole the tramway's trade – a theft the Company seemingly tolerated as owner of a bus company in its own right (Percival's Motor Bus Service). In fact, in 1926 the Company changed its name to the Carlisle & District Transport Co. Ltd to reflect its wider interests.

Also taking an interest in the existing public transport situation was the City Council who, in 1931, purchased the Company's tram and bus undertakings, plus a number of other bus companies, in order to provide a modern, unified service for the city and surrounding districts. The trams did not figure in the Council's grand scheme of things and, in November that year, they made their last journeys. Some mystery surrounds the final composition of the car fleet: it is thought that after the First World War three open-toppers were obtained second-hand from Ilkeston (another BB operation), of which one, given the number 13, was an ERTCW vehicle. The other two cars had just their trucks reused, under new EE bodies, as Nos 5 (rebuilt 1925) and 14 (1923).

Castleford *see* Yorkshire (West Riding) Electric Tramways

Chester Tramways

Authority: Chester Tramways Act 1878
Gauge: 4ft 8½in.
Traction: Horse, compressed air
Opened: 10 June 1879
Closed: 27 December 1902
System: Single line
Length: 2.38 miles
Stock: 19 dd?
Livery: Crimson lake & cream
Last Car: ?

The purpose of this single-track line was firstly to link Chester General station (used by the GWR and the LNWR) with the city centre, about ½ mile away, via City Road and Foregate Street and, secondly, to traverse the centre via Eastgate Street and Grosvenor Street, then cross the River Dee on Grosvenor Bridge to serve the district of Saltney by way of Hough Green and Chester Street, terminating close to the Welsh border. The operator was the Chester Tramways Co. and the first Manager was T. Lloyd, who was Manager of the horse-worked LIVERPOOL TRAMWAYS and had the initial idea for the Chester line. The depot and stables were opposite the station.

The tramway's original car fleet was made up of eight Eades patent reversible double-deckers, presumably numbered 1–8 and possibly built by Milnes; after that, however, the rolling-stock history becomes somewhat unclear. It seems that these cars did not prove satisfactory – possibly the extra weight of the turntable mechanism upon which the body could swivel made them too heavy for even two horses – and they were soon replaced by eight conventional one-horse double-deckers (also Nos 1–8?) constructed by a local coachbuilder. Two Starbuck cars were bought 1885–86 – again open-top double-deckers – joined later by one built by the Company.

In 1886 car No.9 (one of the Starbuck cars?) was made the subject of a curious experiment conducted by the local engineering firm of Hughes & Lancaster; it was fitted with a four-cylinder compressed-air engine fed by under-floor wrought-iron reservoir cylinders. Proudly emblazoned 'HUGHES & LANCASTER'S PATENT LOW PRESSURE COMPRESSED AIR TRAMCAR', it was found to suffer from severe leakage problems, to overcome which an ingenious system was devised: at certain places along the route the driver operated an automatic coupling device to engage an air-feed mechanism from a cast-iron supply pipe laid beside the track. When the car was restarted the coupling disengaged and the feed to the reservoirs closed. It is not certain whether the whole of the line was so equipped, or merely the Saltney–Grosvenor Bridge section; certainly by early 1890 the car had been cut down to a single-decker and, astonishingly, survived in this state until 1961, having spent most of its life as a cricket pavilion near Wrexham.

Carlisle Market Place with passengers boarding No.8 of 1900, bound for Newtown. This system was Cumberland's only passenger tramway. *(Author's Collection)*

By the end of the century Chester Corporation was ready to purchase the line, extend and electrify it and, in 1901, obtained the necessary Act of Parliament to allow it to do so (see below). On 1 January 1902 the tramway came under Corporation control, having been bought for £19,866; on 10 November that year reconstruction work began at the station end, on 27 December the remaining services ceased and on New Year's Day 1903 what was left was sold.

Chester Corporation Tramways

Authority: Chester Corporation Act 1901
Gauge: 3ft 6in.
Traction: Overhead electric
Opened: 6 April 1903
Closed: 15 February 1930
System: Branching
Length: 3.58 miles
Stock: 1 sd, 17 dd
Livery: Apple green & ivory
Last Car: No.10

Following the closure of the Chester horse line (see above) the reconstruction work went speedily ahead, and by the end of March 1903 twelve Milnes open-top double-deckers (Nos 1–12) had arrived in the rebuilt horse tram depot. The route of the old line was faithfully adhered to, with the addition of a 77yd-extension at Saltney, which brought the tramway to an abrupt halt in front of a low railway bridge, effectively blocking any hopes of running double-deckers into Wales. The new line was double-tracked throughout (except for a short stretch in Eastgate), this being made possible by the narrower gauge used.

In 1906 work began on an extension on the eastern side of the city to serve the district of Broughton. Branching off the existing line at the bottom of City Road (where a full double-track triangular junction was laid), a double-track line ran eastwards along Broughton Road for just over ½ mile to the Fountain Inn; here it divided into two single-track routes to the city boundary, along Tarvin Road and Chrisleton Road respectively, each again roughly ½ mile in length. (An authorised line to link the two termini was never built.) Both routes opened on 22 November 1906, with normal workings operated by cars from St Werburgh Street in the city centre only.

To help cope with the extra traffic generated by the new routes, a one-man-operated demi-car (No.13) was bought from Bush in 1906 and five open-top double-deckers (Nos 14–18) from UEC the following year. No.13 was not an operational success – it needed a two-man crew to run to time – and was relegated to odds and ends duties, such as helping out when the Chester Races were on and being used as a snowplough.

Above left: Chester Corporation No.3 of 1903 in Eastgate Street, about to pass under the Eastgate on its way out of the city centre. *(Author's Collection)*

Above right: Chester Corporation No.2, sister car to No.3, at the Saltney terminus in Chester Street, close to the Welsh border. *(Author's Collection)*

No further extensions to the system, or additions to the car fleet, were made thereafter and the tramway settled down to a quiet life; during the 1920s the system was allowed to gradually wear itself out as it appeared increasingly likely that the future belonged to the motor bus. In 1929 the Chester Corporation Act empowered the city to run its own buses and abandon the tramways, which it did the following year.

Colne & Trawden Light Railways

Authority: Colne and Trawden Light Railways Order 1901
Gauge: 4ft
Traction: Overhead electric
Opened: 28 November 1903
Closed: 6 January 1934
System: Branching
Length: 5.23 miles
Stock: 18 dd
Livery: Light green & cream pre-1914, royal blue & white to 1923, then maroon & cream
Last Car: ?

Following the successful promotion of electric tramway services in neighbouring NELSON and BURNLEY, moves to do likewise in the north-east Lancashire town of Colne resulted in the granting of an LRO in 1901 for a line linking the town with Nelson to the south-west and the borough of Trawden to the south-east. The gauge chosen was 4ft, in keeping with the systems of Nelson, Burnley, BLACKBURN and ACCRINGTON close by. The operator was the Colne & Trawden Light Railways Co.

The first section opened ran south-westwards from the Heifer Lane Depot down Keighley Road and Market Street, through the centre of Colne and out along Albert Road as far as the junction with Queen Street (about 1¼ miles); the section from here along Burnley Road to the Nelson boundary opened two days later, effectively doubling the length of the mainly single-track line. The 1½ miles of single-track route from the depot down Skipton Road to the Park Hotel in Trawden opened on 22 January 1904 and included a reserved section to bypass a steeper stretch of the roadway. Initial services were worked by cars 1–6, small Milnes open-toppers running from end to end of the tramway.

On an unknown date in December 1904, a 1¼-mile branch from Heifer Lane north-eastwards along Keighley Road to the village of Laneshaw Bridge was opened (again single-track), and in April 1905 three small Brush open-toppers (Nos 7–9) were introduced to the growing system. The last length of line opened, in December 1905, was an extension of the Trawden route further on through the village to Lane House Lane. Just over 3 furlongs in length, this was also single-track (with another reserved section to avoid a steep hill).

With the system now complete, three further Milnes open-toppers (Nos 10–12) were bought in 1906, and five years later through-running to Nelson commenced (though special excursions had been run from Burnley since 1904 using that system's single-deck cars, together with Nos 1–6 fitted with low 'turtle-back' top covers on account of the low MR bridge over the line in Colne). By now, though, the Company was looking to sell the tramway and, after first approaching Nelson Corporation, sold it to Colne Corporation for £92,830 from 25 March 1914. The new owner promptly bought a UEC balcony car (No.13) and set about rebuilding some of the older cars in an attempt to smarten up the run-down fleet (aided by a new livery). The purchase of further new cars was delayed by the onset of the First World War (though three of the open-toppers were fitted with top covers in 1915), but in 1921 two EE balcony cars were purchased and numbered 2 and 3, the equivalent original cars being withdrawn. From 1919 a new, larger depot in Standroyd Road (across the Trawden route from Heifer Lane Depot) was in use, the old one becoming the home of the Corporation's growing bus fleet.

In 1924–25 cars 6 and 11 (and possibly a third vehicle) were converted to one-man-operated, single-deck vehicles as an economic measure, though three new enclosed double-deckers (Nos 14–16) were bought from Brush in 1926. By now though the growing bus competition and the declining state of the track were irresistible forces, and on 19 October 1926 the Laneshaw Bridge branch closed, followed on 3 June 1928 by the Colne–Trawden section of the main line. From 1 April 1933 the tramway was controlled by the Burnley, Colne & Nelson Joint Transport Committee (see BURNLEY CORPORATION TRAMWAYS) and the car numbers given the suffix C, only for it to be closed – along with the Nelson line – less than a year later.

Darlington Street Railroad

Authority: Local authority permission
Gauge: 4ft 8½in.?
Traction: Horse
Opened: 1 January 1862
Closed: 8 January 1865
System: Branching
Length: c.1 mile
Stock: 2 sd
Livery: ?
Last Car: ?

The first tramway in Darlington was operated by the Darlington Street Railroad Co. Ltd in the wake of G.F. Train's pioneering street railway experiments at BIRKENHEAD and elsewhere, the authority for it being obtained from the local Board of Health. The single-track line was constructed by the contractor Charles Hathaway and ran northwards from the Shambles by the Market Place, along Northgate and North Road to Durham Road, where it terminated at Whessoe Street. A short branch off North Road served the Stockton & Darlington Railway's station (later the NER's North Road station). The two cars used on the tramway were named, in Train's fashion, *Nelson* and *Wellington*.

The line was not a success, largely because of the opposition from other road users raised by its use of Train's step rails, and it was closed suddenly in 1865 by the local authority – according to one account, because of the amount of compensation paid out when one of the cars ran over a valuable greyhound.

Darlington: Stockton & Darlington Steam Tramways

Authority: Darlington Tramways Order 1880
Gauge: 3ft
Traction: Horse
Opened: 10 October 1880
Closed: 18 August 1903
System: Single line
Length: 2.13 miles
Stock: 12 sd & dd
Livery: Chocolate & ivory/white/cream
Last Car: ?

Despite its title, the Stockton & Darlington Steam Tramways Co.'s only steam tramway was in STOCKTON, the Darlington line always being horse-worked. Its single track ran across the town from the NER's Darlington Bank Top station in the south-east, via Victoria Road and Feethams, to the Market Place and, from there, north-west via Bondgate and Woodland Road to Cockerton, terminating at Carmel Road on the borough boundary. The depot was in Woodland Road and the line was worked as two routes from the Market Place with seven cars in service at any one time.

The Bank Top station half of the tramway was closed as unprofitable in 1885, and eleven years later (following the Company's financial collapse in 1893 when control passed to the Stockton & District Tramways Co.) the remainder was acquired by IMPERIAL TRAMWAYS, who wished to electrify it – but then decided otherwise. Accordingly, on 24 January 1902 it was sold for £7,600 to Darlington Corporation, who leased it to a Mr C.J. O'Dowd until it was ready to convert the line to electric working as a municipally owned operation. The tramway was then closed to allow reconstruction to take place (see below), O'Dowd becoming the new Traffic Superintendent.

Darlington Corporation Light Railways

Authority: Darlington Corporation Light Railways Order 1902
Gauge: 3ft 6in.
Traction: Overhead electric
Opened: 1 June 1904
Closed: 10 April 1926*
System: Radial
Length: 4.87 miles
Stock: 16 sd, 8 dd
Livery: Dark blue & ivory/white/cream
Last Car: ?

Darlington Corporation had built its own power station in 1900 and, when it acquired the town's horse tramway two years later (see above), sought the necessary powers to extend and electrify the line. As laid by J.G. White & Co. Ltd, the new system comprised four mainly double-track routes radiating from the Market Place: north-west to Forcett Street, Cockerton (an extension of the horse line), north up North Road and Durham Road to Harrowgate Hill (an extension of the original 1862 line), north-east along Freemans Place, past the depot, then along Haughton Road to Barton Street, and finally east along Parkgate past Bank Top station to Cobden Street in Eastbourne. (The first route opened was the Harrowgate Hill line, which was followed the next day by that to Cockerton, then shortly after by the other two.)

Services were worked initially by single-deck combination cars 1–16 from Milnes; these were joined in 1913 by Nos 17 and 18, UEC top-covered cars. The only others added, Nos 19–24, were open-top Brush cars bought from the Sheerness & District Tramways in 1918 (plus a further two for their spare parts). By the end of the First World War though the ageing track was not so easily replaced and it was decided to switch over to trolleybuses. The Haughton Road route was converted on 16 January 1926, and the line to Cockerton on 20 February, with the last day of tramcar operation over the Eastbourne–Harrowgate Hill through route officially being 10 April 1926 (although the cars remained in use at peak periods for a while longer). After withdrawal, Nos 17 and 18 were sold to Dover Corporation and the other survivors scrapped.

Above left: Photographic postcard of the opening of the Darlington Corporation Light Railways, on 1 June 1904, with the town's Mayoress Mrs A. Henderson at the controls of a Milnes single-decker. *(Author's Collection)*

Above right: Car No.10, another of Darlington's original Milnes single-deckers, at Cockerton, the system's western terminus. *(Author's Collection)*

Darwen Corporation Tramways

Authority: Blackburn and Over Darwen Tramways Act 1879
Gauge: 4ft
Traction: Steam/overhead electric
Took over: 1 January 1899
Closed: 5 October 1946
System: Branching
Length: 4.36 miles
Stock: 3 locos, 3 dd steam; 3 sd, 22 dd electric
Livery: Vermillion & purple lake, later vermillion & cream
Last Car: No.3

Following its purchase of the section of the BLACKBURN & OVER DARWEN TRAMWAY within its boundaries from the start of 1899, Darwen Corporation ran it as a steam line until the electrification work was completed, reopening it as a mainly double-track line on 17 October 1900 – the day after the last steam trams ran – with ten Milnes open-top double-deck cars. A year later, on 11 October 1901, a single-track branch of 1¼ miles eastwards across the moors to Hoddlesden was opened and the car fleet expanded by the purchase of Nos 11–14, again Milnes open-toppers. (Several of these early cars were later given top covers and/or rebuilt.)

Although a small system compared with many of the others in south Lancashire, it formed part of an extensive 4ft gauge network through its connection with BLACKBURN to the north and the car fleet was kept up to date with a series of replacement vehicle purchases. These were MV single-deck demi-cars 15–17 of 1905–06 (No.15 was later converted into a works car and No.17 rebuilt as double-deck No.10), UEC open-toppers 18 and 19 of 1915, and Nos 20–22, EE open-toppers of 1921 construction.

In 1933 the Corporation bought two ex-RAWTENSTALL double-deckers, numbering them 9 (fully enclosed) and 11 (a balcony car) and, three years later, purchased new EE streamlined double-deckers 23 and 24, which were slimmed-down versions of that company's BLACKPOOL 'Balloon' cars.

On 13 October 1937 the Hoddlesden branch closed, but the main Whitehall–Blackburn route survived intact for nearly three years, until 31 March 1940, when the southern-most mile, from Whitehall to Circus, was abandoned. In 1945 the two streamliners were withdrawn, leaving only Nos 3, 7 and 10 to work the final year's services. Nos 23 and 24 were then sold to the Llandudno & Colwyn Bay Electric Railway in Wales and the other cars scrapped.

Dearne District Light Railways

Authority: Dearne District Light Railways Order 1915
Gauge: 4ft 8½in.
Traction: Overhead electric
Opened: 14 July 1924
Closed: 30 September 1933
System: Branching
Length: 14.18 miles
Stock: 30 sd
Livery: Bright red & cream
Last Car: ?

This single-track tramway was a latecomer to the British scene and filled the wide gap in the south Yorkshire network between BARNSLEY to the north-west, and MEXBOROUGH & SWINTON to the south. It was, in fact, the last system to be opened in the British Isles until that at Seaton in Devon (which is hardly comparable) in the 1970s and the MANCHESTER METRO in the 1990s (which is). But for the intervention of the First World War, the tramway would have been constructed earlier, for several years of negotiations between the various local authorities affected (the Wath-upon-Dearne, Wombwell, Bolton-upon-Dearne and Thurnscoe UDCs) had resulted in the 1915 LRO authorising the project.

Construction did not begin until 1923, with the whole system opening the following year. As built, the tramway was unusual in that it was laid with sleepered track throughout, ballasted on the roadside sections and paved in the streets, the theory being that such track would be easier to repair or re-align than more conventional constructions as and when the mining subsidence prevalent in the area necessitated it.

The main route ran from the Alhambra Theatre by the Market Place in Barnsley (though, because of mutual antagonism, no physical connection was ever made with that town's neighbouring track) and ran out south-eastwards along the Barnsley Road through Stairfoot and Wombwell, past the depot (known officially by the American term 'Car Barns') and on through West Melton to Wath-upon-Dearne. Here a branch of 1½ miles, opened in September 1924, led south to the Woodman Inn at Swinton on the M&S system, whilst a second branch, of some 5 miles, led north through Bolton-upon-Dearne to Thurnscoe. The main route continued eastwards from Wath for another mile to Manvers Main Colliery, where it met the M&S trolleybus feeder.

Because of a low railway bridge at Wath, the tramway was restricted to the use of single-deck cars. Thirty of these (Nos 1–30) were constructed for the line by EE between 1923 and 1924 and, following the tramway's closure after just nine years in favour of Yorkshire Traction Co. Ltd buses, five were sold to FALKIRK, four to LYTHAM ST ANNES and the trucks and other parts of the remainder to HULL.

Dewsbury, Batley & Birstal Tramways
Authority: Dewsbury, Batley and Birstal Tramways Order 1873
Gauge: 4ft 8½in.
Traction: Horse, steam
Opened: 25 July 1874
Closed: 26 September 1905?
System: Single line
Length: 4.29 miles
Stock: 11 locos, 18 dd horse & steam
Livery: Locos dark brown/black, later chrome yellow & brown; cars chrome yellow & cream
Last Car: Trailer No.6 (loco unknown)

The DBB was not only one of the first horse tramways to be built after the 1870 Tramways Act, it was one of the very first to make the switch to steam traction. It was promoted by the Dewsbury, Batley & Birstal Tramways Co. (using the archaic spelling of Birstall) to serve those places in the Heavy Woollen District of the West Riding of Yorkshire.

The section from Dewsbury to Batley (1½ miles) was the first opened, then the next mile to Carlington (where the depot was sited) on 25 March 1875, and the final section to Birstall on 23 June that year, the whole line being a single track laid along the highway. In 1879 powers were obtained for a 1-mile extension from Birstall to Moor Lane at Gomersal and this opened in the autumn of 1881 (exact date unknown). Original stock comprised five Starbuck open-top double-deckers, but as these did not arrive until September 1874 services were worked by two large open-top cars borrowed from LEEDS (and purchased two years later as Nos 6 and 7).

In 1876 trials were undertaken on the line with Merryweather and Kitson prototype steam tramway engines and the Company directors were sufficiently impressed to request the BoT to sanction the regular use of this form of traction. (At the time, only the roadside Wantage Tramway in Berkshire, under rather different conditions, was using it.) Steam services began on 10 April 1880, making the line the first street tramway in England to introduce them. Horse working ceased the following year, by which time the line was operating nine locomotives, all from Merryweathers: Nos 1 of 1879, 2–5 of 1880 and 6–9 of 1881; later additions were locos 10 and 11 in 1898, again from Merryweathers. The passenger fleet had been enlarged by 1880 through the addition of six more cars, similar to Nos 6 and 7, for use as trailers, these being numbered 1, 2, 4 and 8–10 (some were later top-covered); the original car No.5 was replaced by a slightly larger open-topper.

The last stock arrivals were bogie top-covered trailers 11–13 c.1886 from Ashbury and similar car No.14 in 1898 from Brush.

In 1902 the Company was acquired by the BET and three years later the relevant local authorities exercised their right to purchase the tramway, leasing it back to the BET in order that it might be electrified. On the first day of 1906 the DBBT Co. went into voluntary liquidation, the refurbished line now the responsibility of a new BET subsidiary, the YORKSHIRE (WOOLLEN DISTRICT) TRAMWAYS Co. Ltd.

Dewsbury, Ossett & Soothill Nether Tramways

Authority: Dewsbury Corporation Tramway Order 1904; Ossett Corporation Tramway Order 1904; Soothill Nether Urban District Tramways Act 1904
Gauge: 4ft 8½in.
Traction: Overhead electric
Opened: 13 November 1908
Closed: 19 October 1933
System: Branching
Length: 3.14 miles
Stock: 12 dd
Livery: Dark red & off-white
Last Car: ?

The DOSNT was one of those grandly named systems whose length of track was in inverse proportion to that of its title; unsurprisingly, it was generally known as the Dewsbury & Ossett Tramways and provided a link between the YORKSHIRE (WEST RIDING) and YORKSHIRE (WOOLLEN DISTRICT) systems centred on Wakefield and Dewsbury respectively.

For such a small system, its promotion and eventual authorisation was complicated and protracted; after several earlier schemes at the beginning of the twentieth century had come to nothing, the three local authorities within whose territory the line would pass finally received the go-ahead, in 1904, to commence construction. This was carried out by the NEC, who then leased the line from the three authorities for operating purposes.

As built, the tramway ran from Ossett Market Place, where it had an end-on connection with the WAKEFIELD & DISTRICT LIGHT RAILWAY, past the depot in Church Street and then, in a roughly north-westerly direction, to Dewsbury Market Place, ½ mile before which a trailing junction into High Road brought in a ½-mile branch from Earlsheaton to the south. Both main line and branch were single-track and incorporated many stiff climbs. An official opening – attended by the usual massed ranks of dignitaries – took place on 12 November 1908, the day after the BoT inspection; public services began the following day.

One of the Deswbury, Ossett & Soothill Nether cars in close-up: Brush open-topper No.3 of 1908 (with a sister car behind) at the Wakefield Road terminus in Dewsbury – apparently on a festive occasion, judging by the displays of flags and other decorations. (Author's Collection)

The tramway's first eight cars were Brush open-top vehicles (later fitted with top covers); in 1911 these were joined by Nos 9 and 10, two more Brush cars, this time ex-MEXBOROUGH & SWINTON (another NEC concern). Both open-toppers, these two were also fitted with top covers at their new home. In 1928 sister cars 11 and 12 were acquired, which arrived with top covers already in place.

Although the line was physically connected to the W&D through-running, which was originally envisaged, was restricted to special occasions (e.g. for Wakefield Trinity *v.* Dewsbury rugby matches). By the late 1920s the NEC was considering replacing the trams with buses or trolleybuses, but the idea was overtaken by events when the BET bought out the Company and, for the last two years of the tramway's life, worked it through the Yorkshire (Woollen District) Electric Tramways Co. Ltd before replacing it with a bus service.

Doncaster Corporation Tramways
Authority: Doncaster Corporation Light Railways Order 1899
Gauge: 4ft 8½in.
Traction: Overhead electric
Opened: 2 June 1902
Closed: 8 June 1935
System: Radial
Length: 14.7 miles
Stock: 1 sd, 46 dd
Livery: Maroon & cream
Last Car: ?

Faced with the threat of a private concern setting up an electric tramway system in this important railway town, Doncaster Corporation decided in the 1890s to construct its own to accompany its municipal electric street lighting (inaugurated in 1899). After an inspection visit to the CITY OF HULL TRAMWAYS, it was decided to use centrally-grooved rails, Doncaster thus becoming the only other British electric tramway to do so.

The first two routes opened ran from Station Road in the town centre, south-west to Balby High Street via St Sepulchre Gate, with a roughly parallel branch off this along Hexthorpe Road to old Hexthorpe; these were followed on 30 June 1902 by a line south-east from the High Street via Hall Gate, South Parade and Bennetthorpe Road to the racecourse. On 1 August a short southern branch off St Sepulchre Gate was opened to Jarratt Street (and extended two months later to Childers Street, Hyde Park), and on 27 October a northern route was opened up Bentley Road to Bentley High Street. This latter line remained isolated from the rest of the system until the long North Bridge was opened in 1911 to carry the Great North Road over the GNR's main-line railway tracks, north of the town centre.

A 1-mile branch north-east from the Station Road/High Street one-way complex was opened in 1903 up Nether Hall Road to Avenue Road (15 January), with a short branch off this along Beckett Road (17 August) whilst, on 25 November, a very short branch was opened off St Sepulchre Gate south into Oxford Street, only to be abandoned two years later because of poor receipts.

The tramway's first cars, Nos 1–15, were ERTCW open-toppers and were followed in 1903 by similar vehicles 16–25; after that there was a gap of ten years before the arrival of top-covered UEC cars 26–32 in 1913 and 33–36 three years later. (Many of the older cars were by now fitted with top covers as well.) Also in 1916, the Corporation purchased MV single-decker demi-car 37 and, four years later, bought EE top-covered cars 38–47 to complete the fleet. The depot and power station were sited in Grey Friars Road by the North Bridge (prior to this a separate depot existed in Marsh Gate to serve the Bentley route).

The last routes opened were a 1½-mile extension of the Balby line south-west along Warmsworth Road to the village of that name on 5 February 1915, and a 3-mile northern route on reserved track beside the Great North Road to Brodsworth on 21 February 1916 to serve the housing development there. All routes were primarily single-track, with the exception of the racecourse line (which ended in a balloon loop) on account of the large crowds it had to cope with on occasion.

 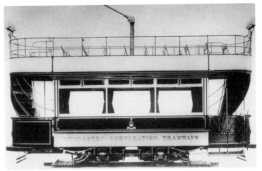

Above left: Postcard view of Doncaster High Street with Corporation open-topper No.2 of 1902 approaching. *(Author's Collection)*

Above right: A close-up works photograph of one of the first Doncaster Corporation cars, an ERTCW open-topper of 1902 or 1903. *(Author's Collection)*

Early in the 1920s the Corporation was once again under commercial pressure, this time from growing bus competition, and decided to abandon the tramways. In 1922 it began running its own motor buses, using them to replace the trams (on 1 May 1925) on the Avenue Road route. On 19 August 1928 the last trams ran to Bentley, replaced by trolleybuses – this route had been extended just four years before to take it to Bentley Colliery – with the Hexthorpe and Beckett Road lines going the following year, the Hyde Park and racecourse routes in 1930 and the Balby line in 1931, leaving just the Brodsworth route to survive another four years.

Drypool & Marfleet Steam Tramway *see* Hull: Drypool & Marfleet Steam Tramway

Farnworth Council Tramways

Authority: Farnworth Urban District Council Act 1900
Gauge: 4ft 8½in.
Traction: Horse/overhead electric
Opened: 9 January 1902
Taken over: 1 April 1906
System: Network
Length: 4.65 miles
Stock: 13 dd
Livery: Chocolate & yellow

The Farnworth system began life as part of the horse tramway promoted by BOLTON CORPORATION and the Astley Bridge, Farnworth and Kearsley local boards to link those towns along the Bolton to Manchester road. The Farnworth section ran as a double-track line from Moses Gate on the edge of Bolton, south-east along the Bolton Road, through Farnworth via Market Street and out to just past the Black Horse in Kearsley, where there was a turning circle (though the use of Eades patent reversible cars rendered this surplus to requirements and it was soon removed), a distance of almost a mile.

Although built by the different authorities, the line was worked originally on a twenty-one-year lease by Edmund Holden & Co. Ltd. Under the Bolton Tramways and Improvements Act of 1897 Holdens agreed to surrender their lease, and on 2 January 1900 electric trams began running from Bolton town centre to Moses Gate, with Holdens providing a replacement horse bus service on the Farnworth and Kearsley section until 13 April 1900, when the electric service was extended to the Black Horse. That same year Farnworth UDC obtained its own Act to construct more than 5½ miles of electric tramways, intended to connect with neighbouring systems.

Construction began in May 1901 and the following year the first section opened. This ran south from Moses Gate (with no connection to the Bolton line), down Egerton Street, Albert Road and Worsley Road to Brookhouse, with an eastern branch from the Albert Road/Worsley Road junction along Longcauseway, terminating just before meeting the Bolton Road south of the Black Horse by the former horse tramway terminus.

The tramway's thirteen cars were supplied by Milnes during 1901–02 and were all open-top bogie vehicles; the depot and generating station were in Albert Road. Also in 1900 Kearsley UDC had secured an Order permitting it to construct just over 1½ miles of electric line and, on 3 October, agreed to lease it to Farnworth. On 20 February 1902 this single-track extension of the Bolton line from the Black Horse through Kearsley to Spindle Point was opened (together with a connection to the Farnworth line at the Black Horse), the last ¼ mile from here to the boundary at Unity Brook following on 13 March that year.

On 1 June 1902 Bolton's powers to operate the former horse line expired and, as that corporation proved unwilling to operate a joint service with Farnworth, on 2 June the electric connection at Moses Gate was broken and Farnworth took control of its portion of the line, linking it to its Egerton Street terminus at Moses Gate shortly afterwards. Even with the addition of this main route, the tramway was not a financial success and the SOUTH LANCASHIRE TRAMWAYS agreed to take over operations from 1 April 1906 on a twenty-one-year lease. The Farnworth cars became SLT Nos 46–58, many of them to be top-covered or otherwise rebuilt in later years.

Fleetwood *see* Blackpool & Fleetwood

Gateshead & District Tramways
Authority: Gateshead and District Tramways Act 1880
Gauge: 4ft 8½in.
Traction: Steam/overhead electric
Opened: 22 October 1883
Closed: 4 August 1951
System: Radial network
Length: 12.47 miles
Stock: 16 locos, 16 dd steam; 50 sd, 49 dd electric
Livery: ? steam; crimson & white electric
Last Car: No.20 (service) and No.16 (official)

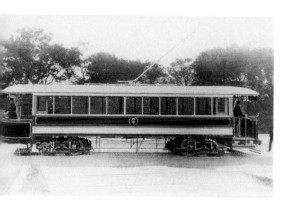

Above left: Gateshead-built No.54 or 55, as new in 1913, both cars being designed for P.A.Y.E. (Pay-As-You-Enter) operation, an idea then being experimented with at Gateshead in the interest of more efficient fare collection. *(Author's Collection)*

Above right: Commemorative postcard of Gateshead & District No.67 of 1923 inaugurating the new tramway (and road) link across the River Tyne. *(Author's Collection)*

A smaller, mirror image of the NEWCASTLE system across the Tyne, the Gateshead tramways differed in that they were always privately owned and went from steam to electric traction without operating any horse lines. Promoted by local business interests, the system was owned by the Gateshead & District Tramways Co. and, after a series of enabling acts, opened in 1883 when the first two locomotives arrived.

Centred on the High Street, the mainly single-track system's three routes ran east along Sunderland Road through Felling to Heworth (just over 2¼ miles), south to Low Fell via the Durham Road (2½ miles), and south-west to Teams via Mulgrave Terrace and Askew Road (just over 1¼ miles). The first tram locos, Nos 1–15, were all supplied by the local firm of BH (and were joined in 1885 by a sixteenth, heavier engine, which proved unsatisfactory and was returned). Passenger cars were Falcon open-top (later enclosed) double-deck bogie trailers Nos 1–14 of 1883–84, followed in 1889 by Nos 15 and 16, enclosed Lancaster bogie vehicles. The depot was in Sunderland Road near the junction with the High Street.

On 12 November 1897 the BET took control of the Company and two years later, under the Gateshead and District Tramways Act 1899, obtained the necessary authority to extend and electrify the system. The steam services were cut back accordingly as reconstruction work proceeded (beginning 12 June 1900), with the last steam cars running on 8 May 1901. The electric cars entered service the next day (a day after the official reopening).

The first electric routes were the three steam lines plus another southerly route to Sheriff Hill via Brunswick Street and the Old Durham Road (1½ miles). This line was extended another mile, to Wrekenton, in October 1903, by which time the mixed single and double-track system was virtually complete, with shorter southern branches to Saltwell Park and Benham (1901) and a western one, off the Teams route, to Dunston (1902) having been added.

The first cars were single-deckers 1–10 and 11–20 (the latter being bogie vehicles), plus open-toppers 21–45, all from ERTCW. These were joined in 1902 by bogie single-deckers 46–50 from Milnes. No further cars were added until 1908, when the Company built bogie single-decker 53, followed in 1913 by Nos 54 and 55, two more of the same. Similar vehicles 56–60 were supplied by Brush in 1921, the Company building, at the same time, four more of this type, which took the numbers 12, 13, 15 and 19 from withdrawn cars. The main depot was on the site as that of the former steam cars.

The only other new cars bought for the tramway were enclosed double-deckers 61–67 and bogie single-deckers 1 and 20 from Brush in 1923; between then and 1928 the Company built Nos 2–11, 14 and 16–18, again all bogie single-deckers. A number of second-hand cars were bought over the years: open-toppers 29, 30 and 38 ex-LIVERPOOL CORPORATION in 1921, top-covered 24, 25, 31, 33, 35–37 and 42 ex-SHEFFIELD CORPORATION in 1922, enclosed double-deckers 35 and 68–72 ex-OLDHAM in 1946, and bogie single-deckers 73–77 ex-Newcastle two years later.

In 1922 work took place on adapting the NER's High Level Bridge over the Tyne to take a tramway link between the Newcastle and Gateshead systems, with the first through services being inaugurated on 12 January the following year. A second link was provided from 10 October 1928, when the New Tyne (road) Bridge was opened with double tram tracks in place.

Tram Terminus, Dunston.

One that got away (at least, from the photographer): the Dunston terminus of the Gateshead system – but with not a tram in sight. *(Author's Collection)*

In 1938 Gateshead Corporation, following Newcastle's example of four years earlier, obtained powers to allow it to operate trolleybuses but, after the intervention of the Second World War, began running (on 5 March 1950) motor buses instead. In June 1950 the (reduced) tramway service over the Wrekenton and Heworth routes was terminated as, on 3 March 1951, were the Salthill Park and Bensham trams. The Lower Fell line closed on 7 April and the Teams route on 14 July, leaving just the Dunston route as the last survivor. It was the last BET-owned tramway to close.

After the closure, bogie cars 1, 3–11, 16–18, 20 and 56–60 were sold to the Grimsby & Immingham Electric Railway and two of these are now preserved in operational Gateshead condition: No.10 of 1925 is at BEAMISH whilst No.5 of 1927 is at the National Tramway Museum, Crich (which also has No.52 – the renumbered 7 of 1901 – currently in store awaiting restoration).

Gateshead Garden Festival

The 1990 Gateshead Garden Festival site (see **Introduction**) occupied 180 acres of formerly derelict land at Dunston on the south bank of the River Tyne, and a 4ft 8½in. gauge electric tramway 660yd in length was laid in the south-west corner, using track and overhead equipment from the GLASGOW GARDEN FESTIVAL tramway. As built, it was a lone line of single track, with a passing loop at each end, and operated from 18 March to 21 October. Four cars in all were used: BLACKPOOL 167, GATESHEAD 5, NEWCASTLE 102 and SUNDERLAND CORPORATION 100, all supplied by the National Tramway Museum at Crich.

Gosforth *see* Newcastle & Gosforth
Gosforth Park Light Railway *see* Newcastle-upon-Tyne Corporation Tramways
Great Crosby *see* Waterloo & Great Crosby

Halifax Corporation Tramways

Authority: Halifax Corporation Tramways Act 1897
Gauge: 3ft 6in.
Traction: Overhead electric
Opened: 29 June 1898*
Closed: 14 February 1939
System: Radial network
Length: 39.07 miles
Stock: 5 sd, 137 dd
Livery: Blue & white to 1924, bright red & yellow to 1927, then dark red & white
Last Car: No.109 (official)

At its fullest extent, Halifax's tramway system was made up of eleven hilly routes radiating from a network of interlinked lines in the town centre, plus an outerlinking line to the south and west. After unsuccessful commercial proposals for a cable tramway system, Halifax Corporation sought the necessary powers to construct its own electric system, and in 1898 opened the first three single-track routes (3½ miles in total) centred on the Post Office: east along Horton Street to Church Street, just short of the LYR's Halifax Old railway station, south-west to King Cross Street, and west to High Road Well via Gibbet Street and the depot.

Though an official opening ceremony was held on 9 June 1898, public services did not begin until 29 June; these were worked by Milnes open-top double-deckers 1–10, joined by similar cars Nos 11–58 over the next two years to keep pace with the succession of new routes being opened. A new depot was built to handle the enlarged fleet south of the town centre off Skircoat Lane, the old one becoming a works facility.

In 1901 Brush open-toppers 59–70 were bought, followed by another dozen (Nos 71–82) in 1902, and a third (Nos 83–94) a year later. In 1904 Brush supplied one-man single-deckers 95 and 96, and by the end of 1905 the system was virtually complete with over 37 miles of routes. Over the next ten years many of the double-deckers were fitted with top covers and windscreens (except No.64, which

Above left: An early photograph of what appears to be Halifax Corporation No.70 or 76, a Brush-built open-topper of 1901, on a Sowerby Bridge working. *(Author's Collection)*

Above right: Beyond Sowerby Bridge, the Halifax system's eventual westernmost route terminus was at Hebden Bridge, pictured here with sister Brush car No.82 of 1902 (in top-covered form) unloading. *(Author's Collection)*

was destroyed in an accident – one of many on the system – in 1907). In 1912 six Brush balcony cars (Nos 97–102) entered service, whilst during the First World War single-decker 95 was used as an army recruiting office and 96 as a mobile kitchen (later converted into an open salt wagon).

The last wholly new route, south to Stainland, was opened on 14 May 1921 and, apart from later extensions and modifications, this completed the system. Between that year – when No.98 was converted into an open-topper – and 1927, the Corporation built a series of cars, these being open-toppers 9, 11, 17, 22, 64 and 80, and top-covered 71, 73, 75, 76, 81 and 92 – all taking the numbers of the withdrawn vehicles they replaced. Also constructed, between 1924 and 1926, were bogie single-deckers 103, 105 and 106, plus a top-covered car, No.104, which introduced a new livery for the fleet. In 1928 these were followed by Corporation-built balcony cars 107–113, followed by similar cars 124–127 three years later; in 1930–31 similar cars 114–123 were supplied by EE.

The first route closure, on 31 March 1929, was the easternmost double-track section along Bradford Road between Brighouse, in the south, and Bailiff Bridge, 1½ miles to the north, which had provided an (unconnected) link between the HUDDERSFIELD and BRADFORD systems. (The Bradford system was also met with at Queensbury and Shelf in the north, and the Huddersfield system at Greetland in the south, but because of gauge differences the Halifax system was always isolated from its neighbours.) The following year, four open-toppers (Nos 128–131) were bought from Exeter Corporation as the last car purchases.

The 1930s saw a succession of further route closures, killed and replaced by Corporation and private bus services, the last to go being the short line from the town centre to the depot.

Hartlepools Steam Tramways

Authority: Hartlepool Tramways Order 1883
Gauge: 3ft 6in.
Traction: Steam
Opened: 2 August 1884
Closed: 21 February 1891
System: Single line
Length: 2.51 miles
Stock: 6? locos, 5 dd
Livery: ?
Last Car: ?

After several proposals in the early 1880s for tramways in the Hartlepools had come to nothing, an Order was secured in 1883 and the Hartlepools Steam Tramways Co. Ltd (registered 16 October 1883) was formed to operate a steam system. Work began that November on the first section, a single-track line running in a broad arc from Northgate in Hartlepool, north-west along Milbank Crescent, west along Cleveland Road (and past the depot at the junction with Hart Road), and on south into Clarence Road before turning east into Church Street, West Hartlepool.

The first tram locomotives were Nos 1 and 2, hauling two top-covered double-deck trailers (presumably also Nos 1 and 2), all from Falcon. These were soon joined by two further locos (Nos 3 and 4) and two more cars (presumably Nos 3 and 4), also from Falcon; in 1885 another Falcon loco and car arrived, both numbered 5, whilst locos 1–3 were withdrawn, presumably because of unsatisfactory performance; one was sold to Birmingham Central Tramways and another to South Staffordshire Tramways. No.6, a similar Falcon loco, is thought to have arrived then or the following year.

The tramway was not a financial success – perhaps because the other authorised routes were never constructed – and in 1891 it closed, by which time, however, the two local authorities affected were ready to consider approving an electric system (see below).

Hartlepool Electric Tramways

Authority: Hartlepool Electric Tramways Order 1895
Gauge: 3ft 6in.
Traction: Overhead electric
Opened: 19 May 1896
Closed: 25 March 1927
System: Branching
Length: 6.98 miles
Stock: 4 sd, 38 dd
Livery: GET green & cream, HET orange & white, Corporation dark red & white
Last Car: ?

On 28 February 1895 the General Electric Tramways Co. Ltd, a subsidiary of the Electric Construction Co. Ltd, was registered to rebuild the defunct HARTLEPOOLS STEAM TRAMWAYS line, services commencing the following year with Milnes open-top double-deckers Nos 1–5 working between Northgate in Hartlepool and the Clarence Road/Church Street junction in West Hartlepool. A new depot was built on Cleveland Road at Greenland, midway along the line.

On 9 October 1897 the last section of former steam line, in Church Street, was reopened (now double-tracked); that year also saw the arrival of another five cars: Nos 8 and 9 (similar to 1–5) and bogie open-topper No.10, all from Milnes, and toastrack trailers 6 and 7 (provenance unknown and used only when called for).

On 15 October 1896 the Hartlepool Electric Tramways Co. Ltd (a BET subsidiary) was registered to construct the 1895-authorised routes in West Hartlepool. Work began in 1897 and on 10 March 1899 the first two of these, a 1-mile continuation of the GET's Clarence Road line past Church Street and along Stockton Street to Foggy Furze, plus a mile-long branch off Stockton Street along Grange Road to Ward Jackson Park, were opened. Both lines were single-track and worked as one route to allow cars to run to and from Church Street. The service was worked initially by Brush open-toppers 11–15, joined later in 1899 by Nos 19 and 20, two ERTCW single-deckers on loan from the BET.

The next route opened, built under the West Hartlepool Light Railways Order of 1897, was a 2¼-mile extension of the Church Street line south, along Mainsforth Terrace and then Seaton Road on the seafront, all the way to the village of Seaton Carew as a single reserved track. Services began on 28 March 1902, four ERTCW open-toppers (Nos 16–19) having been bought to work them. Just after the opening of the new route, Brush bogie open-toppers 20 and 21 were bought (and the single-deck 19 and 20 presumably returned to the BET). These were joined early in 1902 by ERTCW bogie open-toppers 22–25 whilst, at the same time, the two trailers (Nos 6 and 7) were disposed of and cars 8 and 9 given their numbers. Then, in 1904, Nos 1–4 were rebuilt as two bogie open-toppers and given the numbers 8 and 9, the work being carried out by the Company. (The whole system was now operated by the HET Co. Ltd, the BET having bought out the GET Co. Ltd in January 1899.)

After some three years of negotiations, West Hartlepool Corporation took over the system, completing the complicated arrangements from 31 August 1912, buying the lines within its boundaries and leasing the section in Hartlepool. Two years later, five new UEC open-toppers (Nos 1–5) were bought; later that year (on 16 December 1914) the tramway suffered slight damage when German warships shelled the town.

Six new cars (Nos 27–32) arrived in 1920, these being Brush bogie open-toppers but, ominously, that 17 July saw the Corporation commence bus operations. Three years later Nos 8 and 9 were rebuilt with EE open-top bodies – these were the last major alterations to the passenger fleet to take place. More cars were withdrawn and, on 4 October 1923, the Foggy Furze route closed, replaced by a temporary bus service until the planned trolleybuses began running the following year. The Park line closed in November 1925, the Hartlepool line on 22 February 1927 and the Seaton Carew line a month later. Earlier that year cars 1–5 had been sold to Dover Corporation, the others in the fleet being scrapped or otherwise disposed of after the closure.

Haslingden Corporation Tramways

On 1 January 1908 Haslingden Corporation assumed full control of the 2.9 miles of single track within its boundaries, which had previously been leased to the ACCRINGTON CORPORATION STEAM TRAMWAYS Co. At the same time, it purchased eight locomotives and seven cars (fleet numbers unknown) from the Company in order to work the single line itself until 5 September that year, when work began on electrifying the tramway in conjunction with ACCRINGTON CORPORATION who, on 28 September, began services to the Commercial Hotel in the centre of the town and then, on 20 October, through to Lockgate (and on to RAWTENSTALL two years later). From then on this portion of the local network, though nominally independent, was, in practice, run by Accrington (though Haslingden Corporation retained one of the steam locos for use as a works engine). The line closed on 30 April 1930 as part of the abandonment of the whole Accrington–Rawtenstall route in favour of Accrington Corporation-operated motor buses.

Heaton Park Vintage Tramway *see* Manchester: Heaton Park Vintage Tramway

Heywood Corporation Tramways

Authority: Heywood Corporation Tramways Order 1902
Gauge: 3ft 6in.
Traction: Steam
Opened: 10 December 1904
Closed: 20 September 1905
System: Branching
Length: 4.33 miles
Stock: 13 locos, 10 dd
Livery: Locos brown, cars brown & cream?
Last Car: Loco 81

This very short-lived system (and the last municipally owned steam tramway in Britain) provided the final chapter in the MANCHESTER, BURY, ROCHDALE & OLDHAM saga. Caught midway between BURY, which had started running electric cars to the Heywood boundary in April 1904, and ROCHDALE, which had stopped its steam operation on the other side two months later, Heywood Corporation opted to buy some of the old MBRO steam tramway stock and reopen the lines within its boundaries.

Thirteen locomotives and ten trailers (their identities not fully known) were moved by road, in the middle of winter, from Rochdale to Heywood (where a new depot was built in York Street), and on 10 December 1904 the old main line was reopened, followed two days later by the Hopwood branch.

The initiative was not a great success. The stock was decrepit and Rochdale Corporation would not let Heywood run it over the mile or so of former steam tramway track from its boundary to Sudden, where its electric service terminated. By April 1905 this gap had been closed with the extension of the electric line, and that August Bury Corporation began reconstructing Heywood's main line back from the boundary in order to link Rochdale's system with its own; on 15 September steam services over this eastern portion of the tramway were halted altogether. Five days later, a satisfactory agreement having been reached with Rochdale, the remaining services were terminated and the rolling-stock was sold for scrap.

Hoylake & Birkenhead Tramway *see* Birkenhead: Hoylake & Birkenhead Tramway

Huddersfield Corporation Tramways
Authority: Huddersfield Improvement Act 1880
Gauge: 4ft 7¾in.
Traction: Steam, horse, overhead electric
Opened: 11 January 1883
Closed: 29 June 1940
System: Radial network
Length: 39.12 miles
Stock: 36 locos, 37 dd horse & steam; 144 dd electric
Livery: Locos crimson, cars red/maroon & cream
Last Car: No.132 (official)

To Huddersfield Corporation goes the honour of owning the first municipally operated tramway in the British Isles – if only because it could not find anyone who would lease it. Empowered by its 1880 Act, work began in June 1881 on track laying with a gauge of 4ft 7¾in., the Corporation's intentions being to allow for the running of railway wagons over the system. This, however, never came about; instead, the choice of gauge meant that connections could not be made with the tramway's West Riding neighbours (HALIFAX, to the north, and DEWSBURY, to the south). The authority to work the system was granted by the Huddersfield Corporation Act 1882, and on 11 January the following year the first two lines opened: north from St George's Square in the town centre, along Northgate and the Bradford Road to Fartown Bar, and south from St George's Square along New Street, Buxton Road, Chapel Hill and Lockwood Road to Lockwood Bar in the district of Salford. The two lines were worked as one route with Wilkinson tram locomotives 1–6 (arriving in batches from 1882 to January 1884) hauling open-top double-deck trailers Nos 1 (an Eades patent reversible car from Ashbury, a curious choice for a steam trailer) and 2–6 (from Starbuck).

Huddersfield Corporation No.18, one of the tramway's original Milnes open-toppers of 1900, in New Street in the town centre. *(Author's Collection)*

Huddersfield No.74 of 1910,
a UEC balcony car captured
here outside the system's Great
Northern Street Depot. *(Author's
Collection)*

Other routes followed slowly: north-west to Lindley (9 June 1883) and Edgerton (10 January 1884), and east to Moldgreen (9 May 1885) – this last route being horse-worked, on account of a narrow roadway, with Ashbury cars 7 and 8 (again Eades open-toppers). On 11 October 1886 the Lindley and Edgerton routes were linked via Holly Bank to form a loop, and on 15 February 1889 a south-eastern line was opened to Almondbury via Kidroyd, followed on 23 May 1890 by a short western line to Crosland Moor. The Moldgreen route was extended to the Waterloo Inn on the Wakefield Road on 26 September that year, and by the end of 1899 the single-track system was virtually complete, with no fewer than nine radial routes, plus two out-and-back loops, to serve almost all areas of the town and its periphery.

The tramway's stock fleet had, meanwhile, continued to grow to keep pace with the new routes and extensions. Locos 7–9 were bought from BH in 1885–86, Nos 10–18, 21 and 22 from Kitsons in 1887–89, Nos 19, 20 and 23–30 from Greens in 1891–92, and Nos 31 and 32 from Kitsons again in 1894; the only other engines added were Nos 7–9 in 1897 and No.6 in 1898, assembled by the Corporation from Kitson parts. Open-top bogie trailers Nos 9 (from Lancaster), and 10 and 11 (Starbuck), and Eades four-wheeled open-toppers 12 and 13 (from Ashbury) were bought in 1885, followed in 1887 by bogie open-toppers 14 and 15 from Milnes – who supplied, over the next twelve years, twenty-one bogie top-covered cars to take the number series up to 26 (including replacements for lower-numbered vehicles).

The depot was located just north of St George's Square in Northumberland Street, until 1887 when a new one was built off Viaduct Street to the east of Northgate. On 21 May 1900 a 3-mile extension of the Marsden Road route, south-west of the town, was opened from the municipal boundary out along the Manchester Road through Linthwaite to the Star Hotel in Slaithwaite. This was authorised by the Huddersfield Corporation Tramways Order and the Linthwaite Tramways Order of 1898 and, although owned by Linthwaite UDC, was worked by Huddersfield.

By 1899 the Corporation was planning the electrification of the system, with new routes authorised by the Huddersfield Corporation Act of the following year. On 14 February 1901 the first two converted routes were opened: the Lindley Circular (the loop via Edgerton) and the long western line out on the New Hey Road to Outlane. The last steam trams ran on the Far Town route on 21 June 1902, marking the end of the conversion work.

The system continued to grow until 1923, when the last route, an extension of the Far Town route northwards through Rastrick to Brighouse, was opened on 12 March. As completed, the network was the old steam tramway system enlarged to some fourteen, mainly double-track, radial routes with a large fleet of cars based on the old steam depot site and a new depot by the Corporation's generating station in St Thomas' Road, off the Manchester Road, just west of the town centre.

The first electric cars were Nos 1–25, Milnes bogie open-toppers of 1900, joined by open-toppers 26–61 from BEC over the next two years (No.40 was renumbered 62 after an accident in 1902), followed, in 1902, by BEC 40 and 63–66, which had top covers. No.67 of 1903 was an open-top American Car Co. import and Nos 68–70 further top-covered BEC vehicles. UEC supplied balcony cars 71–75 in 1909, enclosed 76 a year later and balcony cars 77–106 during 1912–14, whilst the remainder of the fleet were EE products: balcony cars 107–126 of 1919–20 and enclosed 127–144 delivered during the ten years from 1923 onwards. Two powered coal trucks, supplied by MV in 1904 and numbered 71 and 72 (renumbered 1 and 2 in 1909) were employed until 1934 to make deliveries to mills on the Outlane route.

The beginning of the end for the tramway came in 1932 as a result of bus competition, when the Almondbury route was gradually cut back as it was converted for trolleybus operation, closing altogether on 16 April of the following year. On 10 November 1935 the Waterloo, Lindley and Outlane routes were closed, and by 1940 only the Brighouse line was left. All surviving cars were scrapped, the most modern ones (Nos 137–144) having been sold in 1938 to SUNDERLAND CORPORATION.

Hull Street Tramways
Authority: Hull Tramways Order 1872
Gauge: 4ft 8½in.
Traction: Horse
Opened: 9 January 1875
Closed: Autumn 1899
System: Radial
Length: 10.81 miles
Stock: 4 sd, 31 dd
Livery: Dark red-brown & white
Last Car: ?

The first section of Kingston-upon-Hull's tramway system was built and operated by the Continental & General Tramway Co. Ltd. It was a single-track line 1½ miles in length, running northwards from Saville Street, in the city centre, along Beverley Road to Rose Cottage near Queen's Road, worked by two small single-deckers of unknown manufacture (Nos 11 and 12); these were joined over the next four years by six large double-deckers (Nos 51–56) – possibly from Belgium – six small double-deckers (Nos 5–7, 9, 10 and 14), and another single-decker (No.13). The reasoning behind the somewhat bizarre numbering system is not known.

From 1 November 1876 the tramway was owned and worked by the newly formed Hull Street Tramways Co. Ltd, which set about opening other routes to outlying districts thus: on 12 December

1876 north-westwards up Springbank to the Botanic Gardens, and in 1877 south to the Pier on the River Humber, westwards along Hessle Road to Dairycotes, west along Anlaby Road and eastwards on Holderness Road to Mile House. Short extensions the following year completed the single-track system. Depots were sited in Hessle Road, Holderness Road and off Beverley Road.

By the end of 1882 the car fleet was complete with the 1879 purchase of another single-decker, followed by thirteen small and six medium-sized double-deckers; after the 1882 withdrawal of the four single-deckers, all the double-deck cars were renumbered 1–31 in line with more conventional thinking.

The Company failed in 1889 – largely as a result of competition from cheap and speedy wagonette services – and was wound up and put into receivership on 30 November that year. Thereafter, the stock and track fell slowly into disrepair until being taken over by the Corporation on 15 October 1896 and leased out to a local cab proprietor. The Corporation's intention was to replace the horse trams with electric ones (see below), and services on the Hessle Road were withdrawn accordingly at the end of May 1898, the other routes all gradually going the same way by the end of September the following year (though one staff recollection was of a date in early November).

One feature of the system, shared with that of Burton-upon-Trent, was the existence of a number of level crossings over railway lines (seven in the case of Hull) which, as well as frequently disrupting services, had to be protected by catch points and signals.

Hull: Drypool & Marfleet Steam Tramway

Authority: Drypool and Marfleet Steam Tramways Order 1886
Gauge: 4ft 8½in.
Traction: Steam
Opened: 21 May 1889
Closed: 13 January 1901
System: Branching
Length: 1.34 miles
Stock: 7 locos, 8 dd
Livery: Deep crimson & white
Last Car: ?

On 15 January 1886 a local company was incorporated, the Drypool & Marfleet Steam Tramway Co. Ltd, to construct and operate tramways on the eastern side of Kingston-upon-Hull, especially a line along Hedon Road, past the newly built Alexandra Dock and out to the village of Marfleet some 2 miles distant.

Construction did not begin until July 1888 and, as laid, the line ran from the eastern side of North Bridge over the River Hull, south-west along Great Union Street, through Drypool Square then past Victoria Dock and out along Hedon Road only as far as its junction with Lee Smith Street by Alexandra Dock – half the projected route length. The only other line built was a 100yd-spur from the Great Union Street terminus, running back westwards to the more southerly Drypool Bridge (opened 1888) over the Hull, which was, in the early days of the tramway, also used as a terminus for the main line. When opened, not only was the line one of the last steam street tramways to be built in Great Britain (only the ST HELENS & DISTRICT in 1890 came later), it was the shortest.

Four tram locomotives (Nos 1–4) and five trailers (Nos 1–5) were supplied for the opening of the line, with locos 5–7 and trailers 6–8 following by the end of the year; the engines were from Greens and the large, enclosed double-deck bogie trailers from Milnes. (The extra trailer over engine numbers is accounted for by the fact that the Company intended to run a two-car train, if need be, and apparently did so on occasion.) The depot was in Hotham Street, which was reached by a short spur off Hedon Road by the terminus.

From the outset, the tramway's major problem was that its two western termini were some ten minutes' walk from the city centre and, consequently it, like the HULL STREET TRAMWAYS, suffered from wagonette competition. Attempts to solve the problem by either running combined services in conjunction with the horse trams or buying some of the horse lines for conversion to steam working – notably the Mile House line across North Bridge, only yards from the D&M – were strongly opposed on the grounds of the noise and pollution produced by the engines. In any event, the 1896 purchase of the horse tramways by the Corporation effectively quashed any such plans, and about this time the Drypool Bridge spur seems to have been abandoned as an economy measure.

The Company soon found itself bypassed by outside events – notably the electrification of the old horse system – and in 1899 it successfully negotiated the sale of the tramway to the Corporation. The purchase – at a price of £15,500 – was completed on 31 January 1900, after which the Company went into voluntary liquidation. By the time of the sale the engines and cars were showing signs of wear, and by October 1900 one loco and two trailers had been withdrawn; by the following January only two engines were in service.

City of Hull Tramways
Authority: Hull Corporation Tramways Order 1896
Gauge: 4ft 8½in.
Traction: Overhead electric
Opened: 5 July 1899
Closed: 30 June 1945
System: Radial network
Length: 20.48 miles
Stock: 182 dd
Livery: Red & white
Last Car: No.169

The first Kingston-upon-Hull electric tram services began along the former Anlaby Road and Hessle Road routes of the old horse tramway system, using centre-grooved rails; the rest of the horse and steam lines were similarly converted over the next few years (see previous two entries). Services were worked initially by Milnes open-top cars 1–25 hauling open-top trailers 101–125, all built 1898–99. These were joined in 1899 by Brill Nos 26–30, and in 1900 by Brush open-toppers 31–60, plus five of the same from ERTCW (Nos 61–65). The Milnes trailers were thereupon motorised and renumbered 66–90, and joined in 1901 by HN open-top cars Nos 91–100 and Milnes 101, a bogie open-topper.

As can be judged by the size of the car fleet (and the speed at which it was built up), the electric lines were spreading rapidly, and they eventually formed a radial network of lines on the north side of the Humber, stretching westwards to Anlaby Park and along Hessle Road, eastwards to Marfleet and along Holderness Road, northwards through Newland and up Beverley Road. In addition, a double rectangle of lines off to the west of Beverley Road, completed in 1927, served the residential area there. Virtually all the routes were double-tracked throughout, with most of the extremities occupying sleepered roadside reservations. The only southerly route was a short, ¼-mile double-track branch from the city centre down through the Market Place to Victoria Pier.

By the time the last section of tramway opened, the car fleet (known locally as 'Kipper Boxes') was complete. In 1903 Milnes supplied top-covered cars 102–116, with similar vehicles arriving from UEC in 1909 (Nos 117–122) with others built by the Corporation in 1909–10 (Nos 123–136). Meanwhile, in 1909, bogie car 101 was sold to the Erith UDC system in Kent. In 1912 Brush supplied balcony cars 137–160, and 161–180 three years later. Many of these were replacements for withdrawn older vehicles, and many were later rebuilt (and often enclosed). The last car to be bought, rather than modernised, was a new No.101, an enclosed EE double-decker of 1923. This was followed in 1925 by the system's final passenger car, No.113, another enclosed double-decker, this time built by the Corporation.

Cutbacks to the systems began in the 1930s with the closure, on 5 January 1931, of the Victoria Pier branch. In 1934 an agreement was reached with the local bus operator, East Yorkshire Motor Services Ltd, one of the provisions of which was that the Corporation would cut its outermost tramways back, so closing the Anlaby route beyond the Wheeler Street depot, the Hessle Road route beyond Dairycoats (and the Liverpool Street depot), and the northern Cottingham Road route off Beverley Road (again just beyond a depot).

Above left: One of the City of Hull Tramways' first cars, an unidentified open-topper complete with curtains in the lower saloon – one of a batch supplied by several builders in the years around 1900. *(Author's Collection)*

Above right: One of Hull's 1899 Brush-built cars, No.28 of 1899, photographed with its short top cover added in the late 1900s. *(Author's Collection)*

Hull No.96 of 1901, an HN open-topper converted into a stores car and snow plough in 1933, sold to Leeds Corporation in 1945 and now restored to passenger use on the Heaton Park Tramway in Manchester. *(Author)*

On 23 July 1937 trolleybus services began, putting an end to the northern part of the system, whilst the Hedon Road route closed on 31 December that year, its trams replaced by motor buses. This left just the Holderness Road, Anlaby Road and Hessle Road routes to see the start of the Second World War, during which the first of these (on 17 February 1940) and the second (5 September 1942) both closed. Twelve of the surviving tramcars were thereafter sold to LEEDS CITY TRAMWAYS, leaving just twelve to work the last route to Dairycoats until that too was abandoned. Car No.96 of 1901 has been preserved and can be seen operating on the HEATON PARK line in MANCHESTER, albeit in single-deck form, whilst No.132 of 1910 is a static exhibit in the Hull Transport Museum.

Imperial Tramways

The Bristol-based Imperial Tramways Co. Ltd (1878–1930) owned, at one time or another, the tramways at Bristol, DARLINGTON, Gloucester and Reading, as well as the MIDDLESBROUGH, STOCKTON & THORNABY system and the London United Tramways (formerly the West Metropolitan Tramways); in addition, it owned the Dublin Southern District Tramways in Ireland and the narrow-gauge Corris Railway in Wales.

Jarrow & District Electric Tramway

Authority: Jarrow and South Shields Light Railway Order 1901
Gauge: 4ft 8½in.
Traction: Overhead electric
Opened: 29 November 1906
Closed: 30 June 1929
System: Single line
Length: 2.54 miles
Stock: 12 dd
Livery: Maroon & off-white*
Last Car: ?

Promoted by the BET, this tramway was owned and operated by its subsidiary, the Jarrow & District Electric Traction Co. Ltd. It ran eastwards, south of the River Tyne, from Western Road along Ormonde Street, Staple Road, the High Street and Church Bank in Jarrow, after which it occupied a reserved right of way for ¼ mile (crossing the River Don and passing into South Shields) before joining Straker Street and its continuation, Swinburne Street, finally entering Jarrow Road where there was an end-on connection with the SOUTH SHIELDS CORPORATION line. Virtually the whole route was single-track. (The short Western Road–Ormonde Street stretch was not opened until 21 December 1906 as it needed bringing up to an acceptable standard.)

Services began with Brush open-toppers Nos 1–8, which were joined in 1907 by No.9, a second-hand Brush car of similar type built in 1902 for display at that year's Trade Exhibition. Always known at Jarrow as the 'Show Car', it retained its own green livery. In 1908 Nos 5 and 6 were exchanged for two Gravesend & Northfleet bogie cars, these being renumbered accordingly. The last car to arrive was No.10, formerly GATESHEAD 35, which was borrowed then purchased in 1911; this was an ERTCW open-topper of 1901 vintage.

Through-running between the Jarrow and South Shields lines began on 18 June 1908, much to the benefit of the shipyard and other workers who provided the bulk of the trams' passengers, but was discontinued on 17 June 1911 after a dispute over the financial arrangement between the two concerns. (The Jarrow cars were, in effect, hired by South Shields in return for the fares collected.) On 14 July 1922 through-running recommenced, the dispute having been resolved, only to stop again on 13 July 1927, by which time bus competition was seriously affecting the line. Closure was forced two years later, after which cars 5 and 6 were sold to South Shields and the others scrapped.

Ormonde Street, Jarrow, with a Jarrow & District double-decker approaching – an evocative Edwardian street scene now gone from living memory. (Author's Collection)

Keighley Tramways

Authority: Keighley Tramways Order 1888
Gauge: 4ft
Traction: Horse
Opened: 8 May 1889
Closed: 28 May 1904
System: Single line
Length: 2.28 miles
Stock: 7 dd
Livery: ?
Last Car: ?

Promoted by the Keighley Tramways Co. Ltd (a consortium of local businessmen and councillors), Keighley's first tramway was a simple single-track line running south from the Cemetery in the residential district of Utley, down Skipton Road, North Street and South Street past the depot to industrial Ingrow, terminating close to the MR's and GNR's Ingrow stations. The North Street–Ingrow section was the first to open in 1889, the Utley half following on 18 December that year. Very short – around 200yd –

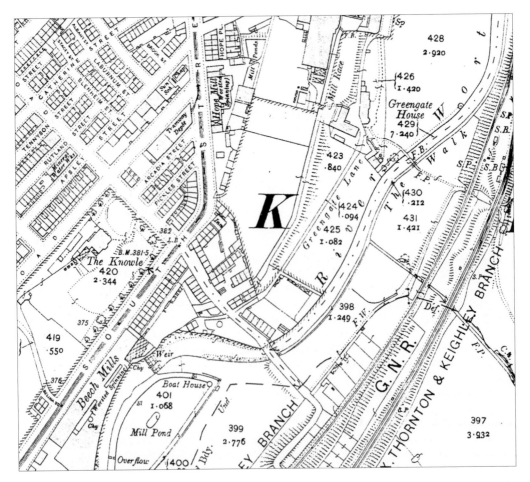

South Street Depot in Keighley, from the 1898 Ordnance Survey 25in. to 1 mile map. Opened in 1889 by the Keighley Tramways Co. Ltd as a horse car depot, it was taken over by the Corporation in 1901 and enlarged to take electric trams (and later both buses and trolleybuses).

extensions at both ends were constructed *c.*1897 (to the Roebuck Inn at Utley and the new railway bridge at Ingrow) and the two halves of the line were, somewhat curiously, normally worked as separate routes. The seven cars, all probably purchased in 1889, were open-top double-deckers by Starbuck.

The tramway was never a financial success, and on 25 November 1896 the Company sold the track to Keighley Corporation for the nominal sum of £5 and leased it back for thirteen years. On 15 January 1901 the Corporation, wishing to extend and electrify the line, became the effective owner after the Company agreed to sell the rest of the concern to them (although municipal operation only began on 21 September 1901 with the formal change of ownership). The Company was wound up that December. Apart from a number of minor improvements and the sale of one of the cars, the tramway continued much as before, under its new ownership, until 1904 when both routes were closed to clear the way for the planned reconstruction (see below).

Keighley Corporation Tramways
Authority: Keighley Corporation Act 1898
Gauge: 4ft
Traction: Overhead electric
Opened: 12 October 1904
Closed: 17 December 1924
System: Radial
Length: 3.44 miles
Stock: 12 dd
Livery: Crimson & white
Last Car: No.6

Even before it began operating the old horse tramway (see above), Keighley Corporation was planning its electrification and, by means of a branch to Stockbridge (authorised by the Keighley Corporation Tramways Act 1903), a link with SHIPLEY and then BRADFORD in conjunction with the Mid-Yorkshire Tramways Co. This company failed, however, and the Corporation never managed to connect its system to any other.

The horse tramway was rebuilt as a double-track line, with the Stockbridge route laid with double tracks from the Institute in North Street, eastwards along Cavendish Street to the MR's Keighley station, where it became a single track along Bradford Road to Victoria Park (about a mile from the Institute). All three routes were opened together and were worked by eight open-top Brush cars, joined by two more (Nos 9 and 10) in 1905 after the 10 February opening of a ½-mile extension of the Stockbridge line to the Dale Street/Bradford Road junction in Stockbridge.

The arrival in 1906 of a pair of top-covered Brush cars (Nos 11 and 12) completed the fleet, as soon after this the Corporation appears to have set its collective heart on introducing trolleybuses to Keighley and, in 1913, did so. The gradual expansion of the new system was interrupted by the First World War, but in the 1920s, faced with the prospect of having to renew the whole track, the Corporation decided to abandon the trams. The Utley route closed on 20 August 1924, followed by the Stockbridge route in mid-November and the Ingrow line a month later, making Keighley the first local authority to close its electric tramway system and replace them with trolleybuses – a dubious double honour indeed.

Kingston-upon-Hull *see* Hull

Lancaster & District Tramways
Authority: Lancaster and District Tramways Order 1889
Gauge: 4ft 8½in.
Traction: Horse
Opened: 2 August 1890
Closed: 31 December 1921
System: Single line

Length: 4.3 miles
Stock: 14 dd
Livery: ?
Last Car: ?

Despite their being linked by both the MR and the LNWR, a horse tramway between Lancaster and Morecambe was promoted and constructed at the end of the 1880s by the Lancaster & District Tramways Co. Ltd. It was a single-track line commencing by the Royalty Theatre in Market Square, Morecambe, close to the MORECAMBE TRAMWAYS terminus there (though no connection was ever put in), from where it ran roughly south-east through Torrisholme to Stonewell in north Lancaster, the terminus being a triangle formed by Cable Street, North Road and Chapel Street. The double-deck stock – hardly surprisingly – was built by Lancaster and the depot was on Lancaster Road, Morecambe. (Some of the cars were converted later to single-deck form.)

As a relatively short, simple system, relying heavily on summer excursion traffic to Morecambe, the line was never taken over for electrification by one of the large tramway groups, nor could it find the money for modernisation itself and consequently, at the end of 1921, after failing to sell out to the local authorities, it closed quietly – another victim of the motor bus and one of the last remaining horse tramways in the British Isles.

Lancaster Corporation Tramway

Authority: Lancaster Corporation Act 1900
Gauge: 4ft 8½in.
Traction: Overhead electric
Opened: 14 January 1903
Closed: 4 April 1930
System: Radial
Length: 2.99 miles
Stock: 12 dd
Livery: Chocolate & primrose
Last Car: No.8

Promoted and operated by Lancaster Corporation, the first section of this small system to be opened ran from the Boot & Shoe Inn, in the southernmost district of Scotforth (then a separate village), north along Scotforth Road, Greaves Road and Thurnham Street to Dalton Square in the centre of the city, whilst a second route ran back from Thurnham Street in a south-easterly direction down Quarry Road, Dale Street and Bowerham Road to the village of that name, where it doubled back northwards up Golgotha Road to the Williamson Park Gates. Both lines were single-track, though part of the Bowerham route was almost immediately doubled. The original cars were ten Lancaster open-top double-deckers, housed in a depot at the top of Thurnham Street. Early in 1905 a third route was opened, this being a short line from Dalton Square, running westwards via Market Street and Meeting House Lane to terminate in County Street by the LNWR's Lancaster Castle station; to augment the car fleet two more open-toppers were bought (Nos 11 and 12), this time from MV.

From the beginning the tramway operated at a loss, and planned extra lines never materialised; instead, efforts were made to attract more passengers by fitting top covers to four of the cars in 1911, and to a further pair two years later, whilst in 1917 an attempt at economy was made by converting No.11 into a one-man single-decker. The measure was judged a success and by July 1920 the remaining five open-toppers had been treated similarly. The following year the idea of purchasing the LANCASTER & DISTRICT TRAMWAYS was raised (see above), but came to nothing, and in April 1922 the station line was lifted. Two years later the Corporation began petrol bus operations (abandoning its Brush battery electric buses, first used in December 1916), in view of which it is surprising that the trams lasted as long as they did. The Bowerham route closed on 18 January 1930 and the Scotforth line that April.

Leeds Tramways

Authority: Leeds Tramways Order 1871
Gauge: 4ft 8½in.
Traction: Horse, steam
Opened: 16 September 1871
Taken over: 2 February 1894
System: Radial
Length: 14.16 miles
Stock: 37 sd, 40 dd horse; 32 locos, 24 dd steam
Livery: Chocolate & white/primrose

Owned by the Leeds Tramways Co. until municipalised in 1894, the Leeds system grew to be the largest in Yorkshire. The first route opened ran from Boar Lane in the town centre (Leeds did not become a city until 1893) via Park Row, Cookridge Street and Woodhouse Lane to the Oak Inn at Headingley, 3 miles away. Roughly half the line was double-track and the first cars, Starbuck double-deckers 1–4, were each hauled by three horses.

A second route, north-east from Boar Lane up Wellington Street to the Cardigan Arms on Kirstall Road, opened on 1 April 1872 and was extended on 18 May along Commercial Road as far as Kirkstall village (3 miles), terminating by the Star & Garter. Three more routes followed in 1874 – north to Meanwood Road and Chapeltown, east to York Road via Marsh Lane, and south-east across the River Aire to Hunslet via the Hunslet Road – whilst the Headingley line was extended the following year to the Three Horse Shoes. Further openings came in 1878 and 1879, by which time steam traction was about to be introduced after successful trials. Three Kitson locomotives (Nos 1–3) were hired in 1880 and used to haul double-deck horse cars until 1882–83, when they were purchased together with trailers from Ashbury (Eades reversible No.55) and Starbuck (Nos 59 and 60).

During 1883–84, two Green locos (Nos 1 and 2) were hired, and from then until 1890 twenty-five more Green and Kitson locos (Nos 4–28) were bought along with another twenty-one Starbuck, Ashbury and Milnes trailers. Meanwhile, the horse car fleet was not neglected as the system expanded again in the late 1880s and early 1890s, with eventually seventy-seven cars (by Stephensons, Starbuck, Ashbury, Milnes and the Company itself) operating from six depots. By this time the Corporation was running its own electric tramcars (see below) and the Company was perfectly willing to sell out after its initial twenty-one years were up. The only problem was agreeing a price, this being fixed by arbitration at £112,225 in 1893, with the transfer of the whole concern taking place the following year.

Leeds City Tramways

Authority: Leeds Corporation Tramways Order 1888
Gauge: 4ft 8½in.
Traction: Overhead electric, horse, steam
Opened: 11 November 1891*
Closed: 7 November 1959
System: Radial network
Length: 72.05 miles
Stock: 31 sd, 36 dd horse; 27 locos, 24 dd steam; 10 sd, 869 dd electric
Livery: Blue & ivory to 1901, chocolate, yellow & white to 1925, blue & cream to 1950, then crimson
& cream
Last Car: No.160

In 1889 Leeds Corporation constructed a line off Chapeltown Road at Sheepscar (just north of the junction with the LEEDS TRAMWAYS' Meanwood Road line), running north-east along Roundhay Road to the gates of Roundhay Park (opened 1873), and tried to interest the Leeds Tramways Co. in working it, though it was not until 15 May 1891 that a proper (steam) service was started. By then, though, the Company was nearing the end of its existence and the Corporation had already decided to electrify the line. This was done the same year by the Thomson-Houston International Co. of America, working the line on concession from the Corporation with six Stephenson single-deck cars, licence numbers 75–80, collecting current from an overhead wire. Its official opening, on 29 October 1891, made it the first street tramway to collect its current solely in this fashion in the whole of Europe.

Public services recommenced on 11 November 1891 and eight days later a second route was opened, from midway along Roundhay Road south via Harehills Road (and depot) to Beckett Street. Three years later the Corporation took over the existing horse and steam tramways (see above) in order to electrify them. While the conversion was still being planned, however, further horse and steam routes were opened, for which locos 29 and 30 were bought in 1897 from Greens and, between 1897 and 1899, single-deck horse cars 111–120 and double-deckers 50, 78, 93–97 and 105–110 were bought from Milnes.

On 31 July 1896 the Thomson-Houston concession ended and the electric cars stopped running, though on 2 August the following year they were re-introduced by the Corporation and now ran all the way through to Kirkstall Abbey. Other routes were similarly converted, with the last horse services (on Whitehall Road) ending on 13 October 1901 and the last steam services (on Armley Road) on 1 April following. The system continued to expand right up to the end of the 1940s, with the completion on 28 August 1949 of a long southern loop to Middleton Park and back – much of it on a private right of way – matching the long northern loop past Roundhay Park and back via Moorstown and Chapeltown.

Inevitably, this expansion was accompanied by the occasional abandonment of unprofitable routes, the first of which (on 15 June 1922) was a short line from City Square south-west across the River Aire, via Whitehall Road, to the Cattle Market. The system was also well-connected to its neighbours, with through-running over YORKSHIRE (WEST RIDING) tracks south to Rothwell, via Hunslet, commencing on 1 June 1905, whilst on 9 June 1909 through-running to BRADFORD began. In this latter case, where the two systems met at Stanningley, a 30ft tapering section of track was laid to connect the 4ft 8½in. and 4ft gauge tramways, each system equipping ten cars with specially designed sliding axle sleeves to enable them to run on either gauge line.

Corporation bus services began on 31 March 1906 and were joined on 21 June 1911 by trolleybuses; the Corporation kept faith with the tramways, though, as the long expansion and improvement programmes indicate. (The trolleybuses were replaced by motor buses during the late 1920s, after the former had brought about the closure of the Whitehall Road route.)

The next route closure did not come for another ten years when, on 31 May 1932, the YWD closed its Rothwell branch, whereupon the Leeds services were cut back to Thwaite Gate, Hunslet, on the city boundary. More closures followed each year from 1934 to 1938, with only the Second World War temporarily halting the abandonments. In 1947 they recommenced, with the very last route to go being that from the Corn Exchange in the city centre out along York Road to Crossgates, plus its branch to Templenewsam Park.

One of the early Leeds City electric cars, No.164 of 1899, on a 1914-franked postcard. (Author's Collection)

Left: Leeds City enclosed double-deckers 237 and 111, the latter demonstrating just how tight a curve a tramcar could negotiate. Note also Leeds' distinctive pattern of current collector. *(Author's Collection)*

Below: General route map of the Leeds City Tramways, from the 1904 *Manual of Electrical Undertakings.*

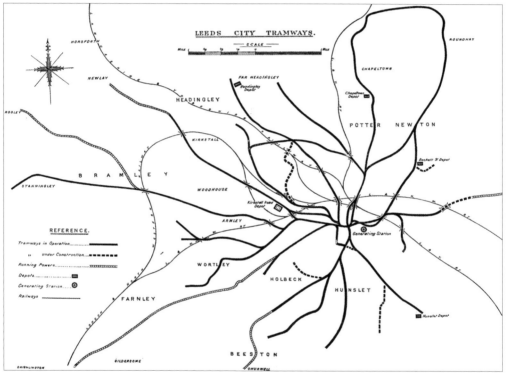

From the very beginning, the Leeds car fleet reflected the latest development in tramcar design. In all, the Corporation operated nearly 900 electric cars, including the original six Stephenson vehicles (which were bought in 1898, used as trailers, and two years later converted into salt cars). The first Corporation-owned cars were Nos 1–25, Milnes open-top double-deckers of 1897, which were followed by a succession of new cars until 1953, from a number of manufacturers (including the Corporation itself). These are listed below and, unless otherwise described, were four-wheeled double-deck vehicles:

Nos 85, 90, 133–182: Brush open-toppers of 1899
Nos 98–103, 128–132: ditto trailers of 1897 (motorised 1900)
Nos 44, 46, 55, 79, 83: Brush open-toppers of 1900 (built originally for LIVERPOOL)
No.49: Brush single-decker of 1900
No.52: Brush bogie open-topper of 1900

Nos 183–282: ERTCW open-toppers of 1901
Nos 27–32, 34, 39, 40, 42, 43, 45, 47, 48, 50, 51, 55–58, 67–70, 74–78, 80, 82, 84, 86, 87, 91–97, 104–113:
    Brush open-toppers of 1902
Nos 26, 33, 35, 41, 53, 54, 59–66, 71–73, 81, 88, 89, 114, 127: Brush top-covered cars of 1904
Nos 115–126, 283–369: Corporation balcony cars of 1908–23
Nos 370–405: Corporation enclosed cars of 1923–26, No.400 being the prototype for:
Nos 76–150: EE enclosed 'Chamberlains' (named after the then General Manager) of 1926–27
Nos 1–75: Brush ditto of 1926–27
Nos 411–445: Corporation ditto of 1926–27
Nos 406–410: Corporation enclosed cars of 1928
Nos 151–154: Corporation ditto of 1930
Nos 155–254: Brush ditto of 1931–32
No.255: Brush experimental high-speed bogie enclosed car of 1933
Nos 256–271: Brush and EE ditto of 1935
Nos 272–274: Corporation streamlined cars of 1935
No.104: Corporation replacement 'Austerity' enclosed car of 1943
No.276: Corporation prototype enclosed car of 1948
Nos 601, 602: Chas. H. Roe Ltd of Leeds bogie single-deckers of 1953

Many of the above cars differed within their batches, as well as being top-covered or otherwise modified
and modernised during their lifetime.
    Second-hand cars acquired by Leeds were:

Nos 446–477: ex-HULL enclosed double-deckers bought 1942
Nos 478–487: ditto 1945
Nos 281–287: ex-MANCHESTER 'Pilchers' bought 1946–49
Nos 290–300: ex-Southampton enclosed double-deckers bought 1949–50
No.301: ex-London Transport 'Bluebird' bought 1951
Nos 501–590: ex-London Transport enclosed bogie double-deckers bought 1949–52
No.600: ex-SUNDERLAND CORPORATION bogie single-decker bought 1944 and numbered 288,
    but not used until 1953, when rebuilt as centre-exit railcar 600

Car No.600 is now preserved at the National Tramway Museum, Crich, along with Nos 180, 345, 399,
602 and 301 (this last car restored as No.1 of London Transport).

Liverpool: Old Swan Tramway
Authority: Turnpike Trust permission
Gauge: 4ft 8½in.*
Traction: Horse
Opened: 2 July 1861
Closed: May 1862?
System: Single line
Length: 1.3 miles
Stock: 1 dd?
Livery: ?
Last Car: ?

The British street tramway was born on Merseyside but, as with many such technological births, it is
rather difficult to put a precise date to the occasion; rather, a series of events marked the evolution of
the railway proper into the tramway proper. One of these events was undoubtedly the construction of
G.F. Train's street railway in BIRKENHEAD in 1860, though a year earlier a significant development
in the genesis of the tramway had occurred just across the Mersey in Liverpool.

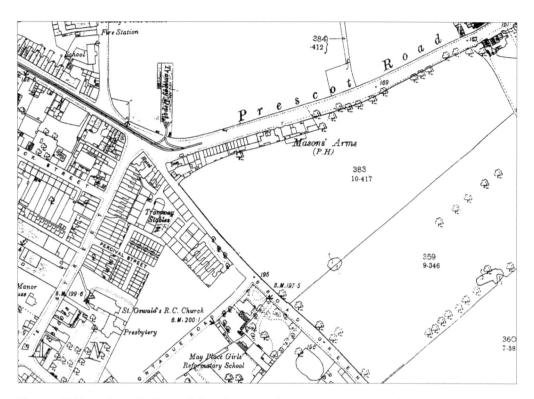

The two Old Swan depots in Liverpool, from the 1893 Ordnance Survey 25in. to 1 mile map. The 1861 depot was on the site marked 'Tramway Stables' whilst the depot to the north was the one opened by the LUT&O Co. in 1881 and taken over six years later by Liverpool Corporation (and later converted to house electric cars).

The story really begins in 1856 when, on 7 May that year, William Joseph Curtis of London was granted patent number 1071 in respect of a device to be fitted to the wheels of horse-drawn vehicles, which, controlled by the driver, enabled the wheels to run plain (on roads) or flanged (on railway tracks). In 1859 he began running horse buses thus equipped along the paved double tracks of the Line of Docks Railway in Liverpool (so called because it ran from Brunswick Dock in the south to Huskisson Dock in the north) used to move wagons in and out of the docks all along that side of the river. The only problem was that other bus operators pirated his invention, introducing rival services, and Curtis' buses lasted only a few months.

Two of Curtis' main rivals were William and Daniel Busby who, inspired by Train's pioneering line across the river, constructed their own street railway from the Old Swan westwards along the Liverpool–Prescot road as far as the then Liverpool boundary at Fairfield, a distance of just under 1½ miles. Permission for the line was given by the Liverpool & Prescot Turnpike Trust, and the single track was laid down the centre of the road with 4in.-wide sleepered plate rails with a slightly convex running surface between the two low flanges. The gauge was given as 4ft 8½in., but exactly how this was measured is uncertain.

Services were worked apparently by an ornate open-top double-deck car built by Oldbury (at a cost of £200), housed in the Busbys' horse bus stables at the Old Swan, though possibly one or more converted buses were also used. The line was not a success, though – possibly because of the type of rails used and its poor construction – and at the end of May 1862 the Turnpike Trustees began to lift it, the cost of this being borne by the operators, the Liverpool Road & Railway Omnibus Co. (registered 14 May 1860). By the beginning of September the whole track had been taken up, so ending the life of the city's first genuine tramway. The Company continued in the bus business though until 1876, when it merged with the LIVERPOOL TRAMWAYS Co. (see below). As for the Line of Docks special buses, these continued to run until at least 1872 – and possibly for another twenty years after that.

Liverpool Tramways

Authority: Liverpool Tramways Act 1868
Gauge: 4ft 8½in.
Traction: Horse
Opened: 1 November 1869
Taken over: 1 January 1897
System: Radial network
Length: 42.78 miles
Stock: 300+ dd?
Livery: Maroon/crimson lake & white/cream; route colour added c.1884

Following the failure of the OLD SWAN TRAMWAY (see above) a second attempt to provide Liverpool with a tramway system was made a few years later with the registration, on 12 December 1865, of the Liverpool Tramways Co. Ltd. Nothing concrete happened, however, until 1868 when an empowering Act was obtained and a new statutory Liverpool Tramways Co. incorporated.

The 1868 Act authorised the construction of a north–south line across the city, plus a circular system – the Inner Circle – in the city centre. Construction began in May 1869 with the Inner Circle, and the line south to Dingle via Renshaw Street, Great George Street and Park Road (just over 3¼ miles in total) opening that November; the 2½-mile northern route to Walton via Byrom Street, Scotland Road, Kirkdale Road and Walton Road opened 1 September following. Exactly one year later the Dingle route was extended just over a mile along Aigburth Road, through Toxteth Park to Aigburth Vale. (The depot had already been built on this section, in Tramway Road off Aigburth Road.)

In 1869 the Liverpool Road & Railway Omnibus Co. (see previous entry) tried to promote a tramways Bill of its own, but was opposed by Liverpool Corporation. The following year it accordingly decided to try to join forces with the LT Co. and on 8 February 1871 a new concern, the Liverpool Omnibus & Tramways Co. Ltd, was registered, the LRR Co. being wound up a year later; in February 1876 this, in turn, merged with the LT Co. to form the Liverpool United Tramways & Omnibus Co., the aim being to secure a profitable monopoly of the city's public transport as far as its roads were concerned.

The original rails used on the tramway had very wide side grooves, but from 1877 onwards they were replaced with centre-grooved ones and the cars were fitted gradually with centre-flanged wheels that could run on both types of track. Always concerned about the condition of the tramway, the Corporation purchased it under the provisions of the Liverpool Tramways (Purchase) Act 1872 on 1 January 1880 for the sum of £30,000 and leased it back to the Company until the end of 1896 – by which date the system had expanded considerably, with lines extending north, east and south beyond the city limits to Bootle, West Derby and Wavertree, and west from the city centre to the Pier Head. The tramway's financial position had now improved greatly with receipts overtaking those from the buses in 1882 (despite a Company programme of buying out rival operators).

Detailed information regarding the cars is lacking. Services began with sixteen open-toppers (from an initial order of twenty-four) from Starbuck, possibly assembled from components supplied by Stephenson. By June 1880 thirty cars were at work, with later vehicles being supplied by Starbuck and Ashbury (Eades reversible cars). From 1883 onwards the Company built its own cars – again all double-deckers – and by the time of the Corporation's purchase of the remainder of the system in 1896, for £567,375, there were 281 in service, though how many had been withdrawn previously is not known. Trials were also conducted with steam (1879), cable (1883) and compressed air vehicles (1884–86), but not followed up.

Liverpool Corporation Tramways

Authority: Liverpool Tramways Transfer Act 1897*
Gauge: 4ft 8½in.
Traction: Horse, overhead electric
Took over: 1 January 1897
Closed: 14 September 1957

System: Radial network
Length: 97.37 miles
Stock: 281 dd horse; 45 sd, 1,260 dd electric
Livery: Crimson lake & cream to 1933, then privet green & ivory
Last Car: No.293

In November 1895 Liverpool's boundaries were enlarged to include areas previously in neighbouring authorities, which were also served by the Liverpool United Tramways & Omnibus Co. (see above); the Corporation took over the powers of the Company in those areas (though Bootle Corporation was empowered by Liverpool's 1897 Act to convert the lines in its borough and lease them to Liverpool). In all, the Corporation acquired 281 horse cars and 69 miles of track in Liverpool, 6 in Bootle and ¾ mile in Litherland, on a total of seventeen routes.

Left: Liverpool's famous Pier Head, where many of the city's tramway routes terminated. The car in the centre of the photograph is fitted with a Bellamy roof, a distinctive pattern of top cover named after one of the system's (1899–1905) general managers. *(Author's Collection)*

Below: Map of Liverpool Corporation Tramways from the 1920–21 *Manual of Electrical Undertakings.*

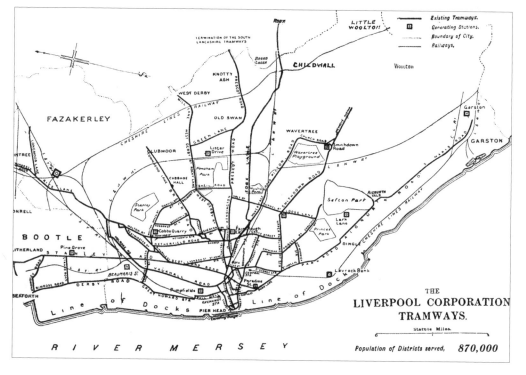

THE
LIVERPOOL CORPORATION TRAMWAYS.

Statute Miles.

Population of Districts served, **870,000**

The first electric route, to Dingle via Park Road, was opened on 16 November 1898 and from then on the other lines were converted quickly so that, by October 1901, only one horse car was left in service (until 25 August 1903), working a shuttle service from the boundary at Linacre to Litherland Canal Bridge. The other horse cars were scrapped as they were withdrawn (with the exception of seven that were sold to ABERDEEN CORPORATION in 1900 and three that went to WALLASEY a year later).

The system continued to expand over the decades up to and including the 1940s, with lines extending eventually as far as Bootle, Litherland, Aintree, Fazakerley and Kirkby in the north, and Garston and Woolton in the south. Eastwards, the system was connected in 1902 with that of ST HELENS via Knotty Ash and the LIVERPOOL & PRESCOT LIGHT RAILWAY which, in 1919, was taken over by Liverpool. (This was the system's only connection with a neighbouring tramway, but through it a link was made with the rest of the south Lancashire network.) Modernisation came in the 1930s and 1940s when several outlying routes were opened (the final extension, to Kirkby, on 12 April 1944), mainly on sections of reserved track – this coming to account for a third of Liverpool's route mileage. At the end of the Second World War the Corporation decided to replace the trams – many of them of relatively modern design – with buses, a programme hastened along by the destruction of sixty-six cars in a fire on 7 November 1947 at Green Lane Depot.

Piecemeal route closures began in June 1948, with services and cars withdrawn gradually over the next nine years, the last day of operation seeing the closure of the routes from the Pier Head to Bowring Park and from Castle Street to Page Moss Avenue.

The first electric cars introduced by the Corporation were Nos 400–429, single-deck powered cars (even numbers) and trailers (odd numbers) of 1898 from W.C.F. Busch of Eimsbuttel, Hamburg. These were all withdrawn by 1901 and broken up in 1914 (with the exception of some converted into works cars). They were joined in 1898 by Nos 432–446, Brill single-deck bogie vehicles, later renumbered 6–20, of which Nos 6, 8 and 12 were rebuilt as double-deckers in 1900–01 and survived until 1933, whilst the others were scrapped in the early 1920s. Thereafter, the car fleet grew as follows (with later numbers in brackets):

Nos 447–458 (21–32): Milnes open-toppers of 1899
Nos 459–463 (43–47): Brush ditto
Nos 464–468: Brush ditto, but never paid for and returned (then delivered to LEEDS)
Nos 469–478 (33–42), 54–133, 141: ERTCW ditto of 1899–1900
Nos 479–484 (48–53): Corporation ditto of 1899
Nos 1–4, 134–140: Corporation open-toppers of 1899–1900 (known as 'Bellamys' after the then General
    Manager)
No.5: Corporation open-topper of 1901
Nos 142–441: ERTCW 'Bellamys' of 1900–01
Nos 442–447: Corporation ditto, but top–covered of 1902–03
Nos 448–452: ERTCW ditto, but open-topped of 1902–03
Nos 453–477: ditto, but top-covered
Nos 478–483: Corporation ditto, but open-topped of 1902–03
Nos 1–4, 484–570: ditto, but top-covered of 1907–12
No.571: UEC top-covered car of 1912
No.572: UEC bogie enclosed car of 1912
Nos 573–576: Corporation 1st class 'Bellamys' of 1913
No.44: Corporation top-covered 'Exhibition' car of 1914
Nos 577–599: Corporation top-covered cars of 1913–15
Nos 600–605: ditto of 1919–20
Nos 609–633: EE ditto of 1919–20
Nos 606–608, 634–636: Corporation balcony 'Birdcages', 1921
Twenty–seven cars: ditto rebuilds of 'Bellamys', 1920–22
Nos 637–756 + 201 cars: Corporation new enclosed top cars and rebuilds of older cars, 1924–1933
No.757: EE long bogie single-decker of 1929 for possible Mersey tunnel line

Above left: Liverpool's 'Last Car', 'Baby Grand' No.293 (now resident in the USA), complete with a parallel procession of cars and a motorcycle escort. *(Author's Collection)*

Above right: Two souvenir tickets issued to mark the closing of Liverpool's tramways, and their common back design.

Nos 758–769: EE enclosed bogie cars of 1931–32
Nos 770–781: Corporation ditto of 1933
Nos 782–817: ditto of 1933–34 (known as 'Robinsons' after the then Chief Electrical Engineer)
Nos 818–867: Corporation bogie enclosed cars of 1935–36 (known as 'Marks' after the then General
   Manager)
Nos 868–992, 151–200: Corporation bogie streamlined cars of 1936–37 (known as 'Liners' or 'Streamliners')
Nos 201–300: Corporation streamlined 'Baby Grands' of 1937–42

Many of the open-topped vehicles were later top-covered and/or rebuilt, a fact which perhaps explains why so few Liverpool cars were ever sold to other operators, the only sales being of the bodies of Nos 48, 49 and 50, which were sold to TYNEMOUTH & DISTRICT in 1920 (but used on the GATESHEAD & DISTRICT system instead) and of forty-six 'Green Goddesses' (as the streamliners were collectively known) in 1953–54 to GLASGOW CORPORATION. The only working preserved Liverpool cars in Britain are Nos 762 of 1931, at the Pacific Road Transport Museum – see BIRKENHEAD: WIRRAL TRAMWAY (2) – and 869 of 1936 (latterly Glasgow 1055), at the National Tramway Museum, Crich, though 'Last Car' No.293 now resides at the Seashore Trolley Museum, Maine, in the USA.

Liverpool & Prescot Light Railway
Authority: Liverpool and Prescot Light Railway Order 1898
Gauge: 4ft 8½in.
Traction: Overhead electric
Opened: 24 June 1902*
Taken over: 1 October 1919
System: Single line
Length: 3.11 miles
Stock: 7 dd
Livery: As for ST HELENS

Owned by the Lancashire Light Railways Co. Ltd (registered 21 April 1898), the LPLR was the only part constructed of a grand scheme of some 24 miles of tramways proposed for the south Lancashire area. The Company had common board links with the SOUTH LANCASHIRE TRAMWAYS, its shares being bought by the South Lancashire Electric Traction Power Co. Ltd before construction began.

The tramway ran, as a single track in a then rural area, from the (then) Liverpool boundary at Berry's Bridge, Knotty Ash, eastwards along Prescot Road and Liverpool Road to Brook Bridge, Prescot, where it connected end-on with the ST HELENS system. It was ready for opening some months before it was due to as the Company was waiting for the LIVERPOOL CORPORATION route to Knotty Ash to be completed (and connected to the light railway); the first cars ran on 24 June 1902 to allow the crews to learn the road, with passengers being carried, though regular services did not begin until the following day, with through-running from Knotty Ash to St Helens. It is thought the line was worked by South Lancs cars for a brief period, its own open-toppers not arriving until later in 1902; these latter vehicles were numbered 37–41 (from Milnes) and 42 and 43 (BEC) in the St Helens fleet (and housed there). On the same day that the St Helens Corporation took over the St Helens tramways (1 October 1919), the Company – owned by Lancashire United Tramways Ltd since 1905 – sold the light railway to Liverpool for £18,000 for incorporation into that system, and the cars to South Lancs.

Lytham St Annes Corporation Tramways

Authority: Blackpool St Anne's Lytham Tramways Act 1893
Gauge: 4ft 8½in.
Traction: Gas, horse/overhead electric
Opened: 11 July 1896
Closed: 28 April 1937
System: Single line
Length: 7.51 miles
Stock: 16 dd gas; 3 sd, 17 dd horse; 4 sd, 52 dd electric
Livery: Light blue & cream to 1920, blue & ivory to 1933, then blue & white
Last Car: ?

This simple system on the north shore of the Ribble estuary, just south of Blackpool, had a far from simple history. It was opened in 1896 by the Blackpool, St Anne's & Lytham Tramway Co. and was built to link Lytham with Blackpool using a coastal route through the new development of St Anne's-on-the-Sea midway between them, there being no coast road at that time. The idea was to connect the line to BLACKPOOL's Lytham Road route (opened 1895) to permit through-running, but in the event the first mainly single-track section ran from St Anne's to close to Blackpool's Station Road terminus, with the 1-mile stretch from here back to the joint boundary at Squires Gate being owned by Blackpool Corporation. The line was operated, on lease from the Company, by the British Gas Traction Co. Ltd, using open-top double-deck cars Nos 1–4 built by Ashbury and fitted with 15hp German-built Otto gas engines. The tramway was extended to Lytham on 21 February 1897 and another twelve cars put into service (these being equipped with 15hp Crossley engines).

In 1898 a new concern, the Blackpool, St Anne's & Lytham Trammings Co. Ltd (registered 15 October 1898) bought out the interests of the BGT Co. for £115,000, including the cars. It would appear that the latter did not prove entirely successful for Blackpool Corporation refused to allow them over its portion of the line from 1900 onwards, and until 1902 this section was worked by horse cars (possibly obtained from BOLTON). By now, though, the Company had obtained the Blackpool St Anne's and Lytham Tramways Act 1900 to authorise electric working – and, early in 1901, was bought out for £111,000 by the Electric Tramways Construction & Maintenance Co. Ltd, who began reconstruction work in December 1902; the gas trams were sold the next year to TRAFFORD PARK and Neath Corporation in Wales. The tramway reopened on 30 May 1903 as a double-track line following the route of the gas and horse line along the sand dunes from Blackpool to St Anne's and then via Clifton Road South to Ansdell, then along Church Road into Lytham and through the Market Square, past the old gas tram depot, where it turned south towards the shore, terminating in Dicconson Terrace, opposite the pier. That September a 1-mile extension east from the Market Square along Clifton Street and Walton Street took the line to a new terminus by the East Beach, close to the Cottage Hospital. The depot was in Squires Gate Lane by the northern terminus, housing new cars Nos 1–30, all BEC open-toppers.

Lytham St Annes Corporation No.12 of 1903 by the 'Golden Sandhills' on the seaside section that made up most of this tramway's one route. *(Author's Collection)*

Through-running to Blackpool began in July 1905 after the two systems had been connected, with ten open-sided crossbench cars (Nos 31–40) being bought from Brush for summer workings. These proved so popular that the following year Nos 21–30 were converted by UEC to a similar configuration. On 28 October 1920 the tramway was purchased for £132,279 by St Anne's UDC; this body, in 1922, became part of the newly incorporated borough of Lytham St Anne's – which began motor bus operations the following year. (The apostrophe in the name was later generally dropped.) Ten new top-covered cars (Nos 41–50) were bought in 1924 from EE; however, just two years later, on 23 July 1926, the eastern end of the line was cut back to Market Square in Lytham. The future of the rest of the tramway appeared bright though, and cars and track were kept in good order with minor rebuilds of the former taking place. In 1930 No.26 was converted to a works car to sweep sand from the line – always a serious problem on the tramway's exposed northern section.

In 1933 four relatively new (1924) single-deck EE cars were bought from the DEARNE DISTRICT system for winter workings and numbered 51–54; these were followed the next year by No.55, a 1915-vintage double-deck enclosed Brush bogie car ex-ACCRINGTON. The last car purchased, No.56 in 1934, was an ex-PRESTON enclosed vehicle (No.42 there). By now, though, the Corporation was looking to sell the line to Blackpool, but to no avail and, as its bus fleet grew, so the tram fleet was reduced until 1936, when it was decided to abandon the trams entirely. The southern section to St Anne's closed on 15 December that year, with the original, northern part of the line going the same way the following spring – and, with it, the chance of as superb scenic run all the way from Lytham to Fleetwood.

Manchester Tramways

Authority: Manchester Corporation Tramways Order 1875; Salford Tramways and Improvement Act 1875
Gauge: 4ft 8½in.
Traction: Horse
Opened: 18 May 1877
Closed: 31 March 1903
System: Network
Length: 27.63 miles
Stock: 84 sd? 431 dd?
Livery: Red & cream
Last Car: ?

This extensive system grew piecemeal during the 1870s and 1880s following the unsuccessful experiment of Haworth's patent track (see SALFORD TRAMWAYS). The history of the system is an immensely complicated one, partly because of the large number of routes and extensions involved and partly because of the number of local authorities who owned and leased track to the tramway operator. In the beginning, this was the Manchester Carriage Co. Ltd, who opened the first line from the Pack Horse Inn, Pendleton, south-eastwards into the city centre, along the route of the original Salford tramway via Broad Street and Chapel Street as far as Bridge Street (2 miles), then back out northwards via Deansgate and the Bury New Road to the Grove Inn, Higher Broughton (another mile), the two sections being leased respectively from Salford and Manchester corporations. The line was extended from the Grove to the toll bar at Kersal on 30 July 1877, with each route being worked by fifteen Starbuck open-top double-deckers (Nos 1–30 in all) based on two depots at Church Street, Pendleton, and Knoll Street, Higher Broughton. At least some of these cars carried the legend 'MANCHESTER & SALFORD TRAMWAYS'.

Surrounding local authorities wished to get in on the act, and a succession of Orders were obtained to expand the system, whilst the Manchester Suburban Tramways Act of 1878 authorised a new concern, the Manchester Suburban Tramways Co., to construct a string of outlying lines and which, in 1880, merged with the MC Co. Ltd to form the Manchester Carriage & Tramways Co. Two years later the system was virtually complete. The western routes converged on Deansgate and the eastern on Piccadilly, the two being connected via Market Street. Routes were a mixture of single and double tracks (with a depot on most of them), running out as far as Stockport in the south-east, Ashton-under-Lyne and Stalybridge to the east, and Oldham to the north-east.

Full details of the passenger stock are not known, though it is certain that well over 500 cars were used, these being lettered and numbered according to their usual route; the vast majority were reversible-bodied cars built from 1877–1890 by the Company at its Pendleton works, to the patented designs of John Eades, the Works Manager. (The basic design was that of a single-ended body that could be rotated on its truck at a terminus in order to avoid unhitching the horses.) Some idea of the scale of the Manchester operation can be gauged by the fact that at one time the Company was the biggest single purchaser of horses in the north of England, with over 5,000 in the stud in 1900, each animal having a working life expectancy of only five years.

As Manchester expanded its boundaries in the 1880 and 1890s, so the Corporation turned its thoughts to running the tramway system itself. There then followed a protracted round of disputes, negotiations, 'horse-trading' and non-agreements between the Company and the various local authorities involved, culminating finally in arbitration in 1901–03 to settle matters. As from 2 May 1901 SALFORD CORPORATION took over its portion of the system (and ninety-four cars), and on 30 October that year the Company stopped its services in OLDHAM, the Corporation there having already introduced electric trams. The Manchester lines were handed over to the Corporation as and when horse-working ceased, the last such transfers being the Oldham Road and Ashton routes.

Manchester Corporation Tramways

Authority: Manchester Corporation Act 1897
Gauge: 4ft 8½in.
Traction: Overhead electric
Opened: 6 June 1901
Closed: 10 January 1949
System: Network
Length: 119.23 miles
Stock: 73 sd, 1,028 dd
Livery: Red & cream
Last Car: No.1007

Manchester Corporation's first electric route was the Cheetham Hill Road line from Albert Square to Hightown, after which the remainder of the horse system (see above) was converted and new routes and extensions added until, by the end of the 1900s, the system was one of the largest in the country and closely linked to the surrounding tramways of SALFORD, STOCKTON, ASHTON, OLDHAM and MIDDLETON. Through-running to Salford began on 31 May 1903, to Oldham on 21 January 1907 and to Ashton on 4 March that year. To the south, Altrincham was reached on 10 May 1907 and, to the west, the TRAFFORD PARK electric tramway had been taken over (on 31 October 1905) jointly with Salford Corporation.

The First World War occasioned a pause in this relentless expansion, but it began again in the 1920s when the end of the lease of the OLDHAM, ASHTON & HYDE system on 24 June 1921 opened the way for new through services to Ashton and Hyde. The takeover of the Middleton system on 9 August 1925 by the surrounding local authorities (including Manchester) led to a new through service to ROCHDALE commencing that same day; three years later, on 19 May 1928, through-running began to BURY via Middleton and HEYWOOD. The system was now at its peak, with nearly a thousand trams out on the roads, a fleet third only in size to those of London and GLASGOW.

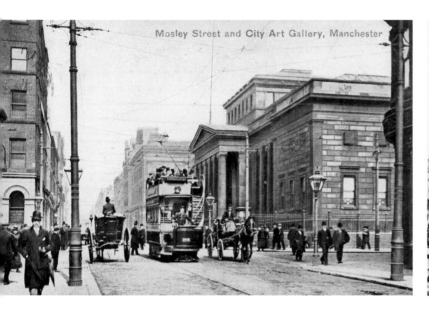

Above left: The evolution of the Manchester Corporation tramcar: Brush open-topper No.186 of 1903 on a 1904-franked postcard of Mosley Street … *(Author's Collection)*

Above right: … sister car 245 in Market Street on a 1909-franked card … *(Author's Collection)*

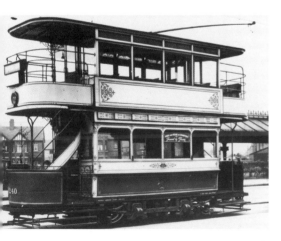
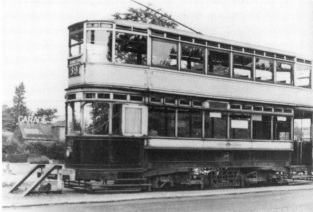

Above left: … and sister car 240 after having a top cover fitted pre-First World War. The notice in the window says: 'READ AND RIDE IN COMFORT. Travel by Tram.' *(Author's Collection)*

Above right: Finally, fully enclosed Manchester Corporation No.427 of the series of replacement bogie cars built in the 1920s and given fleet numbers vacated by older, withdrawn vehicles. *(Author's Collection)*

The 1930s were very different. It was now the turn of the buses – the Corporation's own fleet having grown to well over a hundred by 1930 – and on 6 April that year tramway route 53 from Cheetham Hill to Stretford Road was closed, and on 26 October route 25 (Bradford Road) was treated likewise. The long south-western route down Chester Road, Washway Road and Manchester Road to Altrincham (and the short branch to Sale) went the following year, and in 1932 the through service to Rochdale was another casualty.

On 1 March 1938 the Ashton Old Road line to the east was converted to trolleybus operation, and on 8 February 1939 the Corporation agreed a three-year plan to abandon the tramways altogether. As elsewhere, the Second World War put the plan on hold, though not before further cutbacks had occurred (and some reinstatements made during the war in order to save motor fuel). By the end of 1945 only the Oldham route remained to the north of the city. The abandonment programme now resumed in earnest, the last route to go being the 35 from Exchange to Hazel Grove. The story does not end there, though, for the city has pioneered the resurrection of the British tramway – literally in the case of HEATON PARK (see below), where the only genuine preserved tramway in these islands runs. Far more importantly, the modern MANCHESTER METROLINK is set to serve the city's residents for many years to come (see below).

Because the car fleet was so large, only the briefest details can be given here (ignoring later modifications). The first six cars arrived in 1899 as samples of their manufacturers' products so that the Tramways Committee could decide where to place its initial large order: No.101 was a Manchester Carriage & Tramways open-topper and No.102 was the same from HN; No.103 was a bogie open-topper from Brush, No.104 an Ashbury open-topper and Nos 105 and 106 two Milnes cars, an open-topper and a single-deck saloon. After this, the fleet was assembled as follows:

Nos 107–187, 238–276: Brush open-toppers of 1901–03
Nos 227–436, 487–511: Milnes ditto
Nos 437–486: Brush bogie open-toppers of 1901
Nos 188–237, 537–548: ditto of 1902–04
Nos 512–536: Milnes bogie single-deckers of 1903
Nos 549–648: Brush top-covered bogie cars of 1904–05
Nos 649–668: UEC bogie single-deckers of 1907
Nos 669–679: Corporation balcony cars of 1909
Nos 680–717, 748–762: ditto bogie cars of 1909–14
Nos 718–747: Corporation balcony cars of 1912
Nos 763–767: Corporation bogie single-deckers of 1914
Nos 768–792: Corporation bogie balcony cars of 1914–19
Nos 793–797: Corporation bogie enclosed cars of 1920
Nos 798–835: EE ditto of 1920
Nos 836–847: EE bogie single-deckers of 1920–21
Nos 848–897: EE bogie enclosed cars of 1920–22
Nos 898–933: Corporation ditto of 1920–22
Nos 934–993: EE ditto of 1925–26
Nos 994–1003: Brush bogie single-deckers ex-Middleton 1925
Nos 1001–1005: EE bogie enclosed cars of 1927–28

In addition, between 1924 and 1930 the Corporation built 110 bogie enclosed double-deckers, giving them the numbers from withdrawn vehicles, and between 1927 and 1930 thirty-eight enclosed double-deckers (known as 'Pilchers' after the then General Manager) were similarly added to the fleet.

The system's four depots were at Queens Road in Hightown, Princess Road in Moss Side, Birchfields Road in Levenshulme and at Hyde Road (the main depot and works), just east of the city centre.

At the final closure thirty-five passenger cars still survived, only to be burnt *en masse* on 16 March following. Sadly, out of such a large fleet, only one car – No.765 of 1914 – can be seen working today, on the Heaton Park line.

The mainstay of the Heaton Park Tramway is Manchester Corporation No.765 of 1914, seen here on the preserved original section of the line in the company of Leeds Corporation No.6 (see p.70), on August Bank Holiday Monday 2009. *(Author)*

Manchester: Heaton Park Tramway

The Heaton Park line is unique amongst British pleasure tramways in that it operates on a stretch of original tramway restored for the running of preserved tramcars, the special circumstances of it not being on a public highway making this possible.

This surviving portion of the former MANCHESTER CORPORATION TRAMWAYS was a 380yd-long double-track branch off Middleton Road into Heaton Park itself. The Middleton Road route opened on 1 April 1904 and on 21 April of the following year the branch opened as sidings to cope with cars bringing large numbers of visitors to the park (one of Britain's biggest at 600 acres). On 19 January 1934, during the Manchester closures of the 1930s, the branch was disconnected and the rails tarred over as part of a car park. (A third track was lifted.)

There the matter – and the rails – rested until the 1970s, when the Manchester Transport Museum Society proposed reopening the branch for the operation of preserved vehicles on loan from elsewhere, adapting a large and conveniently sited park shelter as a depot. Refurbishment work took place during 1978, with a trial opening that summer and a formal opening on 28 March of the following year (though public services did not commence until 1 September).

Such was the immediate popularity of the line, even though it is operated (by volunteers) primarily on summer Sundays and Bank Holidays only, that in 1984 work began on extending it to the boating lake, making for a total length of 810yd. The trial opening of the extension took place at the end of the 1985 season, with the formal opening at the beginning of the next.

The current service is provided by HULL 96 of 1901 and Manchester Corporation 765 of 1914, both on long-term loan from the National Tramway Museum at Crich. On display – and occasionally operated – is Manchester horse car L53 of 1879.

Manchester Metrolink

Authority: Greater Manchester (Light Rapid Transit System) Act 1988
Gauge: 4ft 8½in.
Traction: Overhead electric
Opened: 6 April 1992
System: Branching
Length: 22.2 miles
Stock: 72 sd*
Livery: Aquamarine & pale grey*

More than forty years after the last Corporation trams ran in Manchester (see earlier), a new, high-technology system was opened to herald a new age of British street tramway construction. Inspired by light rail developments elsewhere in Europe and America and, closer to home, by the 1980s' successes of the Tyne & Wear Metro in Newcastle and the Docklands Light Railway in London, this historic project was promoted by a Rail Study Group made up of representatives from BR, the Greater Manchester Council and the Greater Manchester Passenger Transport Executive, set up in 1982 to plan for the city's future local rail needs. Six years of analyses, planning and lobbying finally led to parliamentary approval for the first stages of an envisaged city-wide light rail network to include purpose-built street sections in the centre and the use of existing BR lines to serve the peripheral areas.

The first, northern half of the system opened on 6 April 1992 and ran from the past Queens Road Depot and BR Manchester Victoria station, along a refurbished double-track (formerly third-rail) line, through Crumpsall, Heaton Park, Prestwich, Whiteford and Radcliffe, to a new interchange station at Bury, with nine intermediate stations *en route*. On 27 April the double-track street section back from Victoria to BR's Manchester Piccadilly station opened, followed by a south-western line out from Piccadilly to Altrincham. The city centre portion of this, from Piccadilly to the new G-MEX exhibition and conference centre (converted from the former Central station) is a street tramway occupying the High Street, Market Street, Piccadilly Gardens, Mosley Street (where there is a connection to the Bury line), St Peter's Square and Lower Mosley Street. From G-MEX to Altrincham, the cars travel over the refurbished BR line through Old Trafford, Stretford, Sale (and five other stations) to BR's Altrincham station. The official opening of the system, on 17 July 1992, was conducted by HM the Queen.

The initial car fleet was made up of articulated three-bogie vehicles Nos 1001–26, built by the Firema Consortium of Italian rolling-stock manufacturers; each double-body unit is 30m long and can seat eighty-six passengers. With a top speed of 50mph, they represented the latest in such vehicle design and technology at the time of construction, though today they appear very dated in comparison with the more modern vehicles used on later metro systems. (For one thing, they have no low-floor sections.)

Operated by the Greater Manchester Metro Ltd (later Serco Metrolink Ltd), and funded largely by the government, the total cost of the tramway was some £135 million. On 6 December 1999 a short, north-western branch was opened from Cornbrook to Broadway in the Salford Quays area (formerly Manchester Docks) branch, extended on 21 July 2000 to Eccles (with an official opening by HRH the Princess Royal on 9 January 2001). This 4.3-mile line, costing £160 million, and with nine intermediate stops, is a mixture of street and reserved sections, not former railway alignments. The contract to construct and operate it was awarded to the Altram consortium and another six Firema units, numbered 2001–06 and technologically more advanced than the earlier cars, were purchased. Certain trams, from the whole fleet, have been given a strange assortment of names, not all of which have an obvious local connection.

Above left: The former BR station at Bowker Vale, now a Manchester Metrolink halt, with tram unit No.1005 heading out towards Bury on 31 August 2009. *(Author)*

Above right: Tramway maintenance is a never-ending task, though it is usually only major projects – such as relaying the Metrolink track in the whole centre of Manchester – that get noticed by the general public. This is St Peter's Square on 31 August 2009, with tidying-up work underway in readiness for the resumption of cross-city services. *(Author)*

On 15 July 2007 operation (and maintenance) of the tramway was taken over by the Stagecoach Group – operator of the SOUTH YORKSHIRE SUPERTRAM in SHEFFIELD – on a ten-year contract. Also in 2007, a total of twelve new tramcar units were ordered from Bombardier to be built on the Continent, and the following year a further twenty-eight were ordered – all high-floor units with seating for 200 passengers. The thinking behind the orders was to increase capacity on the network and to have stock in readiness for future extensions and new routes as and when they open, current proposals being to enlarge the system to 64 miles/103km, including conversion of railway lines to Oldham and Rochdale, as well as a line to Manchester Airport and a second depot. The first of the new cars, numbered, in a new series, 3001 and sporting a striking silver and yellow livery, arrived in Manchester from Vienna on 13 July 2009, heralding a new tramway era for the city.

Manchester, Bury, Rochdale & Oldham Steam Tramways

Authority: Bury and District Tramways Order 1881; Rochdale Tramways Order 1881
Gauge: 4ft 8½in., 3ft 6in.
Traction: Steam, horse
Opened: 12 March 183
Closed: 30 May 1904*
System: Branching
Length: 30.28 miles
Stock: 91 locos, 72 dd steam; 3 dd? horse
Livery: Locos brown; cars oak & white, later brown & cream
Last Cars: Locos 46 and 87, cars?

Despite its name, this impressive system – of which just a third of the planned lines were constructed – never served Manchester, only the three other towns of its title. Because of the number of different local authorities involved, the promotion was a complicated affair for the owner and operator, the Manchester, Bury, Rochdale & Oldham Steam Tramways Co. (a subsidiary of the City of London Contract Corporation). Matters were not helped by having the two ends of the system laid to standard gauge (with an eye on future through-running with its neighbours) whilst the central portion had to employ 3ft 6in. gauge track on account of the narrow roadways encountered.

The first, standard-gauge section opened ran northwards from Moor Lane in Broughton, just inside the SALFORD boundary north of Manchester, through Whitefield on Bury New Road and Manchester Road to the Derby Hotel in the centre of Bury, a distance of some 6 miles (and later extended as a narrow-gauge branch north-west up the Tottington Road). The first three engines (Nos 1–3) were by Wilkinsons, hauling the first arrivals of a batch of sixteen standard and narrow-gauge six-wheeled open-top cars (Nos 1–16) from Starbuck.

On 20 March 1883 a second route opened: a 2½-mile continuation of the line northwards to Limefield which, until road-widening work was completed, had to be worked by horses with (most likely) three Starbuck double-deckers Nos 33–35 being bought for this purpose. The third section opened, on 7 May 1883, was an isolated route in the east, running south from the Wellington Hotel in the centre of Rochdale down the Oldham Road to the village of Buersil, with a north-eastern branch from Rochdale along Entwistle Road and Halifax Road, through Smallbridge to Littleborough. Both of these lines were narrow gauge and worked by tram locos from a fleet of twenty-six based at Rochdale and supplied by Greens (Nos 9–12, 18–20 and 27–34), Wilkinsons (Nos 13–17) and BP (Nos 21–26), hauling trailers 17–26, more six-wheeled open-toppers from Starbuck. These cars were joined in 1883–84 by Nos 31, 32 and 36–39, conventional Starbuck bogie open-toppers. Locos 4–8 and 35–38 were further Wilkinson standard-gauge engines of 1883, and later that year the Tottington Road branch north-west from Bury was extended as far as the village of that name.

March 1884 saw the opening of a narrow-gauge line from Bury eastwards to Heywood Depot, halfway to Rochdale (plus a ¾-mile branch south from Heywood to Hopwood), with the other half of this 7-mile section opening on 30 May. Another northern narrow-gauge branch, from Rochdale to Whitworth via the Whitworth Road through Shawclough, was in operation by July that year and, on

1 March 1885, services began over a southern extension from Buersil to Royton (where another depot was sited). The line from here through Oldham, opened in stages to 1 August, was standard gauge (with a branch opened on 4 July 1889 to Werneth railway station). Further standard-gauge locos were bought in 1885: Nos 52–54 from MW and 55–59 from Falcon. Three more narrow-gauge locos came that year (No.60 from Greens, and 61 and 62 from Wilkinsons) plus Falcon narrow-gauge cars 40–64 (of 1884–85). Thereafter the remaining stock purchases were all in 1886: standard-gauge BP locos 83–88 and 91, bogie top-covered cars 65–70 from Lancaster and 71–74 from Falcon, plus narrow-gauge locos 63–82 from BP and 89 and 90 from Wilkinsons, with bogie top-covered cars 75–81 from Falcon.

In December 1887 the Company went into receivership and ten months later a new concern, the more appropriately named Bury, Rochdale & Oldham Tramway Co. Ltd, was formed to take over the tramway which, with its lengthy, single-track, largely rural sections, was at one time the longest steam-worked system in the world. The first cutbacks, in the name of economy, were not long in coming, with a mile being lopped off the southern end of the Bury–Broughton route and, on 22 July 1891, the Whitworth branch was cut in half at Henley. On 19 December that year the Hopwood branch was closed (until 18 November 1892), followed by a further truncation of the standard-gauge line south of Bury. These and other measures succeeded in turning the tramway's fortunes round, but by now the local authorities affected were looking towards a more modern, electric future for the line. On 31 October 1901 Oldham Corporation took over the track within its boundaries (which had been leased to the Company) and on 28 June 1902 the last steam trams ran there. The closure of the rest of the system followed in stages until 30 May 1904, when the last standard-gauge stretch (from Royton to the Oldham boundary) and the last narrow-gauge section (from Royton to Summit on the Rochdale boundary) closed. Only the Littleborough branch survived, to be worked by ROCHDALE CORPORATION.

Marfleet *see* Hull: Drypool & Marfleet

Mexborough & Swinton Tramways
Authority: Mexborough and Swinton Tramways Act 1902
Gauge: 4ft 8½in.
Traction: Surface-contact/overhead electric
Opened: 6 February 1907
Closed: 9 March 1929
System: Single line
Length: 6.48 miles
Stock: 20 dd
Livery: Bright red & cream
Last Car: ?

The short, simple M&S tramway provided the vital link between the larger systems of ROTHERHAM and SHEFFIELD to the south and the DEARNE DISTRICT and BARNSLEY to the north. It was constructed by the NEC and worked by a subsidiary, the Mexborough & Swinton Tramways Co. It ran northwards from Rotherham Bridge (where it connected with that town's Effingham Street line), through Parkgate, Rawmarsh and Ryecroft to the Woodman Inn, where it met (from 1924) the Wath Wood Road route of the DD. Here the M&S line swung north-east through Swinton and Mexborough to terminate at the Old Toll Bar at Denaby. The first section opened in 1907 was from Rotherham Bridge to Ryecroft, the remainder following on 3 August with the Dolter surface-contact system being used to supply current to the sixteen Brush open-top cars. These were also equipped for overhead current collection, presumably on the 'belt and braces' principle which, in the event, proved a wise choice for, as elsewhere, the Dolter system was a failure and the Company was in the process of converting the line to an overhead system of supply when, on 30 July 1908, the BoT ordered its closure until the work was completed.

The tramway reopened on 29 August 1908 with another four Brush double-deckers (Nos 17–20) added to the stock; these were top-covered cars and over the next four years all the earlier cars were fitted with top covers with the exception of Nos 10 and 14 which, in 1911, were sold to the DEWSBURY, OSSETT & SOOTHILL NETHER TRAMWAYS. Also in 1908, on 20 October, through-running from Rotherham began. On 31 August 1915 the Company inaugurated two short trolleybus routes as feeders to the tramway and thirteen years later, in January 1928, these vehicles replaced the Mexborough–Denaby trams entirely. The next cutback came in November that year when the stretch from Mexborough back to the Woodman Inn was closed (again replaced by a trolleybus service), with the remaining southern half of the line following the next year. After the closure two more cars (Nos 7 and 15) were sold to the DOSN and the others scrapped.

Mid-Yorkshire Tramways *see* Shipley: Mid-Yorkshire Tramways

Middlesbrough & Stockton Tramways
Authority: Middlesbrough and Stockton Tramways Order 1873
Gauge: 4ft 8½in.
Traction: Horse
Opened: November 1874?
Closed: 24 December 1897
System: Radial
Length: 2.59 miles
Stock: 2 sd, 2 dd?
Livery: Red & cream
Last Car: ?

The history of the tramways of Teesside is a seemingly complicated one involving two counties, three towns, the bridging of a major river and a number of separate lines and companies. Looked at another way though, the story can be seen as the familiar one of a number of concerns slowly coming together, with their lines passing through the common horse-steam-electric traction sequence.

The first line in the area, opened by the Middlesbrough & Stockton Tramways Co., ran from the Wellington Hotel, in Albert Road in the centre of Middlesbrough, south-west along Corporation Road and Newport Road to terminate in Calvert Street, Newport, by the ferry landing stage on the River Tees. Two single-deck and two double-deck cars were supplied by Starbuck and the tramway is thought to have opened in late 1874 sometime after a trial run on 23 November. In August 1878 the line was purchased by IMPERIAL TRAMWAYS, who opened a second route two years later running south from Albert Road, along Linthorpe Road, to the village of that name, terminating by the Cleveland Hotel. The third and shortest route, opened in 1882, ran northwards from Albert Road into Cleveland Street (passing under the railway line by the NER's Middlesbrough station) and on into Durham Street to terminate by Clarence Ferry on the river; this completed the single-track system (which, therefore, never reached Stockton-on-Tees, or indeed left Yorkshire). By this date the STOCKTON & DARLINGTON STEAM TRAMWAYS had been opened across the river in County Durham and this concern too was bought by Imperial in order to pave the way for a linked electric system (see below), both systems being closed accordingly.

Middlesbrough, Stockton & Thornaby Electric Tramways
Authority: Middlesbrough Stockton-on-Tees and Thornaby Tramways Order 1897
Gauge: 3ft 7in.
Traction: Overhead electric
Opened: 21 May 1898*
Taken over: 3 April 1921
System: Radial network*
Length: 9.61 miles
Stock: 10 sd, 50 dd
Livery: Vermillion & white

Following the demise of its STOCKTON & DARLINGTON steam line and its MIDDLESBROUGH & STOCKTON horse line (see above), IMPERIAL TRAMWAYS set about reconstructing and linking the two former tramways via the south Teesside town of Thornaby. Work began at Norton at the western end of the planned system and progressed eastward. As inspected by the BoT on 21 May 1898, the mainly double-track system had a main line running from Norton through Stockton-on-Tees (the former steam tramway route extended from Mandale Road, across the Tees into Thornaby then along Middlesbrough Road and Stockton Road) to Newport Road in Middlesbrough. Here it picked up the former horse tramway route to the junction with Albert Road in the centre of that town, and then continued on in a south-eastwards direction along North Ormesby Road to the district of that name; the Albert Road–Linthorpe branch was also rebuilt, giving a total route length of some 8 miles. It seems that trial journeys were made over the tramway for the purpose of driver training from 21 May onwards, though the official opening was not until 13 July, by which time thirty-five of an order of fifty Milnes open-toppers (Nos 1–50) had been delivered. Depots were provided by the terminus in Norton, by the Victoria Bridge (which opened in 1887) over the Tees in Stockton, and in Parliament Road off the Newport Road in Middlesbrough on a 1-mile link line to the Linthorpe route. After the system's early years, though, this link was used only for special workings and stock movements, reducing the passenger service to a simple cross system in plan when, in August 1901, the former Cleveland Street branch in Middlesbrough was reopened. Ten Milnes single-deckers (Nos 51–60) were purchased that year to work this double-track branch, the bridge by the railway station being too low to take double-deckers. (In 1911 cars 37 and 50 were cut down to single-deck form as well.) In 1918 the local authorities of Middlesbrough, Stockton and Thornaby decided to exercise their right to buy the system and did so from 3 April 1921, allocating twenty-nine of the double-deckers to STOCKTON & THORNABY and the remainder of the car fleet to MIDDLESBROUGH CORPORATION (see below).

Left: Two postcard views of 1898 Milnes open-toppers at work on the Middlesbrough, Stockton & Thornaby Electric Tramways – 1: No.36 in Norton Road, Norton, about to reach the terminus. The spur to the right leads into the depot. *(Author's Collection)*

Below: 2: No.5 in the centre of Thornaby. *(Author's Collection)*

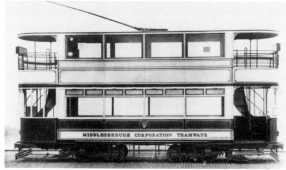

Above: In 1925 one of the cut-down double-deckers was illuminated and used in Middlesbrough's Charity Carnival of that year, the Corporation being the then owner of its portion of the MST system and half its car fleet. *(Author's Collection)*

Left: The last Middlesbrough fleet acquisitions were nine balcony cars (Nos. 132–140) bought from Milnes in 1921, this photograph showing one of them in ex-works condition. *(Author's Collection)*

Middlesbrough Corporation Tramways

Authority: Middlesbrough Corporation Act 1919
Gauge: 3ft 7in.
Traction: Overhead electric
Took over: 3 April 1921
Closed: 9 June 1934
System: Cross
Length: 5.49 miles
Stock: 12 sd, 28 dd
Livery: Dark blue & cream
Last Car: No.103

Following the local authorities' takeover of the MIDDLESBROUGH, STOCKTON & THORNABY system (see above), Middlesbrough Corporation acquired the track within its boundaries and thirty-one passenger cars: single-deckers 51–60 (which were variously renumbered 100–109), double-deckers 37 and 50 (renumbered 110 and 111) and 1–3, 6, 10, 15, 18, 21, 24, 25, 27, 28, 34, 36, 40–42, 46 and 47 (which were variously renumbered 113–131); nine new HN top-covered bogie cars (Nos 132–140) were purchased at the same time.

In 1931 the STOCKTON & THORNABY portion of the system closed down and Middlesbrough accordingly ceased services over the whole of its main line from the Thornaby boundary to North Ormesby – through-running between the two systems had been the norm – leaving just the cross-route between Linthorpe and the famous Transporter Bridge (which had replaced the old ferry in 1911) to survive less than a year and a half until it too was replaced by a bus service.

Middleton Electric Tramways
Authority: Middleton Light Railways Order 1898
Gauge: 4ft 8½in.
Traction: Overhead electric
Opened: 27 March 1902
Taken over: 16 June 1925
System: Branching
Length: 8.51 miles
Stock: 32 sd, 5 dd
Livery: Crimson & primrose

Promoted by the BET and operated by the Middleton Electric Traction Co. Ltd (registered 29 December 1900), this small, single-track system occupied a place in the south Lancashire network between MANCHESTER to the south, OLDHAM to the east and HEYWOOD and ROCHDALE to the north. The first route opened ran east–west from the Oldham boundary, along Middleton Road through Chadderton and on through Mills Hill on the Oldham Road, past the depot and the LYR's Middleton station, through the town centre via Townley Street, Old Hall Street and the Market Place, then out along Manchester Old Road to Rhodes. On 28 March 1902 (Good Friday) the system's other route, north from the Market Place up the Rochdale Road to Castleton, was opened to double the route mileage. (South Middleton was served by two lines operated by the Manchester Corporation. The first of these, from the Market Place south along Manchester New Road, was opened on 24 December 1902 and the second, a branch off this along Oldham Road east to the station then south-east down Grimshaw Lane to Middleton Junction station, followed on 21 September; no connection, however, was made with the Middleton system.)

The first cars were Brush bogie single-deck combination cars 1–20, joined in August 1902 by Nos 22–25 of the same type but different design. (No.21 was a water car.) It would appear that these were not entirely satisfactory, for in 1903 OLDHAM, ASHTON & HYDE open-top double-deckers 39 and 46 were hired, and in late 1903 and early 1904 four of the single-deckers (from Nos 11, 14 and 16–18) were exchanged for OAH single-deck motorised trailer cars 27–34 (which retained those numbers at Middleton), after which Nos 39 and 46 were returned. Then, in 1905, six of the original Brush cars were sold to Swansea and replaced by Brush open-top double-deckers 11–15, the tramway's last acquisitions.

An early postcard view of the long Castleton route of the Middleton Electric Tramways, with single-decker No.5 of 1901 almost the only vehicle in sight. *(Author's Collection)*

The system remained unchanged until the 1920s (apart from the sale of Nos 22–25 to the Potteries system in 1916–20) when, in 1925, an agreement was reached whereby the Middleton, Rochdale and Chadderton local authorities would buy the tramway for £79,000 on 15 June that year. Middleton's portion of the system was then leased to Manchester Corporation and Chadderton's sold to Oldham, after which the tramway quickly became integrated into the area's larger network. As regards the cars, Rochdale ended up with the double-deckers (Nos 11–15), Oldham with the ex-OAH vehicles (Nos 27–34) and Manchester with the remainder.

Morecambe Tramways

Authority: Morecambe Tramways Act 1886
Gauge: 4ft 8½in.
Traction: Horse/internal combustion*
Opened: 3 June 1887
Closed: 24 October 1924
System: Single line
Length: 3.59 miles
Stock: 2 sd, 15 dd horse; 4 sd petrol
Livery: Maroon, teak & white, later green
Last Car: ?

For such a short line, Morecambe's street tramway had a very complicated history. It owed its origin to the rise of the town as a Lancashire holiday resort in the second half of the nineteenth century, and the first 1¼ miles opened fittingly ran from the Central Pier (opened 1869), southwards along the seafront, to the Battery Hotel. On 19 May 1888 a southern continuation from the Battery, along the Heysham Road to Strawberry Gardens (in the borough of Heysham) was opened, followed on 17 June 1895 by a northwards extension from the Central Pier to East View. The depot was on the Heysham Road and the track primarily single, though a doubling programme was soon begun. The line was owned and operated by the Morecambe Tramways Co., originally with four cars supplied by Lancaster: Nos 1 and 2 were open-top double-deckers and Nos 3 and 4 open single-deckers for summer use. In 1888 two similar double-deckers were added (Nos 5 and 6), followed by another (No.7) a year later.

In 1897 Morecambe Corporation received authorisation for its own ¾-mile tramway and this opened the following year as a northwards single-track extension of the existing line on to Bare, leased to the MT Co. To cope with the extra workload four more open-toppers (Nos 8–11) were bought from Lancaster that same year, followed soon after by four smaller cars (Nos 12–15), possibly second-hand vehicles. In 1901 the acquisition of two more open-toppers completed the horse car fleet. On 26 July 1909, however, the Corporation invoked its powers to purchase at least part of the line and bought the section from the Battery Hotel northwards for an arbitrated price of £13,391; the sale included

Postcard of an unidentified Lancaster-built horse car on the Promenade at Morecambe about to pass the West End Pier, probably – judging by the crowds – on a Bank Holiday or similar occasion. *(Author's Collection)*

cars 1–14 and part of the depot, as well as 1.58 miles of the Company's tramway (see below). Although neither half of the line was ever electrified, some modernisation took place when, from 15 January 1912, petrol-driven trams were operated by the Company. These were three closed cars of 1911 and one open car of 1913, all single-deckers built for the line by Leyland Motors (with bodies by UEC) and given the numbers 1–4; the use of this form of motive power on a tramway was a first for Britain. During the First World War these vehicles (which had replaced the horse trams) were converted to run on town gas, a large canvas bag being fitted on the roof as a reservoir. (Many lorries, buses and vans were similarly converted at the time.) They remained in service until the end of the 1924 summer season, when economic circumstances forced the line's closure.

Morecambe Corporation Tramways

Authority: Morecambe Urban District Council Tramways Order 1897
Gauge: 4ft 8½in.
Traction: Horse
Took over: 26 July 1909
Closed: 6 October 1926
System: Single line
Length: 2.4 miles
Stock: 2 sd, 16 dd
Livery: Maroon & white?
Last Car: No.13

Morecambe Corporation's tramway was made up of its own ¾-mile stretch from East View to Bare, plus the part of the MT Co.'s line from East View back to the Battery Hotel acquired in 1909 (see above). It remained faithful to horse traction, which meant that, by the time of its closure in 1926, it was the last such survivor on the British mainland. Indeed, until nearly the end, the Corporation was buying replacement cars: Nos 13 (of 1919) and 16 (1922) were double-deckers and Nos 14 (1919) and 15 (1922) toastracks, all from EE.

National Electric Construction Co. Ltd

Established in 1897 (renamed in 1903), the NEC, among its other interests, owned at one time or another, the English tramway systems of DEWSBURY, OSSETT & SOOTHILL NETHER (which it operated directly), Oxford, MEXBOROUGH & SWINTON and Torquay. In addition, it owned the Rhondda system in Wales and that at MUSSELBURGH in Scotland.

Nelson Corporation Tramways

Authority: Nelson Light Railways Order 1901
Gauge: 4ft
Traction: Overhead electric
Opened: 23 February 1903
Closed: 6 January 1934
System: Branching
Length: 2.74 miles
Stock: 3 sd, 17 dd
Livery: Red & white, then brown & cream
Last Car: ?

This short line formed the central portion of the BURNLEY–COLNE multiple-ownership tramway route and was the northern end of the former BURNLEY & DISTRICT steam tramway, plus it had a short single-track branch northwards from Nelson Centre, along Scotland Road past the depot, then through Barrowford to Higherford Bridge. The old line was relaid to Burnley's 4ft gauge to permit through-running (that system having opened in 1901) and the southern ¾ mile of double-tracks from Nelson Centre to the Burnley boundary was leased to that Corporation. In practice, Burnley cars usually terminated at Nelson Centre on account of a low bridge in Colne, whilst Nelson cars normally worked only from Higherford Bridge to Colne (after that system opened in 1903) via the Centre. Through-working by Colne cars began in 1911 as part of a joint service.

The first Nelson cars were Brush open-toppers Nos 1–6 and ERTCW bogie single-deck combination cars 7 and 8 (joined in 1909 by similar car 9). In 1912 two top-covered UEC low bridge cars were bought and numbered 10 and 11, followed in 1916 by Nos 1–6, six more of the same to replace the original cars with those numbers. Finally, three similar cars (Nos 7–9) were purchased in 1925, this time from Brush.

From 1 April 1933 the line was run briefly by the Burnley, Colne & Nelson Joint Transport Committee (and the cars' numbers given the suffix N) until it and the Colne system closed together.

Newcastle & Gosforth Tramways
Authority: Newcastle-upon-Tyne Tramways and Improvement Act 1877
Gauge: 4ft 8½in.
Traction: Horse, steam
Opened: 5 December 1878
Closed: 13 April 1901
System: Network
Length: 12.19 miles
Stock: 4 locos, 44 horse & steam
Livery: ?
Last Car: ?

The Newcastle & Gosforth Tramways & Carriage Co. Ltd operated its own 2-mile line from Newcastle's northern boundary up North Road to the centre of Gosforth, plus a city network of lines leased from Newcastle Corporation in 1878 for a period of twenty-one years. The cars – details unknown – were principally horse-drawn, with four Hawthorn tramway locomotives being bought in 1879 to work the Gosforth to Westgate in Newcastle route, but sold to SUNDERLAND TRAMWAYS three years later.

In 1899 the Corporation obtained the necessary powers to extend and electrify its own lines – and purchase compulsorily connecting tramways outside its boundaries. When it informed the Company of its decision to electrify the horse lines on expiry of the lease, the Company promptly closed the whole system, leaving the way clear for the Corporation's own network (see below). Car No.49 of 1873 is preserved at the North of England Open Air Museum, BEAMISH.

Newcastle-Upon-Tyne Corporation Tramways
Authority: Newcastle-upon-Tyne Tramways and Improvement Act 1899
Gauge: 4ft 8½in.
Traction: Overhead electric
Opened: 16 December 1901
Closed: 4 March 1950*
System: Network
Length: 51.27 miles
Stock: 110 sd, 218 dd
Livery: Dark maroon & orange
Last Car: ?

In 1899 Newcastle Corporation obtained the necessary powers to construct and operate its own electric tramways and purchase the NEWCASTLE & GOSFORTH routes outside its boundary (see above), with work on the new system commencing the following year. In its final form, this was a network of radial and cross-routes on the north bank of the River Tyne, extending as far as Wallsend and Walker in the east, north on a long loop through Gosforth Park and out on a long route along Westmorland Road past the other western termini to Throckley.

Some 14½ route miles opened in 1901 with an impressively large fleet of cars. (Both system and fleet grew to become the largest in north-east England.) Nos 1–20 were from HN, Nos 21–28 from Brush and Nos 29–110 bogie cars from HN again – all single-deckers. Nos 111–130 were from HN and 131–165 from Brush – all open-toppers.

More cars soon followed: Nos 170–191 were Corporation-built open-toppers of 1904–05, joined in 1906–14 by top-covered cars 1–28 and 192–209; Brush supplied similar cars 210–224 in 1914. After that the Corporation built top-covered cars 225–229 during 1915–18 and enclosed cars 232–236 in 1917–18, after which Brush provided enclosed cars 240–309 from 1921–26 to complete the fleet – surprisingly early for a system that lasted so long (though many of the trams were subsequently rebuilt and modernised).

The predominantly double-track system continued to expand before, during and after the First World War, with two important lines across the Tyne opening on 12 January 1923 and 10 October 1928 to provide links with GATESHEAD. Gosforth had been reached on 8 April 1921 and three years later the construction by the Corporation of a 1½-mile northern loop through Gosforth Park, known as the Gosforth Park Light Railway, secured a connection with the TYNESIDE TRAMWAYS. When the latter system closed on 6 April 1930, Newcastle Corporation took over that company's track on the Great North Road in order to keep the service going (and also ran trams over its line to Wallsend, until 25 May when a bus service was substituted). This was not the network's first cutback though: on 3 June 1929 the line to Denton Burn, only opened in 1926, had been similarly treated.

From then on Corporation policy was to replace the trams with buses or trolleybuses as and when the tracks became worn out, and from 1935 to 1939 two fifths of the system was abandoned. After the Second World War this programme was resumed with the last route – the long one across the river and right through Gateshead to Wrekenton – closing in 1950 (though Gateshead cars still ran into the city until that system closed the following year).

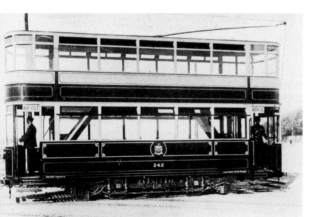

Above left: Outside Central station in Newcastle-upon-Tyne, at the heart of the city's tramway network, with three different types of tramcar in view. *(Author's Collection)*

Above right: Grainger Street, with one of the Corporation's 'C' Class cars (Nos 29–88) threading its way through the pedestrians. *(Author's Collection)*

Left: Newcastle Corporation No.242 of 1921, as new and with a token crew posing formally for the camera. *(Author's Collection)*

Over the years the car fleet, based at Byker Depot east of the city centre, was slimmed down as new cars were added and in later years several were sold to other operators: in 1941 Nos 112–114, 116–119, 122–126, 128 and 129 were sold to SHEFFIELD, in 1948 Nos 29, 42 and 77 to BR for its Grimsby & Immingham line and Nos 43, 52, 54, 80 and 88 to Gateshead.

Car No.102 is preserved and running at the National Tramway Museum, Crich and No.114 is similarly in service at the North of England Open Air Museum, BEAMISH.

North of England Open Air Museum *see* Beamish: North of England Open Air Museum
North Shields *see* Tynemouth

Oldham Corporation Tramways
Authority: Oldham Corporation Act 1899*
Gauge: 4ft 8½in.
Traction: Overhead electric
Opened: 15 December 1900
Closed: 3 August 1946
System: Network
Length: 25.18 miles
Stock: 33 sd, 117 dd*
Livery: Maroon & white
Last Car: No.4

The first tramway in Oldham, although built by the Corporation under the Oldham Borough Tramways Order of 1878 and opened 16 September 1880, was operated on lease by the Manchester Carriage & Tramways Co. (see MANCHESTER TRAMWAYS) and ran from Waterhead, west along the Huddersfield Road and Manchester Road through the town to Hollinwood on the boundary with Manchester to the south-west. This was followed in 1885 by two lines of the MANCHESTER, BURY, ROCHDALE & OLDHAM steam system.

The first line operated by the Corporation opened on 15 December 1900 and ran east from Chadderton along Middleton Road to Rochdale Road (and the MBRO line). Other routes followed, though these were separated by the older horse and steam lines until the horse cars ceased to run, on 31 October 1901, with the expiry of the lease; at the same time, the Corporation took over the steam routes by agreement and began converting them all to electric traction. The Waterhead–Hollinwood line reopened on 17 May 1902, with the former steam routes reopening in stages that year.

The last route of the mainly single-track system to be constructed was a north-easterly branch off the Huddersfield Road, along the Ripponden Road through Moorside to Grains Bar; this opened on 4 June 1914 with the last extension to the tramways, in August 1925, coming with the purchase of the stretch of 1.55 miles from Chadderton to Mills Hill Bridge from MIDDLETON. (Other connections for through-running were made, at one time or another, with ROCHDALE in the north, Manchester to the south-west and ASHTON-UNDER-LYNE to the south via the OLDHAM, ASHTON & HYDE ELECTRIC TRAMWAY (see below).

Services began with single-deckers Nos 1 and 4 and open-top double-deckers 2 and 3, all from ERTCW, of which Nos 3 and 4 were bogie vehicles. These were followed in 1901 by bogie single-deckers 5–16 and, in 1902–03, by single-deckers 17–26 and open-toppers 27–80, again all from ERTCW. No further cars were bought until 1911, when UEC supplied balcony cars 81–92, followed by similar vehicles 93–111 over the next four years. EE balcony cars 4–12 and 14–16 were bought in 1921 as replacements for those numbered vehicles sold to ROTHERHAM in 1916, with enclosed cars 17–20, 22 and 24 coming from the same firm three years later. In 1925 Brush single-deckers 113–120 were bought from Middleton, and enclosed cars 121–132 from EE a year later.

The only other passenger vehicle in the fleet was No.112, built by the Corporation in 1921 from the body of No.3 as a balcony car. The two depots were at Hollinwood and Wallshaw (just east of the town centre).

Oldham Corporation No.119 of 1903 acquired in 1925 from Middleton – and before that, it was an Oldham, Ashton & Hyde trailer. *(Author's Collection)*

The eastern route along Lees Road to Lees closed on 2 May 1928 and the Grains Bar route that 24 December. In 1934 the Corporation decided to abandon the remaining routes over the next five years but, as elsewhere, the Second World War delayed the closure programme with the last line – the original horse route from Waterhead to Hollinwood – surviving until 1946, after which cars 17, 18, 24, 122, 125 and 128 were sold to GATESHEAD.

Oldham, Ashton & Hyde Electric Tramway

Authority: Oldham Ashton-under-Lyne Hyde and District Electric Tramways Order 1896
Gauge: 4ft 8½in.
Traction: Overhead electric
Opened: 12 June 1899
Taken over: 2 July 1921
System: Single line
Length: 9.1 miles
Stock: 56 sd, 12 dd
Livery: Dark green & white

After a separate steam tramway proposal of the 1880s had failed, the early 1890s saw the promotion of an electric tramway linking the south-east Lancashire towns of its title by the Oldham, Ashton-under-Lyne & Hyde Tramways Co. Ltd. This scheme also failed (after ¼ mile of track had been laid in Ashton), only to be revived in 1896 by the BET through its subsidiary, the Oldham, Ashton-under-Lyne & Hyde Electric Tramway Ltd. Construction began in early 1898 with services commencing the following year, using sixteen small Brush single-deckers (possibly Nos 1–16). These proved inadequate to cope with the traffic – only twelve were put into service at first – and eight open-toppers built by Brush for LEEDS CORPORATION were bought instead (after the initial plan to merely hire them was changed) and possibly given the numbers 19–26; later numbered 39–46, they arrived with Leeds fleet numbers and had their staircases and top seats removed to work as single-deckers on account of a low bridge in Hyde (though they were restored from 1902–04 onwards).

By the middle of 1900 the stock situation had improved markedly, with Brush having supplied single-deckers 1–26 and single-deck trailers 27–38 – though these latter vehicles also proved to be no great success in their original form, with Nos 35–38 consequently being motorised in 1900 and Nos 27–34 sold to MIDDLETON three years later. The tramway's other passenger cars were Nos 47–50, Brush open-toppers supplied in 1903, and Nos 27–30, ERTCW single-deck combination cars bought from Middleton a year later (and which ran for a while with the suffix B added to their Middleton numbers 11, 14, 17 and 18). Power was supplied by Ashton Corporation.

In layout, the tramway's northern section was a single-track north–south line running from Hathershaw, at the Oldham boundary, in a straight line south, down the Oldham Road through Waterloo to Ashton Market Place. From the terminal stub there (connected to the ASHTON CORPORATION system) the tramway's second route ran south-west along Katherine Street and the Stockport Road to Audenshaw, then out south along Denton Road (past the depot) and Ashton Road to Denton, where it turned east to reach Hyde via Hyde Road and Manchester Road. In Hyde, the line swung south again along Market Street, Lumb Street and Back Lane through Gee Cross, to terminate at Pole Bank on the boundary with Bredbury. This last mile-long section was leased from Hyde Corporation and opened on 1 January 1903, connecting with STOCKPORT CORPORATION TRAMWAYS; that authority's cars immediately began running into Hyde from here and the Company cut its own services back to the Grapes Hotel at Gee Cross shortly after. The system's only other section of line, a short connecting link between the two routes in Ashton just west of the Market, was never used for passenger workings.

By 1910 it was clear that the relevant local authorities were wanting to purchase the tramway at the end of the customary twenty-one-year period, and in 1921 they did so, by which time the Company had allowed the cars and track to become decrepit. After arbitration, Ashton paid £62,875 for its tracks and acquired cars 1–9, 18, 21, 26–28, 35–39 and 44–48, whilst Hyde paid £26,600 and received cars 19, 20, 22–25, 29, 30, 49 and 50 to be operated by the STALYBRIDGE, HYDE, MOSSLEY & DUKINFIELD TRAMWAYS. Audenshaw paid £13,550 and got cars 14–17 and 40, whilst Denton paid £21,975 and received Nos 10–13 and 41–43, their lines in both cases to be worked by MANCHESTER CORPORATION (with four of the cars being sold to AYR in Scotland and the remainder scrapped).

Ossett *see* Dewsbury, Ossett & Soothill Nether
Over Darwen *see* Blackburn & Over Darwen
Phoenix Tramway *see* Bradford City Tramways
Prescot *see* Liverpool & Prescot

Preston Tramways
Authority: Preston Tramways Act 1876
Gauge: 3ft 6in.
Traction: Horse
Opened: 20 March 1879
Closed: 31 December 1903
System: Radial
Length: 7.01 miles
Stock: 6 sd, 8 dd
Livery: Yellow & cream
Last Car: ?

Preston's first tramway was opened by the Preston Tramways Co. and ran for nearly 2½ miles from the Town Hall northwards on Lancaster Road, North Road and Garstang Road, then eastwards along Victoria Road and Watling Street Road to Fulwood Barracks, where the depot was sited. It was a single-track line worked by six single-deckers and was joined in 1882 by two further routes, this time built by Preston Corporation and leased to a local horse bus operator by the name of Harding. The first of these routes (2 miles of single track) ran north-west from the Town Hall along Friargate, Fylde Street, Fylde Road and Tulketh Road to a terminus in Newton Road in Ashton-on-Ribble, whilst the second (nearly 3 miles of single track) ran eastwards up Fishergate Hill from the River Ribble, along Fishergate past the Corporation's depot and the main railway station, past the Town Hall and out along Church Street, Newhall Lane and Blackburn Road to Farringdon Park. The new routes were worked by eight open-top double-deckers.

In 1886 the Corporation bought the Company's line and this too was worked by W. Harding & Co. Ltd from 1 January 1887 until the lease expired at the end of 1903, whereupon Harding substituted horse buses for the trams whilst the Corporation pressed ahead with plans for an electric system (see below).

Further details of the horse tramways are tantalisingly sketchy, especially as regards the stock. It is known, though, that in later years the (main) depot was sited in Old Vicarage, off Lancaster Road; it later became Hardings Furniture Stores.

Preston Corporation Tramways

Authority: Preston Corporation Act 1900
Gauge: 4ft 8½in.
Traction: Overhead electric
Opened: 7 June 1904
Closed: 15 December 1935
System: Radial network
Length: 10.53 miles
Stock: 12 sd, 42 dd
Livery: Maroon & yellow*
Last Car: No.4?

Constructed under 1900 and 1902 Acts, the first two electric routes to open in Preston were conversions of the horse lines from the Town Hall to Fulwood Barracks and to Farringdon Park (see above), the former being modified slightly by using a longer stretch of Watling Street Road to avoid Victoria Road. Shortly after the opening, on 30 June 1904, a southern link between Fulwood and Church Street was opened along Deepdale Road off which, in Holmbrook Road, the depot and generating station had been built. From the Town Hall, this line followed the old horse tramway route down Fishergate Hill, and then turned south along the river bank (Broadgate) to Penwortham Bridge. All three routes were mainly double-track with services worked by open-toppers 1–30 (the last four being bogie vehicles) built – hardly surprisingly – by local manufacturers ERTCW for DK who had constructed the tramways.

The penultimate route opened – on 1 July 1904 – was the reconstructed Ashton horse route (again slightly modified at its extremity to terminate in Long Lane), with the final line, a new north-east route to Ribbleton via Ribbleton Road and Ribbleton Avenue, opening on 26 June the following year to serve the district between the Fulwood and Farringdon Park lines. Both these later lines were mainly single-track.

Three new cars, bogie single-deckers 31–33, were bought in 1912 from UEC, followed two years later by Nos 34–39, six UEC balcony cars. The only other passenger cars purchased were single-deckers 40–48, bought from SHEFFIELD CORPORATION (and retaining their blue livery) just after the

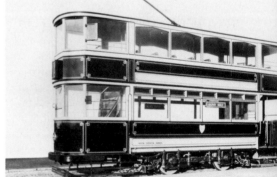

Above left: Preston Corporation No.20 of 1904 in Fishergate, shortly after the opening of the system, complete with attendant policeman keeping a watchful eye on the photographer. *(Author's Collection)*

Above right: Preston double-decker No.42 built by the Corporation in 1929 and given the fleet number vacated by one of its ex-Sheffield single-deckers. *(Author's Collection)*

First World War to replace some of the older cars, and balcony cars 13, 18 and 22, bought in 1929 from the City of Lincoln Tramways; at the same time, the Corporation constructed three enclosed double-deckers of its own (Nos 30, 40 and 42) from parts of withdrawn vehicles.

On 4 July 1932 the Farringdon Park and Penwortham Bridge routes closed, replaced by Corporation bus services. The Ashton route went on 6 August 1934, whilst the Ribbleton services had withered away earlier that summer. All that remained was the circular route from the Town Hall to Fullwood and back, and that too had gone by the end of the following year. The surviving cars were sold off with one – the rebuilt No.42 – gaining a new lease of life at LYTHAM ST ANNES.

Rawtenstall Corporation Tramways

Authority: Rawtenstall Corporation Act 1907
Gauge: 4ft
Traction: Steam/overhead electric
Took over: 1 October 1908
Closed: 31 March 1932*
System: Radial
Length: 11.75 miles
Stock: 12 locos, 12 dd steam; 6 sd, 26 dd electric
Livery: Maroon & cream
Last Car: ?

Following the 1908 takeover of the ROSSENDALE VALLEY TRAMWAYS, Rawtenstall Corporation set about electrifying and adding to that line, with sixteen UEC top-covered cars entering service the next year. The resulting single-track system, focussed on Queen's Square in the town centre, was made up of four routes: west to Lockgate, where it connected end-on with HASLINGDEN CORPORATION's portion of ACCRINGTON CORPORATION's route from Baxenden, north up the former steam line to Crawshawbooth and on to Loveclough, and east along the former steam line to Bacup, with a branch off this at Waterfoot running north through Lumb to Water. The steam service ended on 22 July 1909, after which the routes were switched over to electric working and the old rolling-stock disposed of (with the exception of two locos kept for use as snowploughs).

In 1912 another two UEC top-covered cars (Nos 17 and 18) were bought, together with UEC single-deckers 19–24 for use on the Water route. The last cars acquired were Nos 25–32 in 1921, Brush enclosed double-deckers. The depot was in the centre of Rawtenstall off the Bacup Road. The system died eleven years later, killed by bus competition, with an official closing ceremony on 7 April 1932, a week after public services ceased.

Rochdale Corporation Tramways

Authority: Rochdale Corporation Act 1900
Gauge: 4ft 8½in.
Traction: Overhead electric, steam
Opened: 22 May 1902
Closed: 12 November 1932
System: Network
Length: 28.71 miles
Stock: 10 locos, 8 dd steam; 35 sd, 64 dd electric*
Livery: Dark brown & yellow
Last Car: No.80

As with many of the components of the Lancashire tramway network centred on Manchester, the history of Rochdale's system is a complicated one. Briefly, what happened was that at the end of the nineteenth century Rochdale Corporation decided to purchase the MANCHESTER, BURY, ROCHDALE & OLDHAM routes within its boundaries, then electrify and extend them as a standard-gauge system linked to its neighbours. In the event, the latter part of the scheme came first when, in May 1902, the Corporation opened a short line from the end of Manchester Road, on the west of the town centre, westwards along Bury Road to the Cemetery, followed on 17 June by another westward branch, this time to Norden via Spotland Road and Edenfield Road, and on 21 July by a short northern branch off this to Spotland. (All these routes passed close to the main depot in Mellor Street before diverging.)

Just as some other operators did, the Corporation ordered six sample cars initially, with follow-up orders to be placed in the light of their performance. These were bogie single-decker No.1, bogie open-topper No.2 and single-truck open-topper No.3 from DK, and bogie open-toppers Nos 4–6 from Milnes.

On 10 July 1904 the Corporation purchased the MBRO routes it wanted for the (arbitrated) price of £74,769 and thereafter set about converting them to electric working (as well as continuing to build new routes). The last steam tram ran on 11 May 1905, on the Littleborough route during its reconstruction, the Corporation having purchased ten locos and eight trailers from the MBRO to work the route until its conversion. After that, the stock was sold at auction, though one car body – possibly not one of the eight service vehicles? – reportedly became a tram shelter in Milnrow.

By 1 August 1925, when it took over the northern portion of the MIDDLETON route through Castleton to Sudden, the Corporation had built up a network of routes within the town centre and a number of radial routes in all directions, including connections into OLDHAM and Middleton to the south, HEYWOOD to the west, and a long northern route to Bacup where it met the (4ft gauge) RAWTENSTALL system.

The first cutback came just five years later when, on 18 October 1930, the long, exposed, mainly single-track route north-east through Littleborough and along the Todmorden Road to an isolated terminus by the Summit Inn, was abandoned. More closures came in 1931 and by mid-1932 only a jointly operated through service to MANCHESTER remained; this too went on 12 November of that year as Manchester, in turn, cut back its services. Once again, the buses were the victors.

Arriving after cars 1–6, the following trams made up the Rochdale fleet:

Nos 7–9: ERTCW open-toppers of 1902
Nos 10–29: Brush open-toppers of 1903–05
Nos 30–43: Brush bogie single-deckers of 1905
Nos 44–49: Brush bogie open-toppers of 1905
Nos 50–59: Brush single-deckers of 1906
Nos 60–69: ditto of 1912

Above left: Commemorative postcard of the opening of Rochdale Corporation's north-eastern route towards Todmorden, terminating at the Summit Inn. Brush open-topper No.19 of 1903 does the honours. *(Author's Collection)*

Above right: Rotherham Corporation No.26 of 1903, in post-First World War top-covered form, in Main Street – a postcard street scene that could be of almost any northern industrial town between the wars. *(Author's Collection)*

Nos 70–79: EE top-covered double-deckers of 1920
Nos 80–92: EE enclosed double-deckers of 1925–26
Nos 93, 94: EE/Corporation enclosed double-deckers of 1927–28

In addition, Middleton cars 11–15 were taken into the fleet in 1925, but they were probably never used in service in view of their poor condition (though they were allocated fleet numbers 2 and 12–15).

Rossendale Valley Tramways

Authority: Rossendale Valley Tramways Act 1888
Gauge: 4ft
Traction: Steam
Opened: 31 January 1889
Taken over: 1 October 1908
System: Single line
Length: 6.35 miles
Stock: 13 locos? 12 dd?
Livery: ?

One of the last of Britain's urban steam tramways to open, this was a single-track line, owned and operated by the Rossendale Valley Tramways Co., running south from Crawshawbooth, south of Burnley, down the Burnley Road and through Holmfield to Rawtenstall, where it connected with the ACCRINGTON CORPORATION steam line coming in from the north-west. It then swung east to follow the River Irwell and the road and railway in the valley of its title for 4½ miles to Bacup. Part of this latter section (Rawtenstall to Waterfoot) opened first, followed by the Waterfoot to Bacup (3 August) and Rawtenstall to Holmfield (8 August) sections that same year. Finally, on 5 August 1891, the final extension to Crawshawbooth opened (prior to the official BoT inspection) with a free service, the official public opening being one week later.

Services began with Green locomotives 1–3 (1888) hauling bogie double-deck trailers 1–10 from (probably) Milnes as they were delivered; the locos were joined in 1889 by Nos 4–9, also from Greens. Additions to the stock made after that are believed to have been four more Green locos (No.10 in 1893, 11 in 1894, and 12 and 13? ex-BLACKBURN CORPORATION in 1901) and two Ashbury trailers (No.11 in 1901 and 12 in 1903), both probably also ex-Blackburn. The depot was in Rawtenstall, on the Bacup Road.

In 1900 the concern was acquired by the BET who wished to electrify it, but co-operation was not forthcoming from the two local authorities involved, Bacup and Rawtenstall – or even between each other – until 1 October 1908 when they purchased the line jointly in preparation for building their own electric tramway between the two towns (to be worked by RAWTENSTALL CORPORATION).

Rotherham Corporation Tramways

Authority: Rotherham Corporation Act 1900
Gauge: 4ft 8½in.
Traction: Overhead electric
Opened: 31 January 1903
Closed: 13 November 1949
System: Radial
Length: 11.55 miles
Stock: 15 sd, 68 dd
Livery: Chocolate & yellow
Last Car: No.11

The Rotherham system formed a key part of the south Yorkshire tramway network, being connected to SHEFFIELD in the south-west and MEXBOROUGH & SWINTON in the north. After early horse tramway proposals had come to nothing, Rotherham Corporation successfully promoted an electric line that opened with twelve open-toppers (Nos 1–12) and three single-deckers (Nos 13–15) from ERTCW.

The first two routes opened ran from College Square in the town centre, north up Effingham Street for just over 1 mile to the local authority boundary (and depot in Rawmarsh Road), and north-east along Fitzwilliam Road from the start of Effingham Street to the Pumping Station, a distance of about 1½ miles. A third, westerly route from College Square along the High Street, Main Street and Masbrough Street to Kimberworth was opened on 8 April 1903, followed on 6 June by a southern route down Cranklow Road to Cranklow (1½ miles) and, on 8 June, by a south-western line of about the same length to Templeborough (extended, on 21 July, another mile to Tinsley, where the rails stopped just short of those of the Sheffield system). That year also saw the arrival of cars 16–30, more ERTCW open-toppers.

With a connection between the two systems having been put in, through-running with Sheffield began in September 1905, whilst in the following year, on 1 October, the Fitzwilliam Road line was extended for ¾ mile to Dalton and, on 6 February 1907, through-running with Mexborough & Swinton began via Effingham Street. The tramway was proving a success, and a programme of fitting top covers to the cars was well under way; in 1908 the three single-deckers were rebuilt as roofed balcony cars and in 1909 six UEC balcony cars (Nos 32–37) were bought and a track-doubling programme began on the single-track system. A new, 1-mile route from the High Street south-east along Wellgate was opened on 2 March 1910; in 1912 this was extended along Broom Road and Wickersley Road whilst, in the same year, the Dalton route was extended another mile up the Doncaster Road to Thrybergh to complete the system. That year also saw the introduction of trolleybus feeder services.

By the time of the First World War more cars were needed and the Corporation was forced to shop around for second-hand vehicles, eventually buying twelve ERTCW single-deckers (Nos 38–49) from OLDHAM in 1916 and ten ERTCW closed cars (Nos 50–59) from London County Council a year later. The war also brought an unexpected disruption to services: in 1902 Tinsley had become part of Sheffield and disputes between the two corporations over the affected section of track meant that, on 30 September 1914, through-running ceased, not to be reinstated until 15 May 1915 (with Sheffield finally taking over that piece of track from 1 January 1926).

After the war the car fleet was increased by the 1920 purchase of thirteen EE top-covered cars (Nos 1–4 and 60–68); no further vehicles were bought until 1934–35 when Nos 1–11, enclosed EE cars, were added to the stock, followed in 1942 by the hire, and subsequent purchase, of No.14, formerly enclosed car 125 of LEEDS CITY TRAMWAYS. By this latter date much of the system had been abandoned, the closures beginning with the Broom Road route – always a loss-maker – on 10 June 1929 (replaced by trolleybuses), followed on 16 May 1931 by the Kimberworth–Thrybergh cross-town route. The last trams to Canklow ran on 9 July 1934 leaving just the Templeborough (and Sheffield) service to survive the Second World War; the through service ceased on 11 December 1948 with the Rotherham section of the route closing less than a year later.

St Helens & District Tramways

Authority: St Helens and District Tramways Act 1879
Gauge: 4ft 8½in.
Traction: Horse, steam, overhead electric
Opened: 5 November 1881
Closed: 31 March 1936
System: Radial network
Length: 21.96 miles
Stock: 4 sd?, 9 dd horse; 9 locos, 10 dd steam; 2 sd, 48 dd electric
Livery: ? & cream horse and steam; dark red & white to 1913, green & white to 1919, then red & white electric
Last Car: No.26 (official)

Armed with its empowering Act, the St Helens & District Tramways Co. began construction in October 1880, opening its first horse route just over twelve months later. This ran south-west for 3½ miles from the town centre along Prescot Road and St Helens Road to the King's Arms at the junction of

Warrington Road and Prescot High Street. In May or June 1882 a second cross-town route opened from Denton's Green, running south-east for just over a mile along Denton's Green Lane and Duke Street to the town centre, then onwards for another ½ mile to Peasley Cross to terminate at the junction of Peasley Cross Lane and Sutton Road. A one-way system in the town centre linked the Town Hall, the depot in Hall Street, Coronation Street, Church Street and the railway station. A route to the north-east later ran for 3¾ miles along Park Road, West End Road and Clipsley Lane to Holly Bank Road, just past the GCR's Haydock railway station (opened 1900).

The first services were worked by open-top Eades reversible cars from Ashbury, of which six were bought in 1881 (Nos 1–6?), these soon being joined by three Oldbury single-deckers of *c.*1882, three Metropolitan open-toppers of 1882 and, finally, a single-decker purchased between 1886 and 1890 from Milnes.

The tramway was not an immediate financial success, and in 1883 the Company obtained powers to use steam traction in order to expand the system along other (hilly) routes. The money for this expansion was presumably not forthcoming as nothing happened for another six years. Then, on 22 October 1889, the St Helens & District Tramways Co. Ltd was registered to take over the old company, buying it for £39,750 on 1 January 1890 and commencing steam trials that February. Public steam services began on 4 April over the whole system (with the exception of the last half of the Haydock line from the Ship Inn, Blackbrook, which possibly survived as a horse-worked service for another three years). That April three of the Ashbury cars and the three Oldbury cars were sold to the Birkdale & Southport Tramways Co. at SOUTHPORT, and two of the Metropolitan cars (and the Milnes single-decker?) to the MORECAMBE TRAMWAYS.

The steam services were worked by Green tramway locomotives 1–6 hauling top-covered Milnes bogie trailers, of which seven had been bought by July 1890 (with the passenger fleet increasing to ten over the next three years). Green loco 7 followed in May 1890 and Nos 8 and 9 the year after.

In March 1897 St Helens Corporation agreed to purchase the 9½-mile single-track system for £23,000 from 1 April, leasing it back to the Company which, on 4 November 1898, became the New St Helens & District Tramways Co. Ltd. That year the Corporation obtained an Act enabling it to double the size of the system and electrify it, entering into a new lease with the Company for twenty-one years from 1 October.

On 20 July 1899 electric working began over the Denton's Green route and part of the line to Prescot (which was reached two days later); the official opening was on 3 August. The Peasley Cross line was inspected on 8 December (and presumably opened shortly afterwards) and was extended on 19 September 1900 south along Marshalls Cross Road, then east along Rodins Lane and Station Road to just short of St Helens Junction railway station. (The 111yd gap to the station was not bridged until 1927.) Other extensions included a ½-mile branch south from the Toll Bar on the Prescot line along Lugsmore Lane to Thatto Heath station, extended another ½ mile down Nutgrove Road to Nutgrove, and a ¾-mile extension of the Haydock line to the Ram's Head in Church Road.

St Helens & District electric car No.18 of 1899 in immaculate livery, probably soon after delivery from Brush, its upper-deck decency boards still unsullied by advertisements. (*Author's Collection*)

A 1½-mile branch east along Parr Stocks Road and Oak Road to the Horse Shoe in Parr opened on 2 June 1900, with a 1-mile branch north along North Road and City Road to Windle following on 19 September. The last route opened (sometime after its inspection on 8 January 1901) continued the Nutgrove line south along Rainhill Road to near Rainhill station, then north-west along Warrington Road to meet the Prescot line at its terminus (2¾ miles); this was later extended ½ mile south-west to Derby Street, Brook Bridge, where, on 25 June 1902, it connected with the LIVERPOOL & PRESCOT LIGHT RAILWAY. Earlier, on 4 April 1902, through-running had begun when a connection was made at Haydock with the SOUTH LANCASHIRE TRAMWAYS (in which the Company bought a controlling interest four years later).

Relations between the Company and the Corporation were never good and the latter refused to renew the lease, taking over the tramway on 1 October 1919, thereafter refurbishing the car fleet (which had become neglected). On 1 April 1921 LIVERPOOL CORPORATION began operating through to the King's Arms in Prescot (having taken over the LPLR two years earlier), purchasing for £8,000 the 946yd of track between there and Brook Bridge. On 17 August 1923 the Corporation began its own regular bus services and used them, from March 1927, to replace the trams on the Nutgrove and Prescot section of the tramway. On 8 December 1923 the Parr route closed, again replaced by a bus service (in preparation for the introduction of trolleybuses), whilst on 21 June 1931 trolleybuses took over on the Haydock route. Buses took over on the Windle line on 12 July 1932 and, on 1 May 1935, the St Helens Junction line went.

The original electric car fleet comprised Brush open-toppers taking the odd numbers between 1 and 15 with Brush bogie open-toppers taking the even ones. (One theory is that the shorter, odd-numbered cars were intended originally to be trailers.) Brush bogie cars 17–36 were bought in 1899–1900, some of which were cannibalised during the First World War (and No.24 rebuilt as a works car in 1923) and the others were renumbered when EE open-toppers (top-covered 1920–21) were bought in 1918 and numbered 33–36; these were followed the next year by Nos 37–44, top-covered vehicles from Brush (renumbered 21–28 in 1929). In 1927 two ex-WIGAN single-deckers were bought (ERTCW 1904 cars 68 and 77), which were renumbered (order unknown) 30 and 31 (and 13 and 14 two years later at a time of wholesale scrapping and renumbering).

Between 1910 and at least 1919 various South Lancs cars were borrowed or hired to help out on the tramway, some of which were given the temporary numbers 44–46, whilst the numbers 37–43 were taken originally by the LPLR's fleet of seven cars housed by St Helens, even though they were never officially owned by the St Helens company.

Salford Tramway

Authority: Local authority permission*
Gauge: c.5ft?
Traction: Horse
Opened: Late 1861
Closed: Early 1872?
System: Single line
Length: c.1 mile
Stock: *
Livery: Red & white?
Last Car: ?

Salford's first tramway was a unique affair and one of the few early 1860s pioneering lines. It was laid by John Greenwood, a local bus operator, and used a single three-rail track of a type patented by his brother-in-law, John Haworth, under the name 'Haworth's Patent Perambulating System'. Unlike other tramways of the time, such as G.F. Train's in BIRKENHEAD, the Haworth track did not use step rails but instead used two flat rails or plates, some 3in. wide, set flush into the surface of the road, upon which ran the flangeless wheels of the tramway vehicles. Guidance was provided by a third rail laid down the centre of the track; this had a slot in its top to take a small guide wheel (the 'perambulator') attached to the front of the tramcar (or rather, converted horse omnibus).

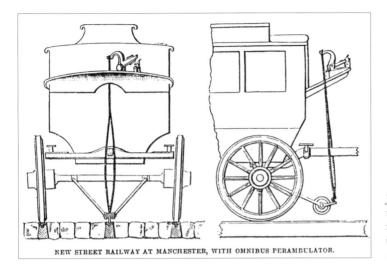

NEW STREET RAILWAY AT MANCHESTER, WITH OMNIBUS PERAMBULATOR.

John Haworth's guided tram mechanism used on Salford's first tramway, as depicted in the *Illustrated London News* of 16 November 1861.

Permission was given by Salford Council and the Pendleton Turnpike Trustees for the line from Pendleton (to the north-west of Manchester) along Broad Street, the Crescent and Chapel Street to a terminus at Albert's Bridge on the Salford/Manchester boundary. Other details of the line are sketchy, but it is thought that the tramway was opened in stages during 1861 and 1862, and was initially well regarded as being smooth, reliable and no hindrance to other road users. The gauge is not known, but it must have been sufficient to accommodate the outside wheels of Greenwood's buses, some of which were fitted with the guide wheels (which could be raised at the end of the tramway section to allow the bus to continue along the road).

On 1 March 1865 Greenwood, Haworth and other local businessmen came together to form the Manchester Carriage Co. Ltd, a concern later to play an important role in the development of horse tramways in MANCHESTER and the surrounding district. By the later 1860s, though, it appears that maintenance of the tramway had been allowed to slip – possibly because the Company was now expressing an interest in laying conventionally railed lines – and in February 1870 the Council ordered the removal of the rails, though this was not done for another two years.

Salford Corporation Tramways
Authority: Salford Corporation Act 1897
Gauge: 4ft 8½in.
Traction: Horse, overhead electric
Took over: 1 May 1901
Closed: 31 March 1947
System: Network
Length: 38.8 miles
Stock: 77 horse?; 10 sd, 231 dd electric
Livery: Chocolate/maroon/red & cream
Last Car: No.350

With its 1901 takeover of part of the MANCHESTER TRAMWAYS for £42,500, Salford Corporation found itself the owner of ninety-four cars, some 35 miles of track within its boundaries and the depots at Weaste, Pendleton and Lower Broughton. It thereupon set about converting the system to electric working with the first route, from Kersal Bar along Bury New Road to Blackfriars Bridge in Manchester, reopening on 4 October. The other lines followed quickly with the last horse trams running in about May 1903, by which date the new services were being worked by Milnes open-toppers 1–100 (1901–02), Milnes bogie open-toppers 101–130 (1903) and similar BEC cars

Salford Corporation Nos 30 and 63 of 1901–02 with the almost inevitable crowd of fascinated small boys. *(Author's Collection)*

131–150 (also 1903), based on a new depot on Frederick Road in the town centre. (Most of these cars were later top-covered and/or rebuilt.)

Three years later, on 2 October 1906, the system's last route opened, north-west to Worsley, to produce a sprawling network of lines connected to those of Manchester to the east, TRAFFORD PARK to the south, SOUTH LANCASHIRE to the west and BURY to the north – though through-running agreements were not fully exploited until the 1920s when bus competition was beginning to pose a serious threat. The Corporation introduced its own bus services in 1920, by which time the tramcar fleet had grown with the purchase of the following vehicles (some renumbering ignored):

Nos 151–160: ERTCW single-deck combination cars of 1905
Nos 161, 162, 173–177: ex-Trafford Park cars bought 1905
Nos 163–172: UEC balcony cars of 1906
Nos 177–196: ditto of 1908
Nos 197–200: HN balcony cars of 1908
Nos 151–160: Brush open-toppers of 1913–14
Nos 201–212: Brush bogie balcony cars of 1915
Nos 213–224: Brush bogie open-toppers of 1915–16

These were followed in 1923–24 by enclosed Brush cars 225–230, the Corporation's last purchases, and eight years later, on 19 March 1932, the through service north-east to MIDDLETON up the Middleton Road to Rhodes and then on via Manchester tracks was withdrawn. This was followed on 9 March 1935 by the closure of the two north-west branches from Irlams O'Th'Height to Swinton and Pendlebury. Other closures followed, accompanied by car withdrawals; by 1938 the Corporation was operating more buses than trams and complete closure was planned for the following year. The outbreak of the Second World War, however, saw this postponed (though cutbacks continued) and it was not until 1947 that the last three routes went, the final service being on the Deansgate and Docks circular.

Scarborough Tramways

Authority: Scarborough Tramways Act 1902
Gauge: 3ft 6in.
Traction: Overhead electric
Opened: 6 May 1904
Closed: 30 September 1931
System: Network
Length: 4.78 miles
Stock: 29 dd
Livery: Dark red & cream
Last Car: No.12?

Owned and operated by the Scarborough Tramways Co., a subsidiary of Edmundson's Electricity Corporation Ltd (although promoted by the Corporation), this compact little system was surprisingly short-lived for so popular a seaside resort. As opened on 6 and 7 May 1904 the route layout resembled a figure 8 on its side, with the West Pier and Foreshore Road on the South Bay seafront to the east, Vernon Place at the central crossroads and Scalby Road Depot on the western inland edge. In addition, a ¾-mile branch northwards from the western loop led via Castle Road and North Marine Road to the entrance to Alexandra Park in the area known as North Side, whilst a ¼-mile southern branch continued the Foreshore Road line southwards past the Aquarium and along a private toll road to the Spa; a link via Barwick Street and Hanover Road provided a shortcut across the western loop. Route length was of just 4½ miles, of which roughly half was double-tracked.

Services were worked by a fleet of open-top cars, Nos 1–15 being from Brush and 16–18 from BEC; these were joined in 1905 by Nos 19–22, four similar Brush vehicles.

A ¼-mile extension eastwards, from the West Pier along Sand Side to the Marine Drive toll gate, opened at the start of the 1906 summer season and completed the system, which remained intact until receipts were hard-hit by the First World War. Consequently, immediately after the war minor trimmings of the network began, though in 1925 seven Brush open-toppers were bought from Ipswich Corporation and renumbered 21 and 23–28, the first of these taking an Ipswich body and the truck from Scarborough 21 after that car had been damaged in a serious accident on 16 September that year.

In March 1931 the Corporation decided to buy the tramways (for £20,000) in order to close them and, under the Scarborough Corporation Act of that year, took them over on 30 September to do just that, immediately scrapping the trams in favour of a profit-sharing bus service operated by United Automobile Services Ltd.

Left: Scarborough: Where the holidaymakers arrived – a 1905-franked postcard of the railway station in Westborough, with the Grand Hotel dominating the scene … *(Author's Collection)*

Below left: … and where they went – the South Bay seafront with its myriad attractions … *(Author's Collection)*

Below right: … and the cars they rode on – Nos 2 of 1904 and 24 of 1903 vintage, bought from Ipswich in 1925. As befitting a seaside resort, all the system's cars were open-top double-deckers. *(Author's Collection)*

Arguably the most important component of a tramway is its track. This is Scarborough's Vernon Place junction being laid, with conventional grooved tramway rails, prior to the system's 1904 opening. Westborough is to the left and Newborough Street to the right. *(Author's Collection)*

Scarborough: Central Tramway

Not a tramway, but a standard-gauge funicular railway, 254ft in length on Scarborough's South Bay. Still operational (during spring and summer), it opened in 1881 using steam-powered winding gear, but was converted in 1920 to electric winding.

Scarborough: Queen's Parade Tramway

Not a tramway, but a funicular railway running from Queen's Parade down to the Royal Albert Drive on Scarborough's North Bay. It had a track length of approximately 218ft, a gauge thought to have been 4ft and was operated on the water-balance system. Opened in 1881, recurrent landslips led to its closure just six years later.

Scarborough: South Cliff Tramway

Again, not a tramway, but another of this Yorkshire town's cliff railways (of which there have been five in all). Opened in 1875 – making it the first such line in Britain – it was built to railway standard gauge and was 284ft in length. Originally worked as a water-balance funicular, in the winter of 1934–35 it was converted to electric winding. Sited at the southern end of the South Bay, it is still operational during the spring and summer months.

Sheffield Tramways

Authority: Sheffield Tramways Act 1872
Gauge: 4ft 8½in.
Traction: Horse
Opened: 7 October 1873
Taken over: 11 July 1896
System: Branching + branching
Length: 9.43 miles
Stock: 18 sd, 35 dd
Livery: Route colour

Built by Thomas Lightfoot, a local contractor, the first Sheffield horse tramway was owned by the Corporation but leased to its promoters, the Sheffield Tramways Co. The official opening of the mainly double-track route, from the Wicker, on the edge of the city centre, north-east up Savile Street and the Attercliffe Road to the Golden Ball in Attercliffe (about 2¼ miles), was on 6 October 1873 with public services commencing the next day with double-deck Starbuck cars Nos 1–12. On 7 May 1874 the line was extended another mile to Carbrook (where Tinsley Depot was built). A year later, on 26 May 1875, a parallel route was opened to the north of the first line, off Savile Street and along Brightside Lane to the district of that name (where a second depot was later constructed). To work the enlarged system cars 13–20 were purchased, all Starbuck single-deckers.

On 19 May 1877 a third route was opened, west of the Wicker, running north-west along Infirmary Road and Langsett Road to Hillsborough (2½ miles), and to work this ten more Starbuck double-deckers (Nos 22–31) were bought; No.21 is thought to have been a Falcon single-decker used on trials with a Hughes steam tramway locomotive and subsequently kept.

Also in 1877, the last two Company-operated routes were opened. Running south down the Moor from the Moorhead (south of and unconnected to the Wicker terminus), the line then divided with one branch (opened 29 October) continuing south down the London Road to Heeley, and the other (opened 24 December) veering south-west down Washington Road and Wostenhome Road to Nether Edge. Depots were provided at both these southern termini with the Heeley line worked by (probably) Starbuck double-deckers 32–40 with (most likely) Starbuck single-deckers 41–45 on the Nether Edge route.

In 1878 further steam trials were carried out, this time with a loco supplied by a local firm, the Yorkshire Engine Co. Ltd of Sheffield, but again nothing came of them. By now Company-Corporation relations were not very good and the former was operating horse bus services as well as the trams. In 1882–83 car No.16 was rebuilt as a double-decker and in 1884 (presumably) Ashbury single-deck saloons 46–49 were added to stock (and converted to double-deckers five years later). In 1886 two Ashbury double-deckers on Eades reversible trucks were bought (Nos 1 and 50), followed a year later by Nos 2 and 12, more conventional double-deckers from the same builders. (As these numbers suggest, some of the older cars were now being withdrawn.)

By the 1890s the Corporation was ready to terminate its lease and run the tramways itself and, in 1896, secured the necessary Act to enable it to do so (see below).

Sheffield Tramways horse car No.15 of 1874, now immaculately restored at the National Tramway Museum, Crich – where, back in 1963, it was the first tram to operate. (M. Donnison)

Sheffield Corporation Tramways

Authority: Sheffield Corporation Tramways Act 1896
Gauge: 4ft 8½in.
Traction: Horse, overhead electric
Took over: 11 July 1896
Closed: 8 October 1960
System: Radial network
Length: 52.05 miles
Stock: 68 horse; 69 sd, 820 dd electric
Livery: Route colour horse; royal (later azure) blue & cream electric
Last Car: No.510

Following its 1896 takeover of the SHEFFIELD TRAMWAYS (see above), Sheffield Corporation found itself in possession of forty-four tramcars and four horse buses – and, far more importantly in historical terms, the first clear parliamentary mandate for a municipality to both own and operate a tramway system. A number of the old cars were quickly withdrawn and two dozen new ones purchased, these being double-deck vehicles 6–9, 14, 30 and 51–56, and roofed toastracks 27 and 57–67, all from Milnes.

The intention from the outset was to extend and electrify the tramways, but before this could take place three new routes were opened: north-west to Walkley via West Street and Crookes Valley Road from a terminus in Church Street sited between the other two, south-west along Ecclesall Road from the Nether Edge/Heeley routes junction to Hunter's Bar, and south-west from a point midway along the Heeley route down Abbeydale Road. Conversion work on the original horse lines was also put in hand, including the linking of the three central termini.

The first converted routes to reopen, on 6 September 1899, were to Nether Edge, Heeley and Tinsley (a short extension beyond Carbrook). The first electric cars were short, open-top double-deckers 1–25 and single-deckers 39–52, all from Milnes. More conversions (and new routes) followed, the last horse trams running on 11 November 1902 on the (cut back) Hillingsborough route; by then the car fleet had been augmented by the addition of Milnes open-toppers 26–38, ERTCW single-deckers 53–58, ERTCW open-toppers 59–88, Brush single-deckers 89–103, Brush open-toppers 104–123, Corporation single-deckers 124–129, Milnes open-toppers 131–155, plus single-deckers 156–165 and open-toppers 167–186 from Cravens of Sheffield. A number of horse trams were converted into works cars, one of which – No.15 of 1874, renumbered 166 as a breakdown car – can now be seen restored to its original state at the National Tramway Museum, Crich (and was the first car to run there). Two others were sold to Chesterfield Corporation and the remainder scrapped.

Above left: Sheffield Corporation-built No.213 of 1904 on a pre-First World War service, on a postcard of the Nethergreen terminus. The F on the car indicates the route. (*Author's Collection*)

Above right: The junction of Angel Street and the High Street in the centre of Sheffield, with three Corporation double-deckers in view, No.454 to the fore. (*Author's Collection*)

As the system continued to grow, so more cars were bought or built: Milnes single-deckers 187–192, Corporation open-toppers 193–198, Corporation single-deckers 200–211 (1903), Corporation open-toppers 213–218, Brush open-toppers 219–243 and original horse cars 6 and 7 motorised by the Corporation using Brush trucks (1903–04). These were followed in 1905–06 by Corporation open-toppers 246–257 and, in 1907, by UEC 258–272, the first top-covered cars. (Many of the open-toppers were later top-covered or fully enclosed.) The main depot was originally at Tinsley and then, from 1911 onwards, in Queens Road, south of the city centre; there were several other smaller depots scattered around the system.

No new trams were added until 1912, when the Corporation built top-covered cars 281–295; these were followed by similar Brush vehicles 296–345 and, in 1913–15, similar Nos 346–355 from the Corporation again. The system's other new cars added between the two world wars (all enclosed double-deckers) were:

Nos 367–369, 401–500: Corporation of 1918–21
Nos 376–400: Brush of 1921–22
Nos 36–60: Brush of 1924–25
Nos 2–35, 61–130: Corporation of 1924–33
Nos 1, 451–500: Cravens of 1926–27
Nos 131–155: W.E. Hill Ltd of South Shields of 1929–30
No.370: Corporation of 1931
Nos 156–303: ditto of 1933–39

Between 1941 and 1944 the Corporation constructed fourteen more enclosed double-deckers to replace the ones lost through German bombing; these took the numbers 83, 85, 100, 112, 119, 129, 133, 192, 201, 227, 261, 274, 430 and 483 and were appropriately termed 'Blitz' class cars. A number of second-hand vehicles were also purchased: twenty ex-London County Council ERTCW enclosed double-deckers of 1903 vintage, bought 1917–18 and numbered 356–365 and vacated earlier numbers, eight similar balcony cars from ROTHERHAM in 1926 (of which six were put into service), fourteen ex-NEWCASTLE HN double-deckers of 1901, bought in 1941 and numbered 311–324, and ten EE double-deckers of 1920–21, bought in 1943 from BRADFORD (Nos 325–334).

The only passenger cars bought or constructed after the Second World War were the 'Jubilee' class of streamlined enclosed double-deckers, Nos 501–536, of which the first was built by the Corporation in 1946 and the remainder constructed between 1950 and 1952 by Roberts.

The system continued to expand during the 1920s and 1930s – including the 1926 takeover of 1.28 miles of line from Rotherham (the only connecting system), between Tinsley and Templeborough, when Sheffield's boundaries were enlarged – though by now the tramway was being trimmed elsewhere. It was hit badly by bombing raids during the Second World War and replacement vehicles had to be built or bought (as listed earlier); though in the late 1940s its future seemed bright, things were soon to change. Through-running to Rotherham ceased on 11 December 1948, when a railway bridge needed to be rebuilt, and that route's services were terminated at Tinsley; three years later the Corporation decided to abandon its other routes over the next fifteen years, though, in the event, it took only nine.

Because of the late closure of the tramway, several of its electric cars have been saved for preservation. Currently on view at the National Tramway Museum, Crich, are Nos 46 of 1899, 189 and 264 of 1934, 510 of 1950 and ex-Bradford car 330 (which was converted to a rail grinder in 1951), whilst Nos 264 of 1907 and 513 of 1950 are at the North of England Open Air Museum, BEAMISH (though the latter car has been on loan to BLACKPOOL).

Sheffield: South Yorkshire Supertram
Authority: South Yorkshire Light Rail Transit Act 1988
Gauge: 4ft 8½in.
Traction: Overhead electric
Opened: 21 March 1994
System: Branching

Length: 17.68 miles
Stock: 25 sd
Livery: Grey & blue to 1998, white & orange, red, blue colour bands from 1999 to 2006, then blue, orange and red

Hard on the heels of the MANCHESTER METROLINK project came a similar one centred on Sheffield. Government funding for the scheme was announced on 11 December 1990, although the idea dated back more than twenty years when, not long after the 1960 closure of the city's tramways (see above), proposals were explored for a brand-new system costing some £230 million. Planning and evaluation studies continued up until 1985, when the South Yorkshire Passenger Transport Executive successfully promoted a Bill for a route running from north–west to south–east across the city. This was followed by a second Bill (which became the South Yorkshire Light Rail Transit Act 1989) for a route north-east from the city centre, past the World Student Games arena, to the Meadowhall Shopping Centre as part of the area's regeneration plan, giving the proposed system the shape of a tilted Y. This line was, in fact, the first to be constructed.

Work began immediately after the closing of the World Student Games at the end of July 1991, with the public opening coming less than three years later (the official opening by HRH the Princess Royal being on 23 May 1994). The contractors were BB.

The double-track line begins at Meadowhall Interchange station, at the junction of BR's lines from Sheffield to Barnsley and Rotherham (and actually just over the Sheffield/Rotherham boundary), then circles the shopping centre before running south-west along the trackbed of the former GCR branch to Barnsley. It passes the Sheffield Arena and the Don Valley International Stadium before leaving the old trackbed on its own alignment, past the Woodbourne Athletics Stadium, to reach Nunnery Depot by Sheffield Parkway, which it crosses via a bridge (the number of new bridges is a feature of the route) and then follows to a city centre terminus in Commercial Street, by Haymarket, some 4½ miles from Meadowhall.

An example of modern tramway ticket design (compare with the old-fashioned variety on p.83): a machine-readable ticket of the style issued during the early years of the Sheffield Supertram.

A triangular junction just before the terminus feeds the Phase 2 route to a second interchange, this time behind Sheffield Midland station in Granville Street. (A new, more convenient halt was opened here in October 2001 during ongoing improvement work to the station; the finished interchange was deemed 'Project of the Year' at the 2006 National Rail Awards.) The section south from here (Phases 2 and 5) opened on 5 December 1994 and takes the line on street and reserved sections over Norfolk Park Viaduct, along Park Grange Road, City Road and Ridgeway Road to Gleadless Townend. Here Phase 5 veers westwards as a short branch to Herdings (opened 3 April 1995), whilst the main line carries on as Phases 6 and 7 to Halfway (opened 27 March 1995), some 8¼ miles from the city centre. The north-western branch of the Y opened westwards from Commercial Street/Fitzalan Square to Cathedral (Phase 3) on 20 February 1995, and on to the University of Sheffield, where it swung north to Shalesmoor (Phase 4) on 27 February. Phase 8, opened 23 October, continued this line north-west to Middlewood, with a short branch west from Hillsborough to Malin Bridge. Just under half the system is laid with ballasted sleepered track.

The initial twenty-five cars (single-deck, eight-axle articulated two-car units Nos 1–25, the first modern design trams of this type in the British Isles) were built by Siemens in Düsseldorf, delivered by mid-1994 and finished in a modern version of the city's old blue and cream tramcar livery, the light silver-grey bodywork being finished off with a blue-grey skirting. There is seating for eighty-eight, with level access from the system's medium-height platforms. The operator was South Yorkshire Supertram Ltd, a subsidiary of the SYPTE, but this concern was bought out by Stagecoach Holdings plc, the bus and coach operator, on 19 December 1997.

Shipley Tramways
Authority: Shipley Tramways Order 1881
Gauge: 4ft?
Traction: Horse
Opened: 3 August 1882?
Closed: 9 October 1891
System: Branching
Length: 2.31 miles
Stock: 6 sd?, 1 dd?
Livery: Varnished wood?
Last Car: ?

The first tramway in Shipley, immediately north of Bradford, was a short, unsuccessful single-track horse line running from the Fox & Hounds, at Briggate in the town centre, westwards along Commercial Street and Saltaire Road to its junction with Bingley Road (where the depot was sited in Moorhead Lane behind the Rosse Hotel). It was promoted by the tramway contractor Joseph Speight of Eccleston Park near Prescot who, after the failure of an 1873 scheme, obtained authorisation in 1881 for 1.39 miles of line, of which only 0.8 miles was laid. The line's one single and one double-deck car were from Oldbury. The BoT inspection was on 2 August 1882 and the line possibly opened to the public the following day. Some uncertainty also surrounds the tramway's gauge: it was planned as a 3ft 6in. line, but is believed to have been constructed to a gauge of 4ft at the request of the Shipley Local Board, with an eye on a possible connection to the new system at BRADFORD. (The official returns are of no help in resolving the matter as they give both gauges at different times!)

By 1883 the tramway (and/or Speight) was in financial difficulty, and on 10 May that year the horses and cars were auctioned (though the latter apparently failed to find buyers); later that year ownership of the line passed to a Maurice Jones of Liverpool who, in February 1884, reopened it with two new, lighter cars. Jones' operation was no more successful than Speight's for, on 13 February 1885 (reportedly), the tramway shut once again. Jones then offered it to the local board, which declined to buy it. Horse working resumed, albeit very intermittently, until mid-1887. Rescue was at hand, though; the following March saw the line purchased by Bradford & District Tramways Ltd, who opened a second single-track line on 26 August 1888, this running south-east along the Bradford Road from the Rosse Hotel to the Shipley boundary at Frizinghall, where it met but did not connect with the steam tramway line from

Bradford. Two further cars were obtained to help work the enlarged system, followed by another some months later – presumably all single-deckers once more.

Plans for additional routes came to nothing and in February 1891 the Company went into receivership, services ceasing nine months later. It is thought that two of the cars found their way south to Bradford to join the fleet there and, two years after the tramway closed, the Bradford Road line reopened as part of Bradford's Keighley Road steam route into Shipley. Ten years later, though, a new, electric system began operations in the town (see below).

Shipley: Mid-Yorkshire Tramways

Authority: Shipley Improvement Act 1901
Gauge: 4ft
Traction: Overhead electric
Opened: 23 July 1903
Taken over: 30 April 1904
System: Cross
Length: 3.43 miles
Stock: 10 dd
Livery: Royal red & ivory

Following the failure of Shipley's horse tramway (see above), early in the twentieth century proposals were made for a grand tramway network to link all the major towns of central Yorkshire, but all that came of them was the opening by the Mid-Yorkshire Tramways Co. (on behalf of Shipley UDC) of two short routes through the centre of Shipley. The first ran east–west from the Bradford boundary at Thackley via the Leeds Road, Briggate, Saltaire Road and Bingley Road to Nab Wood Cemetery, whilst the second shorter north–south route (opened 14 November 1903) ran from Baildon Bridge, through Briggate to the Branch Hotel on the Keighley Road. At both Saltaire and the Branch, the lines were connected to the BRADFORD CITY TRAMWAYS' new electric line in Bradford Road.

Ten HN open-toppers were ordered for the tramway, of which four arrived in time for the opening with trials and (probably) some early services being worked by cars borrowed from Bradford. The depot was in Exhibition Road off Saltaire Road – it is a Grade II-listed building and was recently converted into a restaurant. Traffic on the system did not live up to expectations – the Council would not agree to through-running with Bradford – and less than a year after it opened the whole concern was sold to Bradford Corporation to become integrated into the larger system. The cars, renumbered 230–239, stayed loyal to their old home, being used thereafter mainly on Shipley services.

Shipley Glen Pond Tramway

This early pleasure line – gauge unknown, but possibly c.3ft – was laid round Glen Pond in Shipley Glen, a beauty spot to the north of Bradford, in Yorkshire. During the 1880s and 1890s a number of attractions were constructed in the Glen by the owner, Col. Maude, including a boating pool, a switchback railway and an aerial runway. The horse tramway was built by a local engineer and entrepreneur, Sam Wilson, who had purchased the six open toastrack cars used on a temporary line at the 1887 Saltaire Exhibition; two of these, each seating about twenty passengers, were used on the Shipley Glen line and the other four were put into store and later (possibly) made use of on the SHIPLEY GLEN TRAMWAY (see below). It is not known when the line closed – probably sometime before the outbreak of the First World War – nor indeed are many other details known.

Shipley Glen Tramway

Not a tramway, but a funicular railway (with a maximum gradient of 1 in 12, far less steep than its cliff railway counterparts) that serves visitors to the beauty spot of its name near Bradford (see above). Opened 18 May 1895, it is a double line of 1ft 8in. gauge tracks, 386yd long. The original pair of small open cars on each track were built by S. Halliday of Baildon, possibly using parts from the companion cars to the Shipley Glen Pond Tramway (see above); these were heavily rebuilt in 1955–56, though it is thought that some of the original parts (including one underframe) were incorporated into the 'new' cars. The railway runs from Coach Road, at the bottom of the Glen, up to Glen Top, where the cable winding house is situated in standard funicular fashion, and has been restored and operated by volunteers since it foundered as a commercial enterprise in the 1980s.

Soothill Nether *see* Dewsbury, Ossett & Soothill Nether

South Lancashire Tramways
Authority: South Lancashire Tramways Act 1900
Gauge: 4ft 8½in.
Traction: Overhead electric
Opened: 20 October 1902
Closed: 16 December 1933
System: Network
Length: 39.1 miles
Stock: 91 dd
Livery: Red & white/cream
Last Car: No.7

Part of the large, standard-gauge network of tramways stretching across south Lancashire from LIVERPOOL to MANCHESTER, this system was promoted by the brothers Jacob and James Atherton, who had a number of other tramway interests, including the ST HELENS system, and who, after a number of false starts, obtained the necessary empowering Act.

Built by the South Lancashire Electric Traction & Power Co. Ltd (registered 29 November 1900), the first section opened ran for 6½ miles from the Lowton St Mary's boundary north-east through Leigh and Atherton (with the main depot and power station midway between the two) and on to Four Lane Ends, where it connected with the BOLTON system. This was followed on 25 October 1902 by a south-eastern branch of some 2 miles from Atherton to Tyldesley, which was extended north-westwards 3¾ miles from Atherton, on 7 February 1903, through Hindley Green to Hindley, followed on 4 April by a line running south-west from Hindley for 6 miles, through Platt Bridge and Ashton (where it passed close to the WIGAN CORPORATION terminus) to Haydock and a connection with St Helens to complete the northern half of the system.

The first cars were Nos 1–45, Milnes open-toppers of 1902 (many of which were later top-covered). There was also a private directors' single-deck saloon car, possibly by Milnes of 1897, painted white and used briefly on private-hire services, such as weddings and funerals. There were also plans to operate an extensive night-time freight service with special goods trains, but this never materialised.

Milnes-built South Lancashire No.2 of 1902, before its top cover was fitted. *(Author's Collection)*

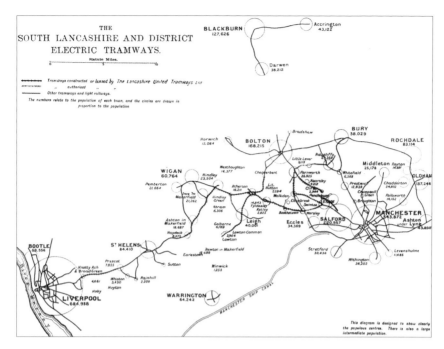

Map of the
South Lancs
system and
connections,
from the
1909 *Manual
of Electrical
Undertakings.*

    The first eastern extension, from Tyldesley through Mosley Common to Boothtown (2 miles), opened on 20 April 1905; by this date, though, the Company was in receivership and on 29 December 1905 a new concern, Lancashire United Tramways Ltd, was registered to take over the tramway, which it did on 2 January of the following year. On 1 April 1906 it took over the FARNWORTH UDC system as well, opening, on 29 June, a 1–mile southern extension of this from Brookhouse to Walkden Memorial, the thirteen Farnworth cars becoming Nos 46–58 in the South Lancs fleet. The network continued to expand, with a ½-mile extension from the Lowton/Leigh boundary to the GCR station in Lowton St Mary's opening on 6 July 1906 and, on 27 September 1906, a 4-mile eastern extension from Boothstown was opened to Swinton Church via Leigh Road through Worsley. That year also saw the arrival of twenty-four Brush and UEC top-covered double-deckers (Nos 59–82), whilst 1907 saw the opening of two more lines: a 1½-mile extension of the former Farnworth line, from Unity Brook to the Oddfellows Arm on the Kearsley/Pendlebury boundary (28 February), and a ½-mile branch from Worsley south to Winton (29 March). Like the rest of the system, these lines were principally single-track.

    On 14 June 1909 through-running to Bolton commenced and that October the St Helens system (which had been controlled by South Lancs since October 1906) took over the operation of the Haydock–Ashton section. The last extension opened on 28 August 1913, running as a single track north-west from the Walkden Memorial along Manchester Road East to Little Hutton, where it swung northwards along Cleggs Lane to meet the Buckley Lane route in Farnworth.

    In 1919 the Company bought seven BEC open-top cars (Nos 83–89) from the LIVERPOOL & PRESCOT LIGHT RAILWAY, the fleet being completed in 1927 with the purchase of EE top-covered bogie cars 44 and 45. A year later, a connection to the SALFORD system had been put in at Swinton, and one (finally) to that of Wigan at Ashton.

    In 1929 the Company obtained an Act to abandon the tramways in favour of trolleybuses – it was already operating motor buses – and changed its name to South Lancashire Transport in anticipation of this event. On 3 August 1930 the Atherton–Ashton route was switched over, followed on 21 June 1931 by the isolated St Helens-worked Ashton–Haydock section (at the same time as the rest of the route to St Helens was converted by that corporation). Other changeovers came quickly with the last tram route, Leigh to Four Ends, being closed two years later. After the abandonment, eight of the surviving bogie cars (Nos 44, 45, 47, 48, 50, 54, 55 and 58) were sold to Bolton and the remainder scrapped.

South Shields Tramways
Authority: South Shields Corporation Tramways Order 1881
Gauge: 3ft 6in.
Traction: Horse
Opened: 1 August 1883
Closed: 31 January 1906
System: Single line
Length: 2.53 miles
Stock: 12 sd, 17 dd?
Livery: ?
Last Car: ?

Owned by South Shields Corporation, this line was leased originally to the South Shields Tramways Co., who began services with five MRCW open-top double-deckers, plus a similar number of vehicles borrowed for the official inspection from the aborted Ramsgate & Margate line (see Volume 1). It was constructed by James Gowans of Edinburgh – but to the unauthorised gauge of 3ft 6in., which meant that a second Order had to be secured in 1883 to permit the use of the narrower gauge. The portion built of the authorised (mainly single-track) line ran from the South Pier, on the sea coast, along Ocean Road and King Street to the Market Place, from where it continued in a zigzag fashion beside the River Tyne to Slake Terrace at Tyne Dock. A short midway branch down Victoria Road led to the depot.

The tramway was not a financial success and, at midnight on 30 April 1886, the cars were driven off the end of the line and along the roadway to a timber yard in East Jarrow – presumably to avoid their seizure by the Corporation or creditors – and promptly sold by auction, going to the DOUGLAS BAY TRAMWAY in the Isle of Man, where they took the numbers 13–18 (of which No.14 is preserved in the Manx Museum). In 1887 the line was rented to a new concern, the South Shields Tramways & Carriage Co. Ltd, and reopened on 28 March. The new car fleet eventually consisted of Nos 1–6 (Milnes single-deckers on Eades patent reversible trucks), Nos 7–10 (Milnes open-top double-deckers), another similar but longer No.8, six Ashbury open toastracks (Nos 11–16?) and possibly six more Milnes open-toppers. At least some of the cars bore names.

In July 1899 the tramway was taken over by the BET but not electrified, presumably because of uncertainty regarding the lease, which the Corporation decided to terminate from 1 February 1906. The line closed the day before this, and its nineteen cars and eleven horse buses were sold by auction. The Company itself was wound up later that year.

South Shields Corporation Tramways
Authority: South Shields Corporation Tramways Act 1903
Gauge: 4ft 8½in.
Traction: Overhead electric
Opened: 30 March 1906
Closed: 31 March 1946
System: Network
Length: 7.51 miles
Stock: 59 dd
Livery: Crimson lake & ivory to 1935, then royal blue & primrose
Last Car: No.39 (official)*

Well before the closing of the town's horse tramway (see above), South Shields Corporation had been planning the extension and electrification of the line, with work commencing in June 1905 on the new routes. The heart of the new system was a figure-8 track plan, the western side of which was formed by the northern part of the former horse route from Tyne Dock up to King Street (though with a more direct route from Green Street down Frederick Street and South Eldon Street), and the eastern side by a line from there, down Fowler Street past the Town Hall, and along Westhoe Road, Dean Road and

South Shields open-topper
No.18, built by UEC
in 1906, posed with its
crew – and apparently
the conductor's young
lady! – by the Woodhave
Memorial at Tyne Dock.
(Author's Collection)

Stanhope Road, where it swung westwards via Bolden Road and Hudson Street to Tyne Dock (and a connection with the JARROW system). The two sides of the 8 were connected midway along Laygate, near the junction of which with Dean Road was the depot.

The first section opened was the stretch from Fowler Street to Stanhope Road, with the remainder following in stages over the next twelve months, including a short extension of the Fowler Street line at the King Street junction up Mile End Road, and a longer extension of the King Street line down Ocean Road to the South Pier (the last portion of the old horse tramway, in fact). This junction was one of the few 'Grand Union' junctions in Britain: two double tracks crossing at right-angles, with double-track connections between them in all the four quadrants so formed. All routes were totally or predominantly double-track and the original car fleet was made up of HN open-toppers 1–10 and similar UEC vehicles 11–20, these being joined in 1907 by UEC Nos 21–25 (virtually identical to the earlier cars) and 26–35 (with top-covers).

In 1913 the Corporation began operating battery electric buses (mainly to counter the threat of competition from neighbouring BET subsidiaries) and the following year they purchased five Brush top-covered cars (Nos 36–40). Improvement and expansion were very much in the Corporation's mind, and suggestions were made to Jarrow Corporation that it should buy the Jarrow line, which would make a more unified system (though running had ceased in 1911), but nothing came of the plan. Instead, in 1920, the Corporation obtained the South Shields Corporation LRO, authorising 1¼ miles of reserved section line from Dean Road south down King George Road to its new, large housing estate at Cleadon. This double-track line, down the centre of a dual carriageway, opened on 1 June 1922 for two-thirds of its length, the final portion to the Ridgeway opening that December. Five 1921 EE bogie enclosed double-deckers (Nos 41–45) were bought to cope with the extra traffic. Plans to continue the line on to link with the SUNDERLAND CORPORATION system, just 2 miles away, sadly never bore fruit.

All further stock acquisitions (with one exception) were of second-hand vehicles: Nos 29 and 48 in 1929 ex-Jarrow, Nos 46 and 47 in 1930 ex-TYNESIDE, Nos 23, 33, 50 and 51 in 1931 ex-WIGAN, Nos 16 and 34 ex-AYR and Nos 18 and 20 ex-YORKSHIRE (WEST RIDING) in 1932; the sole exception was the purchase in 1936 of No.52, a new enclosed car from Brush. (Many of these cars at first carried temporary numbers as rebuilding and withdrawal programmes progressed.) Of special interest is that, in 1929, the Corporation revived the horse tramway practice of naming cars and did so with an odd mixture in honour of local dignitaries, Roman emperors and ocean liners. It is thought that eighteen in all were so treated before the practice ceased in 1934 (and the existing names painted out).

Whilst many other systems were succumbing, in the 1930s, to a combination of bus competition and maintenance costs, that at South Shields stayed open as a result of investment in both cars and track. In 1936, however, the Corporation began trolleybus operations with the intention of eventually replacing the trams which, on 3 May 1937, they did from the Market Place to Stanhope Road. On 1 April 1946 the trolleybuses took over the last tramway route, to the Ridgeway, with a 'Last Car' ceremony the day after public services ceased. All surviving tramcars were then broken up, with the exception of No.52, the fast, streamlined Brush car of 1936, which was sold to Sunderland Corporation for £250 – a tenth of its purchase price.

South Yorkshire Supertram *see* Sheffield: South Yorkshire Supertram

Southport Tramways
Authority: Southport Tramways Order 1872
Gauge: 4ft 8½in.
Traction: Horse, overhead electric
Opened: 31 May 1873
Closed: 31 December 1934
System: Network
Length: 17.35 miles
Stock: 25 horse?; 17 sd, 37 dd electric
Livery: ST Co. green & white, BST Indian red & cream, Corporation maroon & cream
Last Car: ?

Unlike the majority of the Lancashire tramways, Southport's compact network of criss-crossing routes was never connected to any others; as if to make up for this, it had an extremely complicated life of its own. The first (horse) line, operated by the Southport Tramways Co., ran south-west from Churchtown station, in the north, via Mill Lane and Road Lane to Lord Street, thence on to Birkdale station on the LYR. This was soon followed by a second route, closer to the shore, which headed back up Lord Street and Cambridge Street to rejoin the first line by Chruchtown station, before continuing east a short distance to the Botanic Gardens. The length of the single-track system was 6¼ miles, worked by a fleet of (eventually) thirteen trams, all probably open-top double-deckers.

The ST Co.'s monopoly in the town lasted for ten years, until 12 May 1883, when the Birkdale & Southport Tramways Co. opened a separate line to the east of the ST system, running from London Square on Lord Street, south-east to Kew Gardens via Scarisbrook Road, with a short southern branch along Sefton Street to the Crown Hotel, opening on 5 November 1884 (the only part of this company's system actually in Birkdale). A probable total of twelve cars worked this tramway.

Above left: Postcard of Southport Corporation's open-topper No.12 of 1900 in Lord Street, the town's grand thoroughfare. *(Author's Collection)*

Above right: An LYR official postcard of Lord Street, Southport, with two Southport Tramways Co. double-deckers at work. The card has been overprinted for distribution in northern France and Belgium, publicising the railway company's Zeebrugge–Hull ferry service and connections to the Lake District and Lancashire coast resorts. *(Author's Collection)*

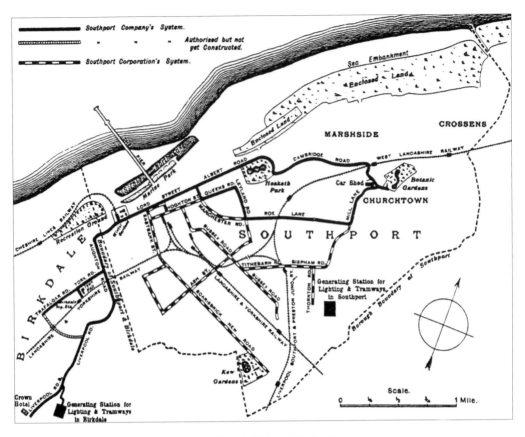

Map of Southport's tramways, from the 1909 *Manual of Electrical Undertakings*.

In 1896 Southport Corporation and Birkdale UDC purchased those portions of the lines within their respective boroughs and leased them back to the ST Co. for twenty-one years (the B&S lines only until electrification, these being taken back on 1 January 1900), Southport Corporation having obtained an Order to electrify its lines (and lay new ones) the year before. Three new electric routes were opened on 18 July 1900 with nine open-top double-deckers (many of which were later top-covered) numbered 2, 4, 6, 8, 10, 12, 14, 16 and 18, six combination single-deckers Nos 1, 3, 5, 7, 9 and 11 and single-deck saloon No.13, all from ERTCW. These were joined in 1901 by Nos 15 and 17, two more combination cars, all based at Crowlands Depot on the east side of the town.

Other routes soon followed, with the last horse trams running on 13 December 1902, by which time eight more ERTCW electric open-toppers had been bought (even numbers 20–34). Meanwhile, the ST Co. had been busy electrifying its leased lines, beginning services on 11 August 1901 on the Botanic Gardens route via Cambridge Street and Lord Street to the Southport/Birkdale boundary, using Brush open-toppers 1–20, based at the former Churchtown horse car depot. A single-deck demi car, No.21, was added two years later, by which time conversion of the Company's 5½-mile system was complete.

In 1912 Birkdale was absorbed into Southport and five years later, from 1 January 1918, the Corporation took ownership of the Company's effects for £35,000 with the expiry of its lease, taking over operations from 1 March that year. Of the newly acquired cars, No.21 was scrapped and the double-deckers renumbered 35–44, plus the odd numbers 1–17, the Corporation's single-deckers having been withdrawn. In 1914 ERTCW had supplied open toastrack 21 for use on a circular tour service, followed by similar bodies 23, 25 and 27 to take the trucks from withdrawn single-deckers (the bodies of four of which had been sold to BARROW-IN-FURNESS). Car No.13 was sold to Grimsby and one of the others withdrawn, but not scrapped, for in 1927 it was rebuilt as an illuminated car. Three new toastrack bodies, Nos 29, 31, and 33, were bought in 1919 and a top-covering programme begun for the double-deckers. This 'make do and mend' policy kept the ageing trams running through the 1920s, with the first route closure not coming until March 1931, when most of the former ST lines were abandoned. Three years later the rest of the system followed likewise, in favour of buses.

Southport Pier Tramway (1)

Authority: -
Gauge: ?
Traction: Manual
Opened: 7 May 1863
Closed: December 1863?
System: Single line
Length: c.0.8 mile
Stock: 1 sd
Livery: ?

Opened in 1860 by the Southport Pier Co., the town's 1,465yd-long pier was the first iron structure of its kind in the British Isles. With such a length – required to reach deep water, due to the shallow slope of the seabed there – the need for a tramway or railway of some sort, to convey steamer passengers and their luggage, and other users of the pier, soon became apparent. Accordingly, three years later a single-track line of unknown gauge was laid down the centre of the decking from shore to pier head; along this was hand-propelled the tramway's single carriage. The line was an immediate success and produced such a rise in the number of people using the pier that the Company decided, in December of the same year, to widen the whole structure, move the tramway to the south side and adopt cable traction. The line accordingly reopened in 1865 as a railway, fenced-off from the rest of the decking and worked on the funicular system. Several incarnations of the railway then followed, the last, which closed with the pier in 1997, being a 2ft gauge line worked by a Severn-Lamb diesel train.

Southport Pier Tramway (2)

Authority: -
Gauge: 3ft 6in.
Traction: Battery electric
Opened: 1 August 2005
System: Single line
Length: 0.51 mile
Stock: 1 sd
Livery: Blue & sand

Its structure seriously degraded, Southport pier closed in 1997 for safety reasons and the railway stock (see above) sold. Thankfully, the following year the National Heritage Lottery Fund awarded £1.7 million to the Southport Pier Trust towards the cost of refurbishing this Grade II-listed structure. Plans for the work provided for a new railway or tramway and, during the reconstruction, 900yd of 3ft 6in. gauge tramway track was laid down the centre of the pier, set into the (widened) decking. Flat-bottom rails were used, together with alloy channel extrusions to form the grooves for the wheel flanges; the line is single, without passing loops. Phase 1 of the project – restoration of the pier up to deck level – was completed in April 2002 at a cost of some £7 million and the pier reopened that May Day Bank Holiday weekend, though with a road train in temporary use; the following year saw the completion of the new pier buildings (and also saw Sefton Council take over responsibility for the pier and tramway), though it was not until July 2005 that the tramway train arrived. The reason for the delay was that the train builder, Severn-Lamb Ltd of Alcester, had collapsed and, in December 2004, had gone into voluntary liquidation; consequently, the £300,000 order had had to be completed by UK Loco Ltd of Cropthorne, Worcestershire, a new concern formed by some of the Severn-Lamb personnel.

The 76-seater tramcar unit, formed of two single-deck bogie coaches, is battery powered (with a stabling and recharging point at the seaward end of the line) and has an operating speed of 5mph. Total length of the unit is 22m and it weighs 18 tons.

Spen Valley Light Railway *see* Yorkshire (Woollen District) Electric Tramways

Stalybridge, Hyde, Mossley & Dukinfield Tramways

Authority: Stalybridge Hyde Mossley and Dukinfield Tramways and Electricity Board Act 1900
Gauge: 4ft 8½in.
Traction: Overhead electric
Opened: 15 October 1903
Closed: 12 May 1945*
System: Network
Length: 21.19 miles
Stock: 20 sd, 44 dd*
Livery: Dark green & white
Last Car: No.18 (official)*

This cumbersomely named tramway, operated by the Stalybridge, Hyde, Mossley & Dukinfield Tramways & Electricity Board, was built to serve the towns of its title immediately to the east of the Lancashire/Cheshire border systems of ASHTON CORPORATION and OLDHAM, ASHTON & HYDE. The Board was set up as a joint venture by the relevant local authorities on 23 October 1899, and between 1902 and 1905 it constructed an intricate network of long and short single-track lines along a north–south axis from Roaches and Haddens, in the north, down through Mossley, Stalybridge, Ashton-under-Lyne and Dukinfield to Hyde.

Services from Stalybridge west to Ashton began in October 1903, using cars borrowed from Ashton Corporation, over the former horse tramway route operated by the Manchester Carriage & Tramways Co. (see MANCHESTER TRAMWAYS); on 22 May 1904, the Board's own cars were introduced with the opening of the next route, from Stalybridge to Hyde. These were open-toppers 1–20, single-deckers 21–30 and single-deck combination cars 31–40, all from BEC and joined, in 1905, by Nos 41–55, open-toppers from HN, who also supplied open-top bogie cars 56–60 two years later. No further trams were added until 1924–25, when the Board constructed balcony cars 61–64 using equipment taken from four of the single-deckers. Most of the open-toppers were fitted later with top covers, No.24 was rebuilt as a balcony car in 1911 and, following the break-up of the OAH system in 1921, ten of its cars were acquired and scrapped after seeing little, if any, service with the Board. Several small depots were scattered around the system to supply cars for the many different services operated.

Hyde Market Place, towards the southern end of the sprawling Stalybridge, Hyde, Mossley & Dukinfield system. The nearest tram is BEC-built combination car 36 of 1904 – note the somewhat unusual high positioning of the headlamp for a single-decker. *(Author's Collection)*

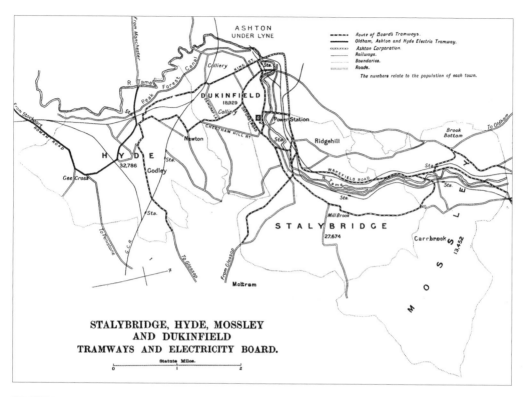

STALYBRIDGE, HYDE, MOSSLEY
AND DUKINFIELD
TRAMWAYS AND ELECTRICITY BOARD.

Above: Map of the SHMD system, oriented with west towards the top, from the 1909 *Manual of Electrical Undertakings.*

Left: A typical, locally produced 'tramway disaster' postcard of a SHMD 1904 single-decker (series 21–30) after running away at Millbrook, north-east of Stalybridge, on 2 April 1908. *(Author's Collection)*

After the break-up of the OAH, through services began to STOCKPORT via Hyde and to Manchester via Denton. In 1923, though, the Board obtained powers to operate buses and, as that fleet grew, so the tram services were slowly run down, with services on many routes reduced to holidays and peak hours only. On 12 January 1928 the Ashton–Hyde service was withdrawn completely, initiating a series of abandonments which left, by 1939, only the Hyde–Manchester and Hyde–Stockton routes in the hands of half a dozen cars (Nos 18, 42, and 61–64). On 12 May 1945 the last Board cars ran from Hyde to Gee Cross on the Stockport route, though No.18 was brought out on 29 May for an official farewell ceremony. This was not quite the end of the story, however, for Stockport cars continued to run to Hyde Market Place until 2 March 1947, and Manchester trams until 30 December that year.

Stockport Corporation No.70 of 1923, built by Cravens of Sheffield, on a Cheadle Heath working. (*Author's Collection*)

Stockport Corporation Tramways

Authority: Stockport Corporation Act 1899
Gauge: 4ft 8½in.
Traction: Overhead electric, horse
Opened: 26 August 1901
Closed: 25 August 1951
System: Radial network
Length: 19.46 miles
Stock: 4 sd, 16 dd horse?; 87 dd electric
Livery: Red & cream
Last Car: Nos 82 (service) and 53 (official)

Stockport's first tramway, promoted by the Manchester Suburban Tramways Co. (see MANCHESTER TRAMWAYS), was a 2¼-mile double-track line opened 7 May 1880, running south from Levenshulme, down the Stockport Road and Wellington Road North to the George Hotel on Mersey Square by the river. The Stockport end of the line was extended by early 1881 to the start of Wellington Road South, where it turned sharply north-east up St Petersgate to St Peter's Square. Services operated through from the Manchester Royal Infirmary, Piccadilly, using cars from a stock of some sixty double-deckers based at Longsight Depot on the corner of Stockport Road and Grey Street. (In the same year as the line opened, the MST Co. became a constituent part of the Manchester Carriage & Tramways Co.)

Under the Stockport Corporation Act 1899, the Corporation obtained the authority to buy the line, electrify it and lease it back to the Company and, under the Stockport Corporation Act 1900, it obtained powers to construct further tramways, the first of which opened the following year. This ran from Lancashire Bridge, north of St Peter's Square, in a north-east direction along Warren Street, Great Portland Street, Carrington Road, Stockport Road (West and East) to Ashton Street, Woodley. On 31 August 1901 a short ½-mile branch north from Lancashire Bridge was opened up Lancashire Hill to Sandy Lane and by the end of the year ten open-top ERTCW double-deckers had been supplied by DK and housed in a new depot in Mersey Square.

Further lines soon followed. On 1 June 1902 a route was opened along Prince's Street to connect Mersey Square with Lancashire Bridge, followed some six months later by a connection between St Peter's Square and Mersey Square via Daw Bank. At the end of January 1902, a 1-mile double-track western branch along Chestergate and Brinksway was opened as far as the then town boundary, extended on 1 August 1903 as a single-track line another 2 miles to the railway bridge at Cheadle Heath, again on 26 January 1904 to Cheadle church and finally, that 25 March, to the Horse & Farrier at Gatley. Meanwhile, other extensions were being opened. The terminus at Sandy Lane was moved northwards, in stages, along Reddish Road, through Reddish and up Gorton Road (25 November 1903) to the Old Bull's Head Inn, where it was connected, five years later, to MANCHESTER CORPORATION'S

Hyde Road route while, on 18 July 1902, the Woodley line was extended to the Hyde boundary with through-running to Hyde Town Hall commencing 1 January 1903 over the OLDHAM, ASHTON & HYDE ELECTRIC TRAMWAY.

The car fleet grew to keep pace with the expanding system with DK supplying ERTCW cars 11–30 in 1902–03, similar vehicles to Nos 1–10. The purchase of the STOCKPORT & HAZEL GROVE TRAMWAY (see below) was completed on 24 January 1905; reconstruction started in April and the single-track line reopened on 5 July. The horse cars were sold off, but two were bought back two years later for conversion to salt cars. UEC top-covered cars 41–45 were bought in 1906, and 46–50 were bought a year later (after which several of the open-toppers were similarly equipped). On 2 October 1906 a short double-track extension from Torkington Road to the Rising Sun Hotel completed the system.

In 1919 five of the older cars were re-bodied and renumbered 61–65, whilst EE enclosed cars 51–60 were bought in 1920, the same year that the Corporation's trolleybus operations, which had begun in 1913, finished. More ominously, 1920 also saw the inauguration of Corporation motor bus services, though the tram fleet continued to grow with the addition, in 1923, of enclosed cars 66–75 from Cravens and, a year later, similar cars 76–85 from the same firm; in 1928–29 the Corporation constructed enclosed cars 6 and 26 to complete the fleet. To help accommodate them all, a new depot was opened in Heaton Lane just north of the river.

On 19 September 1931 the Gatley line was cut back to the town boundary, though the rest of the system survived until 14 January 1950, when the Crossley Road–Hazel Grove through route was axed, followed, on March 1951, by the Edgeley–Vernon Park route. On 10 April the Cheadle route closed entirely, leaving just the Reddish line as the last to go that August. Car No.5 of 1901 is preserved and currently operating at BLACKPOOL.

Stockport & Hazel Grove Tramway
Authority: Stockport and Hazel Grove Tramways Order 1889
Gauge: 4ft 8½in.
Traction: Horse
Opened: 4 April 1890
Taken over: 24 January 1905
System: Branching
Length: 3.45 miles
Stock: 4 sd?, 16 dd?
Livery: ?

The second tramway to be built in Stockport, after the MANCHESTER TRAMWAYS' line from the north (see above), was a southerly route from St Peter's Square, where it shared a terminus with the MT line, back to Wellington Road South and thence, via Buxton Road and the London Road, to the Bull's Head Hotel in Torkington Road, Hazel Grove, some 3 miles away. A ½-mile branch running south-west off Wellington Road South served Edgeley, terminating at Grenville Street. Both lines were single-track, owned and operated by the Stockport & Hazel Grove Carriage & Tramway Co. Ltd. Details of the rolling-stock are patchy, though at least one of the single-deckers was a roofed toastrack, and the depot was at Dialstone Lane behind the Crown Inn on Wellington Road South.

In 1899 the Stockport Corporation Act empowered that body to purchase the tramway (and the MT line), but this was not done until six years later – for a price of £24,000 – by which time the municipal electric system was in operation (see above).

Stockton & Darlington Steam Tramways
Authority: Stockton-on-Tees and District Tramways Order 1880
Gauge: 4ft
Traction: Steam
Opened: November 1881
Closed: November 1897

System: Branching
Length: 3.25 miles
Stock: 8 locos, 15 dd?
Livery: Chocolate & white
Last Car: ?

The Stockton & Darlington Steam Tramways Co. Ltd operated two separate tramways, one in each town of its title, of which only the Stockton system was worked by steam. (The DARLINGTON line, opened in 1880, was horse-worked.) It began as a single line running south from The Green in Norton, along Norton Road and Stockton High Street, where it swung east, past the depot (as an 1887 extension), to cross the River Tees via Victoria Bridge into Mandale Road, terminating by the Harewood Arms. Later extensions were a ½-mile branch from the northern end of the High Street, west along Bishopton Lane to the NER station, and a 1-mile branch from the southern end of the High Street, west and south along Yarm Lane and Yarm Road, to St Peter's church.

Services were worked by Merryweather steam locomotives 1–6, joined in 1883 by Nos 7 and 8, ex-North Staffordshire Tramways, hauling an unknown number of trailers (possibly by Starbuck).

In 1893 the Company went into liquidation and was succeeded by the Stockton & District Tramways Co., until 1896, when the tramway was bought by IMPERIAL TRAMWAYS and closed the following year to make way for reconstruction and electrification. (See MIDDLESBROUGH, STOCKTON & THORNABY.)

Stockton & Thornaby Joint Corporation Tramways

Authority: Stockton-on-Tees Corporation Act 1919; Thornaby-on-Tees Corporation Tramways Order 1919.
Gauge: 3ft 7in.
Traction: Overhead electric
Took over: 3 April 1921
Closed: 31 December 1931
System: Single line
Length: 3.76 miles
Stock: 29 dd
Livery: Vermillion & white
Last Car: Middlesbrough 113

This short line straddling the Durham/Yorkshire boundary was made up of the two sections of the longest route of the former MIDDLESBROUGH, STOCKTON & THORNABY system that lay within the Stockton and Thornaby local authorities' area. When MIDDLESBROUGH CORPORATION took over its part of the system, the other two Corporations did likewise, working the line through a Joint Committee with cars 4, 7, 9, 11, 14, 17, 19, 20, 22, 23, 26, 29–32, 38, 39 and 43–45 owned by Stockton and Nos 5, 8, 12, 13, 16, 33, 35, 48 and 49 owned by Thornaby. Several of these were then renumbered to make a single sequence of 1–29 thus: 30–32 became 1–3, 33 (24), 35 (10), 38 and 39 (27 and 28), 43–45 (18, 25 and 15) and 48 and 49 (6 and 21).

No further cars were added under the new ownership (solely by Stockton from 1 August 1930 onwards), with the line closing at the end of 1931, the trams displaced by Stockton's buses.

Sunderland Tramways

Authority: Sunderland Tramways Order 1878
Gauge: 4ft 8½in.
Traction: Horse
Opened: 28 April 1879
Closed: 19 February 1901
System: Network
Length: 6.41 miles

Stock: 5 sd, 28 dd?
Livery: ? & white?
Last Car: ?

The Sunderland Tramways Co. operated horse tramways on both sides of the mouth of the River Wear in this major Durham town, beginning, in April 1879, with a short line from the Royal Hotel in Monkwearmouth, on the north bank of the river, north-east along Roker Avenue to the district of that name. The first cars were three single-deckers, joined by two double-deckers when, on 11 June, two southern routes opened. The first of these continued the original line south across the river via North Bridge Street, Bridge Street, Fawcett Street and Burdon Road to Christ Church, before swinging east along Gray Road to Tatham Street, then back north to rejoin Fawcett Street; the second was a northwards continuation of the line in Tatham Street, along Nicholson Street and Cousin Street, to form a short branch to the docks, terminating at Adelaide Street. The 3½ miles of routes were principally single-track.

While the above lines were being constructed, Sunderland Corporation was planning to build lines of its own, and in 1880–81 it added a northern branch (North Bridge Street west to Southwick via Southwick Road) and two southern branches (High Street East and New Durham Road) to the system, leasing them to the Company. (During this period steam traction was experimented with, but not adopted.)

By 1894 the car fleet had grown to a total of thirty-three (of which details are sketchy, though several of them were Eades patent reversible cars) and the Corporation was planning to take the system over in 1899, when the Company's lease expired; in that year it obtained the necessary Act of Parliament to enable it to operate its own tramways. The purchase – for £35,000 – of the horse system was completed on 26 March 1900, with the Corporation assuming control of operations from 30 March, shutting down routes as reconstruction work progressed (see below).

Sunderland Corporation Tramways

Authority: Sunderland Corporation Act 1899
Gauge: 4ft 8½in.
Traction: Overhead electric
Opened: 15 August 1900
Closed: 1 October 1954
System: Radial network
Length: 12.24 miles
Stock: 13 sd, 127 dd
Livery: Light maroon & cream
Last Car: No.86

One of the longer-lasting of the English tramways, Sunderland's municipal system was a compact network of three routes north of the River Wear and five south of it, worked by a fleet of new cars, plus a motley assortment of second-hand ones bought as other tramways closed down.

Immediately after taking possession of its leased lines and the Company-owned lines in 1900 (see above), the Corporation set about relaying and electrifying the system, with the first route (Roker to Christ Church) opening that August. Services were worked by open-toppers 1–12 and bogie open-toppers 13–18 of 1900, and single-deckers 19–26 of 1901, all from ERTCW. Later in 1901, ERTCW open-toppers 27–50 were added as further routes were opened (including one north from Roker along the coast via Whitburn Road to Seaburn and south along Ryhope Road to Grangetown), all mainly double-track.

By the end of January 1904 the first flurry of construction was over, with the three northern routes (north-west via Southwick Road and Sunderland Road to Southwick, north via Gladstone Road and Fulwell Lane, plus the Seaburn line) all open. South of the river, via Bridge Street, a line ran south to Grangetown, with a loop along Villette Road, Suffolk Street and Tatham Street, a new branch led off to the docks, and a western circular route occupied Hylton Road and Chester Road. (The former horse lines to the docks and High Street East were abandoned.)

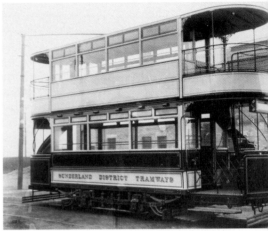

Above left: Sunderland Corporation's Brush-built balcony car No.68, photographed after it was top-covered in 1923, on the system's Circle route. *(Author's Collection)*

Above right: In comparison, Sunderland District balcony car No.32 of 1908, also built by Brush, as new. *(Author's Collection)*

For the next twenty years, the only major changes to the tramway were the additions of new batches of cars. In 1902 ERTCW supplied single-deck combination cars 52–55 and open-toppers 56–65; in 1906 Brush provided balcony cars 66–71 (nicknamed 'Dreadnoughts'); and in 1918 UEC supplied top-covered car No.10, a replacement for the original of that number destroyed in a Zeppelin air raid two years before. (Virtually all these cars were later fitted with top covers and/or fully enclosed.) The trams were based at the Wheatsheaf Depot, where Roker Avenue met North Bridge Street, just north of the river, and at the works (with power station), on Hylton Road south of it.

On 3 January 1921 through-running with the SUNDERLAND DISTRICT line via Grangetown began (see below) and during that year and the next a dozen EE enclosed double-deckers (Nos 72–83) were added to the stock. On 2 December 1925 a new route, south-west along the Durham Road to Barnes Park, was opened, and was extended on 4 August 1929 over Humbledon Hill to serve the residential development there. By this date, though, the first cutback had occurred, with the abandonment of, on 6 February 1928, the Barrack Street (docks) branch – though, for legal reasons, a token car was run over it occasionally for another year.

In 1925 enclosed double-deck cars 22, 23 and 25 emerged from the Corporation's works, followed a year later by No.84, a rebuild of the SD's former parcel car. In 1931 Brush supplied bogie single-decker 85, the Corporation built enclosed cars 86 in 1932 and 96–98 in 1933, whilst EE provided enclosed cars 87–95 (1933) and 99 (1934), the latter a streamlined bogie vehicle. The other new cars added were Corporation-built 26–28 (1935) and 49–54 (1936–40), and Brush 55 (1935), all enclosed vehicles. These were joined by second-hand enclosed double-deckers 19 and 20 (ex-ACCRINGTON in 1931), 52 (ex-Portsmouth Corporation in 1936), 100 (ex-London Transport in 1937), 2–9 (ex-Ilford Council in 1938), 29–36 (ex-HUDDERSFIELD in 1938), 48 (ex-SOUTH SHIELDS in 1946), 37–42 (ex-MANCHESTER in 1947) and 85 (ex-BURY in 1948); in 1933 the Corporation produced enclosed cars 21 and 24, rebuilds of Mansfield & District cars 27 and 28 (EE of 1925).

Further route extensions took place before and after the Second World War: on 10 May 1937 the Fulwell Lane route was extended east along Dykelands Road to Seaburn (where it terminated close to the Whitburn Road route) and, on 21 February 1948, the Durham Road line was extended on a central reservation, first to Grindon Lane and then, on 7 February 1949, to Thorney Close Road to serve new housing estates. The decision, though, had already been taken to close the system in favour of buses: on 5 November 1950 the Villette Road–Suffolk Street loop was closed, followed on 2 September 1951 by the Southwick route. The Grangetown line went on 30 November the following year, with the remaining services going in 1954 – the Chester Road Circle and the Roker line on 3 January, Durham Road on 28 March and the Seaburn via Fullwell route at the beginning of October. The closure was marked by a procession of trams – one carrying a band – with No.86 bearing the official party.

After the system's demise, those trams not already scrapped met that fate, with the exception of three: No.100, which can be seen operating at the National Tramway Museum, Crich – also home to No.85 (sold to LEEDS in 1944 and preserved as that system's No.600) – whilst the veteran No.16 of 1900 is awaiting restoration at the North of England Open Air Museum, BEAMISH.

Sunderland District Electric Tramways

Authority: Houghton-le-Spring and District Tramways Order 1900
Gauge: 4ft 8½in.
Traction: Overhead electric
Opened: 10 June 1905
Closed: 12 July 1925
System: Branching
Length: 14.28 miles
Stock: 57 dd
Livery: Blue & white
Last Car: ?

Built to serve the mining villages to the south-west of Sunderland, this strung-out single-track system had a main line like a letter Z on its side, plus short branches, laid along rural roads. Promotion was by the United Kingdom Tramways, Light Railways & Electrical Syndicate Ltd – the Company was reformed in November 1903 as the Sunderland District Electric Tramways Ltd – with construction, by BPs, commencing in January the following year.

The main line began near the coast at Grangetown, where it connected with the SUNDERLAND CORPORATION system, and ran south to Ryhope before turning westwards for a long run through Tunstall, Silksworth, East Herrington and West Herrington to New Herrington, where it swung south again through Philadelphia (where the depot was sited) and Newbottle to Houghton-le-Spring. The two branches – north-west from New Herrington to New Penshaw via Shiney Row, and west from Houghton to Fencehouses – opened at the same time as the main line, with all services worked by open-top Brush cars 1–15, together with Nos 16–30, top-covered cars from Etablissements Arbel of Paris. Just two days after the opening, on Whit Monday 1905, No.8 was involved in a fatal accident and rebuilt as No.31 two years later.

On 20 October 1905 the main line was extended further south, by 2 miles, to Hetton-le-Hole and, in August 1906, by another mile to Easington Lane to complete the system. Two years later Brush top-covered cars 32–34 were added to stock, followed in 1913 by similar cars 8 and 16–30, the latter batch replacing the worn-out French vehicles. Finally, eight more were bought in 1920 – it is thought these took the numbers 35–38 plus four from withdrawn older cars.

By now the tramway was nearing the end of its relatively short life, for it was particularly vulnerable to bus competition and, on 13 May 1921, the Company replaced the New Penshaw branch service with its own buses. In June 1924 the line south of Houghton was abandoned and later that year the 1920 cars were sold to BOLTON. In January 1925 the Fencehouses branch was closed and the Company changed its name to the Sunderland District Transport Co. Ltd.

The next closure came on 12 March 1925, when the Grangetown–New Herrington section was abandoned, with the final stretch closing four months later. The 1913 cars were sold to Grimsby Corporation and the remainder scrapped, with the exception of No.33 which, after an accident in 1922, had been converted into a single-deck parcels car; this was sold to Sunderland Corporation and rebuilt as a passenger vehicle (see above).

Swinton *see* Mexborough & Swinton

Trafford Park Tramways

Authority: -
Gauge: 4ft 8½in.
Traction: Gas, overhead electric
Opened: 23 July 1897
Closed: 1 May 1908
System: Single line + loop
Length: c.4 miles
Stock: 4 dd gas; 1 sd, 6 dd electric*
Livery: Green & cream gas, blue electric
Last Car: ?

For a short line, this tramway had an astonishingly varied history. Situated in Trafford Park to the west of Manchester, immediately to the south of the Manchester Ship Canal (opened 1894), its function was to help in the conversion of the park from a rural haven into an industrial estate.

The park was purchased in 1896 by the Trafford Park Estates Ltd, who invited the British Gas Traction Co. Ltd (see LYTHAM ST ANNES) to lay and operate a tramway of just under 3 miles in length along its east-west axis. The single-track line (with no passing loops) opened the following year and was laid along or beside the existing roadways between Barton, in the west, and the show ground near the eastern end of the park. Services began with car No.1, an open-top double-decker built by Gas Motorenfabrik Deutz of Cologne and powered by a two-cylinder gas engine complete with a large flywheel in the lower saloon. Three cylindrical tanks stored the town gas used as fuel.

On 28 July 1897, however, a slight accident led to the suspension of services – and a long dispute between the two companies over the state of the track – until 8 April of the following year, when the line reopened to coincide with a visit by Barnum & Bailey's Circus. By now the line had been extended

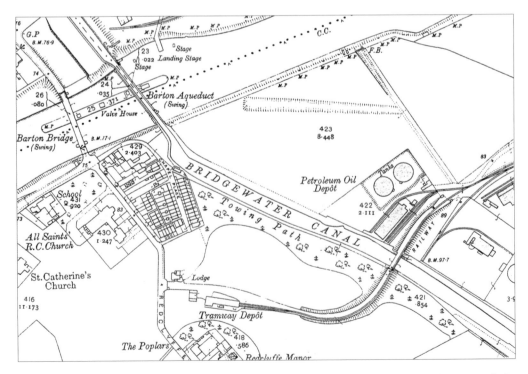

The first Trafford Park Tramways Depot was at Barton, opened in 1897 between the Bridgewater and the Manchester Ship canals to house the gas trams. From the 1908 Ordnance Survey 25in. to 1 mile map.

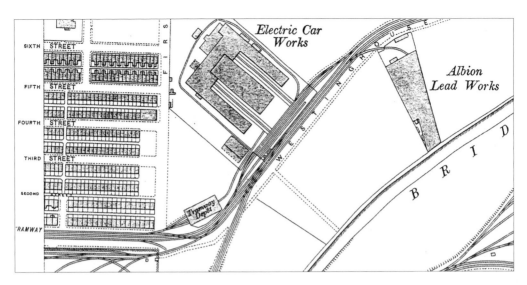

The second Trafford Park Tramways Depot, for the electric cars, close to the BEC's tramcar works. From the 1908 Ordnance Survey 25in. to 1 mile map.

½ mile eastwards to the Trafford Road entrance of the park, a car shed had been erected at Barton, passing loops had been added and three more cars (Nos 2–4), identical to No.1, had been provided. The tramway was now also connected to the park's industrial railway system and used by goods trains as well, it being laid with flat-bottomed railway rails spiked to wooden sleepers.

As more businesses moved to the park, so more workmen were carried on the tramway on weekdays, and the idea was mooted of linking it to the MANCHESTER CORPORATION system at Old Trafford. Before this could be done, though, the BGT Co. went into liquidation at the end of 1899, with the cars stopping on 3 November after the gas supply was cut off. The equipment was purchased by the TPE Ltd for £2,000 and services resumed.

In 1902 it was decided to construct a new electric tramway in the form of an out-and-back loop from the Trafford Road entrance along Trafford Park Road, then along Westinghouse Road to the south-west, past the BEC works and the car shed, north up Third Avenue and then east on Ashburton Road, back to the old Post Office at Hatton's Wood, where it rejoined the Trafford Park Road to run as a double-track back to the starting point. Total length of this 'Westinghouse Loop' was 2.55 miles and included no less than thirty-four railway level crossings! (The gas line now terminated at the old Post Office, with no connection to the new line.)

The electric tramway stock was built by BEC and consisted of Nos 5–9 and bogie car 10, all open-top double-deckers (though No.8 was immediately top-covered), and No.11, a single-deck bogie trailer converted in 1904 to a roofed, double-deck powered car known as the 'Cattle Truck', seating 132 passengers (plus standees) and which, at 16ft 7in. in height, was Britain's tallest tramcar. Three ex-Bristol horse cars were bought in 1903 for use as trailers, but possibly never saw service.

On 30 October 1905 the line was finally connected to the Manchester – and SALFORD – system in Trafford Road. Salford Corporation bought the electric cars and took over the running of the tramway, with the two corporations running alternate trams into the park. Cars 10 and 11 became Salford 161 and 162 and Nos 5–9 became 173–177 respectively. TPE Ltd retained and operated the gas trams – now increasingly decrepit – until 1 May 1908, replacing them the next day with an HC saddle tank railway locomotive and two small carriages from the CLC, whereupon the trams were sold for scrap. The original tramway was now just another part of the estate's railway network and workmen's trains were run until 1921, when they were replaced by three motor buses.

Transperience *see* Bradford: Transperience
Trawden *see* Colne & Trawden

Tynemouth & District Tramways

Authority: Tynemouth and District Tramways Order 1879
Gauge: 3ft
Traction: Horse/steam
Opened: 1883
Closed: 1900
System: Single line
Length: 2.58 miles
Stock: ? horse; 5 locos, 5 sd steam
Livery: ?
Last Car: ?

This short line at the mouth of the River Tyne in Northumberland, linking Prudhoe Street in North Shields with Percy Park in Tynemouth, had a very complicated history. It was opened as a horse line by the Tynemouth & District Tramways Ltd, then sold in 1884 to the North Shields & District Tramways Co. Ltd. That same year the Company began steam working, with five Wilkinson patent design locomotives (Nos 1–3 from BH and 4 and 5 from Greens) and the same number of Lancaster bogie passenger trailers. The depot was in Suez Street, off Northumberland Square, in the centre of North Shields.

In 1890 the line was sold to the North Shields & Tynemouth District Tramways Ltd, which was bought by BET in 1897, changing its name two years later to the Tynemouth & District Electric Traction Co. Ltd in readiness for the planned electrification of the line (see below).

Tynemouth & District Electric Tramways

Authority: Tynemouth and District Tramways Order 1879
Gauge: 3ft 6in.
Traction: Overhead electric
Opened: 18 March 1901
Closed: 4 August 1931
System: Single line
Length: 4.23 miles
Stock: 1 sd, 23 dd*
Livery: Crimson lake & cream
Last Car: ?

Tynemouth & District electric car No.10 of 1901 at the Whitley Bay Links seaside terminus. *(Author's Collection)*

Above left: Tynemouth & District No.12, another ERTCW open-topper of 1901, posed outside the tramway's John Street Depot – note the access track on the left. *(Author's Collection)*

Above right: A blackly comic postcard of Saville Street in North Shields on the Tynemouth & District system. Printed in 1916, this Gateshead-published card alludes to the very real threat faced by the north-east coast of bombardment by the German navy. *(Author's Collection)*

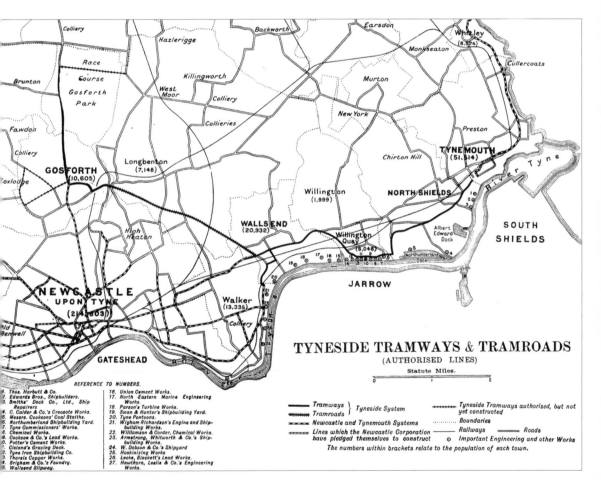

Map of the tramways of north Tyneside, from the 1909 *Manual of Electrical Undertakings.*

Following the closure of the TYNEMOUTH & DISTRICT steam line (see above), the Company set about relaying, extending and electrifying it, the contractor for the work being George Law of Kidderminster. As reopened, the new tramway ran from New Quay in North Shields, up the 1 in 10 gradient of Borough Road to the junction of Prudhoe Street and Saville Street, turning east down the latter to follow the former steam route along Tynemouth Road and Percy Park Road, with an extension along the Grand Parade, through Cullercoats and past the depot in John Street to a terminus in Whitley Road, Whitley Bay.

The tramway's original car fleet was a very mixed bag indeed. The first ten trams were ERTCW open-toppers, No.11 was a Midland single-decker (possibly ordered by the BET-owned Merthyr Tydfil system in Wales, but transferred north) used as a Borough Road shuttle until Nos 12–18, more ERTCW open-toppers, arrived in October 1901, after which it was rebuilt as a works car, whilst Nos 19–22, Milnes open-toppers, were again built for another line (probably the Poole & District) but transferred to Tynemouth.

No further cars were added to the stock from 1901 until 1927, when ten Brush open-toppers were bought from the Burton & Ashby Light Railways, though only four (Nos 21–24) were put into service to replace some of the older cars.

In 1902 the TYNESIDE system was opened as far east as Prudhoe Street (see below), though no physical connection could be made on account of the two tramways' different gauges. Two years later, under the Tynemouth and District Tramways Act 1903, a short northern extension was made from Whitley Road further on up the coast, via Park Avenue and Park Road, terminating by the bandstand on Whitley Bay Links, to complete the mainly single-track line, to which no major changes were made until bus competition, and the age of its track and rolling-stock, brought about its demise.

Tyneside Tramways

Authority: Tyneside Tramways and Tramroad Act 1901
Gauge: 4ft 8½in.
Traction: Overhead electric
Opened: 4 September 1902
Closed: 6 April 1930
System: Branching
Length: 10.99 miles
Stock: 30 dd
Livery: Dark green & cream
Last Car: ?

The gap between the north Tyneside electric systems of NEWCASTLE and TYNEMOUTH was bridged by the Tyneside Tramways & Tramroads Co., the first section of whose system was opened from Prudhoe Street in North Shields, westwards to the boundary of Wallsend with Newcastle. From here, a stretch north-west to Gosforth opened on 18 October 1902 (though the official opening had been on 29 September). The last 2 miles ran north from Gosforth to Gosforth Park Gates and was opened on 18 June 1904, with a ½-mile branch from Wallsend to Neptune Bank completing the system.

The first cars were bogie vehicles Nos 1–4 and single-truck cars 5–18, all open-toppers from Milnes. These were joined in 1903–04 by four single-truck cars (Nos 19–22) and two bogie vehicles (Nos 23 and 24) from Brush, and in 1910 by single-truck cars 25 and 26 from UEC. Again, all were open-toppers. The last arrivals, Nos 27–30 in 1920, were similar EE single-truck vehicles.

Although the tramway abutted the Tynemouth system, no through-running was possible because of the gauge difference; where the two lines met in Prudhoe Street, however, there was some 300yd of mixed gauge track (the only other comparable example of this in the British Isles being on the Blackrock & Kingstown line in Ireland, though Laxey station on the Isle of Man has its short section of mixed gauge MANX ELECTRIC RAILWAY and SNAEFELL MOUNTAIN RAILWAY track used for car-servicing purposes). Leaving North Shields, the single-track line ran south-westwards along Howdon Road to the Howdon Ferry across the Tyne to Jarrow, and then swung westwards along

Ropery Lane into Wallsend, where the branch to Neptune Bank (and the depot) left it. Here the track was doubled along the High Street, before singling again for some 3 miles of reserved sleepered track to Gosforth – the 'tramroad' of the Company's Act. Here it zigzagged (and doubled again), before a second stretch of reserved sleepered track of some 2 miles took it up to Gosforth Park Gates. (This section was soon metalled over to form part of the Great North Road.) Some 350yd before the single terminal stub, a third track was laid to cater for traffic to the racecourse there.

Three links with the Newcastle system were made at Wallsend, Neptune Bank and Henry Street, Gosforth, with through-running to Gosforth Park beginning on 6 August 1904, and to Park Road, Wallsend, on 29 August that same year.

Although several extensions were planned, none were ever built and when the great depression of the 1920s hit the region it was just at the time when much of the track and car fleet needed renewing. Newcastle Corporation declined to buy the undertaking and the Company had very little option but to close it down. All the cars were scrapped, with the exception of Nos 3 and 4, which were sold to SOUTH SHIELDS.

Wakefield & District Light Railway

Authority: Wakefield and District Light Railway Order 1901
Gauge: 4ft 8½in.
Traction: Overhead electric
Opened: 15 August 1904
Closed: 25 July 1932
System: Network
Length: 16.95 miles
Stock: 55 dd
Livery: Crimson lake & cream
Last Car: ?

Several tramway schemes were proposed for the county town of the West Riding of Yorkshire from the late 1870s onwards, to use a variety of traction methods. The one that eventually succeeded was a promotion by a group of businessmen resulting in a 1901 LRO for 10 miles of line and the incorporation of the Wakefield & District Light Railway Co. Ltd. Two further extension LROs brought the length authorised to 22 miles by 1902.

Wakefield & District Light Railway No.22 of 1904, in Station Road, Ossett. *(Author's Collection)*

The situation was complicated by the fact that 25 April 1903 saw the registration of the Yorkshire Electric Tramways Construction Syndicate Ltd to actually build the W&D system (and others in the area) and then take it over completely through a subsidiary set up in 1905, the Yorkshire (West Riding) Electric Tramways Co. Ltd.

As constructed, the W&D had three routes. The longest ran some 9 miles from the Castle Inn, Sandal, north through Wakefield to the Leeds boundary, where it made an end-on connection with the LEEDS system at Thwaite Gate, Hunslet. The second route ran east–west from Agbrigg to Ossett, where it made another end-on connection, this time with the DEWSBURY, OSSETT & SOOTHILL NETHER line; where it crossed the Sandal–Leeds route, the two lines shared a mile of double-track. Both routes were originally single-track, but later doubled for the most part, and both opened on the same day in 1904, with through-running into Leeds commencing 1 June the following year. The W&D's third route was a 1½-mile single-track branch from Rothwell Haigh (1½ miles south of the Leeds boundary), eastwards to the village of Rothwell; this opened around the second week of December 1904 – the exact day is uncertain – and was worked as a service from Thwaite Gate.

To work the system, fifty-five open-top double-deckers were ordered from DK in 1903; the first batch of these (Nos 1–30) were built by ERTCW and delivered during 1904 from the summer onwards, whilst the remainder (Nos 31–55), built by UEC, arrived during the first half of 1905 with top covers fitted (the first batch later being similarly equipped). By this time, the tramway had become part of the YORKSHIRE (WEST RIDING) concern, although it was not until August 1911 that the Company was wound up.

Wallasey Tramways
Authority: Wallasey Tramways Act 1878
Gauge: 4ft 8½in.
Traction: Horse
Opened: 28 June 1879
Closed: 19 March 1902
System: Single line
Length: 3.78 miles
Stock: 7 sd, 15 dd
Livery: Red & ivory, later maroon & cream
Last Car: ?

After a number of fruitless proposals to provide a tramway link between at least some of the towns and villages on the northern part of the Wirral peninsula, the Wallasey Tramways Co. was ultimately successful in doing so. Its one line ran from close to the ferry landing stage on the Mersey at Seacombe, northwards along Brighton Street to Egremont (from where there was another ferry service to Liverpool), then north-west along Liscard Road to Liscard, north along Rake Lane to Upper Brighton and the depot in Field Road, just south of New Brighton (the residents of which did not wish anything so common as a tramway to despoil their streets). Virtually the whole line was single-track, with a long one-way loop in Egremont.

Operation began with Starbuck single-deckers 1–7 – possibly transfers from the neighbouring WIRRAL TRAMWAY (see BIRKENHEAD) – with services commencing from Church Road in Seacombe in June 1879, the 150yd-extension to the ferry not being opened until the autumn. Between 1880 and 1883 five Eades reversible double-deckers (Nos 8–12) were added to the car fleet.

On 8 May 1891 the Company became part of the Wallasey United Tramway & Omnibus Co. Ltd (incorporated 20 April 1888 to bring together the directors' interests of its title), and in 1893 seven Milnes double-deckers were purchased; these took the numbers 13 onwards, with some later taking numbers vacated by withdrawn cars, so that they had become Nos 6, 7 and 10–14 by 1901, when Wallasey UDC purchased the line. The takeover was effective from 1 April 1901 and the arbitrated price was £20,500; on 26 April three ex-LIVERPOOL CORPORATION double-deckers were added to the fleet, presumably as replacement vehicles.

The Council's intention was to replace the tramway with a larger electric system (see below), though the horse cars continued to operate amidst the reconstruction work, often on diverted sections of track. Following the line's total closure the stock was auctioned off, though one of the Milnes cars was retained to become a Corporation works vehicle.

Wallasey Corporation Tramways

Authority: Wallasey Tramways and Improvements Act 1899
Gauge: 4ft 8½in.
Traction: Overhead electric
Opened: 17 March 1902
Closed: 30 November 1933
System: Network
Length: 12.06 miles
Stock: 77 dd
Livery: Green & cream to 1924, then greenish-yellow & cream
Last Car: No.68

Under its empowering Act of 1899, Wallasey UDC was authorised to construct 8½ miles of mainly single-track tramways based on the old horse line (see above), which was the first route to reopen (extended into New Brighton), followed on 19 March 1902 – the system's official opening day – by a second 2½-mile line to Upper Brighton from Egremont, along Seabank Road much closer to the shore. A third, 3¾-mile linking route to the west, from Liscard to New Brighton via Wallasey, opened on 17 May that year. The depot was sited on this route, off Seaview Road between Liscard and Wallasey, and a one-way loop at New Brighton served the ferry and promenade piers there. The landscape traversed was a mixture of residential, industrial and rural areas and traffic was very mixed, with trippers to the northern beaches rubbing shoulders with commuters to Liverpool using the three ferries; for the latter passengers, the short crossing from Seacombe was the most popular, and the trams even carried warning flags when the two more exposed northern Mersey crossings were affected by inclement weather (usually fog).

The system's first cars, Nos 1–25, were ERTCW open-toppers; these were joined in 1903 by five more, Nos 27–31 (No.26 was a works car). All had been fitted with top covers by mid-1905, which also saw the arrival of Nos 32–36, top-covered UEC vehicles. From then on, all Wallasey's new cars – Nos 37–41 (UEC of 1907) and 42–78 (Brush of 1910–20) – were of this type. After the town became

Above left: Wallasey Corporation open-topper No.14 of 1902 captured on an early postcard of Victoria Road, New Brighton, looking eastwards to the adjacent ferry and promenade piers. *(Author's Collection)*

Above right: Wallasey Corporation No.77, a 1920 Brush car fitted, like some of its counterparts across the Mersey, with a Bellamy roof. *(Author's Collection)*

a Municipal Borough in 1910, the 'WALLASEY COUNCIL TRAMWAYS' legend on the cars was changed to 'WALLASEY CORPORATION TRAMWAYS'.

A fourth, even more westerly, route from Seacombe to New Brighton was added in 1910–11, beginning with a 1–mile section westwards from Seacombe, along Poulton Road to St Luke's church in Poulton, opened on 8 July 1910, followed on 7 February 1911 by the remaining 2¼ miles northwards up Marlowe Road and St George's Road, through Wallasey Village, then eastwards along Grove Road to join the Liscard–New Brighton route in Wallasey. This entire route (nicknamed 'the Switchback') was double-tracked and, coupled with a track-doubling programme on the other routes, meant that nearly three-quarters of the system was eventually so laid.

After the First World War the tramway entered a boom period – especially as regards the holidaymaker traffic – but much of the track had reached that critical point in its life when renewal was necessary and, ominously, on 3 April 1920 the Corporation began its first motor bus service. By the end of November 1929, no less than fifty-six buses were being operated and it was only a matter of time before the tramways were abandoned as worn out. (The Seabank Road route had, in fact, closed on 19 June that year.) The last Rake Lane trams ran on 4 February 1933, and those operating on the remaining routes stopped running at the end of November, after which they were sold for scrap (with some bodies retained for a new, ignominious role as bus shelters).

Warrington Corporation Tramways

Authority: Warrington Tramways Act 1900
Gauge: 4ft 8½in.
Traction: Overhead electric
Opened: 21 April 1902
Closed: 28 August 1935
System: Radial
Length: 6.84 miles
Stock: 27 dd
Livery: Munich lake & cream
Last Car: No.1

Planned and operated by Warrington Corporation to serve this large industrial town in south Lancashire, this system grew to form a starfish-shaped layout of five routes, of roughly equal length, radiating from the town centre. The first 1½ miles opened ran east from Rylands Street across the River Mersey via Warrington Bridge and down Knutsford Road to Latchford, terminating on the northern bank of the Manchester Ship Canal. This was double-track throughout, though the second route opened, from Rylands Street west along Sankey Street and Liverpool Road to Sankey Bridge, with a terminus close to Sankey station, was mainly single-track. This half of the original one through route, another 1½ miles in length, was opened on 23 April 1902, with the first services being worked by open-toppers 1–8 from Milnes, quickly joined by Nos 9 and 10, a similar pair. The depot was in Mersey Street, off Rylands Street.

On 4 October 1902 a southern, double-track line to Wilderspool was opened. This left the Latchford line just south of Warrington Bridge and ran south for 1¼ miles along Wilderspool Causeway to terminate by Stafford Road, again just short of the Manchester Ship Canal. (This route was extended a few hundred yards on 7 July 1905, over the canal on the Northwich Road Swing Bridge, to Victoria Square in Stockton Heath, Cheshire, the canal marking the county boundary.)

The last of the five radial routes were north-east to the Cemetery (mainly double-track, opened 22 November 1902) and north down the Winwick Road, past the CLC's Warrington Central station to Longford (mainly single-track, opened 29 October 1902), the car fleet being increased in size accordingly with the purchase of Nos 11–21, another eleven Milnes open-toppers. Between 1904 and 1905 eighteen of the cars were fitted with top covers and, in 1909, No.18 (one of those not so equipped) was cut down to single-deck form to become a one-man car for the financially unrewarding and sparsely populated Longford route.

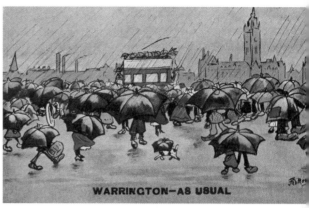

WARRINGTON—AS USUAL

Above left: A 1907-franked postcard of Warrington Bridge, over the Mersey, at the heart of the Warrington system, with the double-deck tram seemingly an insignificant part of the greater industrial landscape. *(Author's Collection)*

Above right: Water of a very different kind: a Manchester-published postcard taking a sly dig at Lancashire's reputation as regards the weather. *(Author's Collection)*

At the beginning of 1920 six new Brush cars were delivered to the tramway. These were Nos 22–27, all top-covered double-deckers, and they were a sign that the system was enjoying a ten-year period of capital expenditure after the war years: new cars were bought, track relaid and doubled, the town centre layout remodelled and new, enclosed top covers fitted to some of the cars.

The beginning of the end came on 17 September 1931, when the Stockton Heath line closed, followed by that to Longford on 31 December. Six of the cars were then withdrawn, followed by a further five some time later. On 27 March 1935 the Cemetery and Sankey Bridge routes closed and seven more cars were withdrawn, leaving the last nine to work the Latchford route for the tramway's final summer.

Waterloo & Great Crosby Tramways

Authority: Great Crosby Tramways Order 1898; Waterloo-with-Seaforth Tramways Order 1898
Gauge: 4ft 8½in.
Traction: Overhead electric
Opened: 19 June 1900
Closed: 31 December 1925
System: Single line
Length: 2.66 miles
Stock: 2 sd, 14 dd
Livery: Green & cream
Last Car: ?

Situated immediately to the north of Bootle, the neighbouring UDCs of Waterloo-with-Seaforth and Great Crosby – both created in 1894 – jointly promoted a single-track tramway running inland from Seaforth Sands, at the mouth of the River Mersey, along Crosby Road South, through Seaforth to Waterloo, then continuing on along Liverpool Road to Great Crosby to terminate in Cook's Road by the police station.

Construction began in 1899 and the southern half of the line, from Seaforth Sands to Five Lamps, Waterloo, opened in June 1900, with the northern half following on 1 September. The main feature of this otherwise undistinguished tramway was that, although built by the two UDCs, it was stocked and worked by the Liverpool Overhead Railway. It is possible that the UDCs hoped that the LIVERPOOL CORPORATION would operate the line for them, but in the event the LOR (which had reached Seaforth Sands on 30 April 1894) agreed to lease the line for twenty-six years from 1 January 1900,

Waterloo & Great Crosby cars 1 and 14 in the passing loop at the junction of South Road and Crosby Road North in Waterloo, roughly halfway along this single-line tramway. *(Author's Collection)*

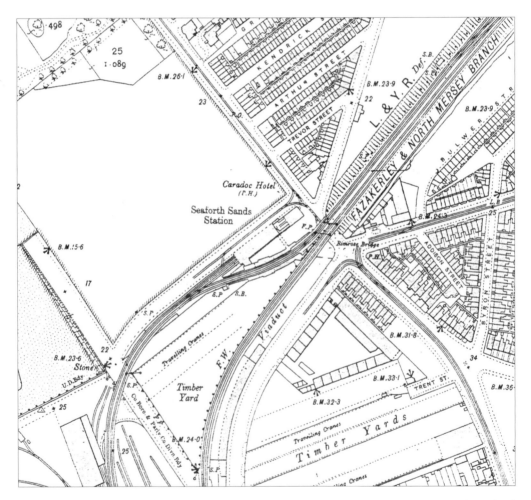

The unusually sited Waterloo & Great Crosby Tramways Depot, opened in 1900 beneath the Liverpool Overhead Railway's Seaforth Sands station; after its closure in 1925 it was let as a bus garage. The tram tracks to the right are those of Liverpool Corporation. From the 1908 Ordnance Survey 25in. to 1 mile map.

working it with ERTCW open-toppers 1–8 (of 1899) and 11–14 (of 1900), plus toastracks 9 and 10 (of 1899) for summer use. The cars were lettered 'LIVERPOOL OVERHEAD RAILWAY CO.' and housed in the depot beside the Seaforth Sands terminus, underneath the LOR station (with passenger transference by one of the very first escalators in England).

In 1903 ERTCW open-toppers 15 and 16 were added to the fleet and nine years later two of the older cars (possibly 5 and 7) were re-bodied; some of the older cars were later top-covered and the single-deckers withdrawn.

After the First World War the LOR, fearing its lease would not be renewed, allowed the tramway to run down and the two councils entered into negotiations with Liverpool Corporation, who expressed an interest in buying the line and connecting it to its neighbouring terminus in Bootle. It was not to be, though, and from 1 January 1926 the trams were replaced by buses.

West Riding *see* Yorkshire (West Riding)
West Yorkshire Transport Discovery Centre *see* Bradford: Transperience

Wigan & District Tramways
Authority: Wigan Tramways Order 1879
Gauge: 3ft 6in.
Traction: Horse, steam
Opened: 2 August 1880
Taken over: 30 September 1902
System: Single line + branching
Length: 5.49 miles
Stock: 8 dd horse & steam; 23 locos, 20 dd steam
Livery: Locos dark brown, cars dark red & cream

Wigan's first tramway system was certainly unusual. Not only did it chop and change between horse and steam traction, it did so on two physically separated lines. It was operated by the Wigan Tramways Co. Ltd and constructed by the contractors Holme & King of the town; the first route ran west from Queen Street, by the LNWR bridge in Wallgate in the town centre, for just over 2 miles to the Black Bull at Lamberhead Green, Pemberton, and was worked by Eades patent reversible double-deck horse cars Nos 1–8 from Ashbury. On 23 September 1880 a short extension taking the line along Wallgate to the Market Place was opened. The small depot was in Smethurst Street, Pemberton, near the terminus.

Steam trials were held on the line in 1881, and on 11 February 1882 the BoT authorised the use of steam locomotives. By the summer of that year, Wilkinson tram locos Nos 1–4 were in service (works Nos 1–4) pulling Starbuck top-covered cars 9–12 as well as the Eades cars (which had been fitted with canvas roofs).

On 13 January 1883 the system's second line opened; this ran eastwards for 2½ miles, from King Street in the centre of Wigan via Darlington Street and Manchester Road through Ince, and from there via the Wigan Road to Market Street, Hindley, terminating by the corner of Bridge Street. Here a small depot was sited off Market Street, in Albert Street. To work the new line, another four Wilkinson locos (Nos 5–8) were purchased, hauling some of the existing cars (which were horse-drawn for about six months until the locos arrived).

In February 1884 the locos were withdrawn from the Pemberton route and horses were reinstated, the direct result of a fatal accident the previous December, but brought back again that August; horse services ceased for good the following spring. In 1886–87 the tram's last four new Wilkinson locos, Nos 9–12, were added to the fleet. The Company's financial problems resulted in a receiver being appointed in 1890, and three years later it was taken over by a new concern, the Wigan & District Tramways Co. Ltd. All the passenger cars and locos 1–4 and 9 were scrapped, replaced by sixteen large, enclosed double-deck bogie cars of unknown origin, two Wilkinson locos of 1884 vintage (Nos 5 and 6) ex-Brighton & Shoreham Tramways and five new Kitson engines (Nos 10–14). The surviving original Wilkinson engines were renumbered 1–4 (the former 5–8) and 7–9 (the former 10–12). Kitson locos 15 and 16 were bought in 1895, and 17 and 18 a year later.

By the early 1890s Wigan Corporation was planning its own tramway system, obtaining, in 1893, the Wigan Corporation Act empowering it to construct two separate lines from the town centre: one north-east to Martland Mill and the other south-east off the Company's line in Darlington Street to Platt Bridge, a total of nearly 4 miles of route. Two years later, before construction had begun, the Company obtained the Wigan and District Tramways Order to authorise a short link between the proposed Corporation lines and its own, plus a short extension at Platt Bridge. In the event, only the line down the Warrington Road to Platt Bridge was constructed, opening on 2 September 1896, with the Company leasing the main Corporation-owned section of the route. A third depot was now necessary, and one was built in Tram Street off Walthew Lane at the Platt Bridge terminus. Soon the Corporation was planning further lines, with electric traction envisaged on a wider gauge (see below). For a short while the two systems co-existed, until 30 September 1902, when the Corporation took over its independent rival.

Wigan Corporation Tramways

Authority: Wigan Corporation Act 1898*
Gauge: 3ft 6in., 4ft 8½in.
Traction: Overhead electric*
Opened: 25 January 1901
Closed: 28 March 1931
System: Radial network
Length: 24.83 miles
Stock: 54 sd, 49 dd
Livery: Crimson lake & cream to 1913, then carmine red & white*
Last Car: ?

As mentioned above, Wigan Corporation entered the tramway fray in 1893, when it obtained powers to construct two lines, though it was not until 1898 that it was empowered to operate its own tramways, the first of which ran north-east from the town centre to Maitland Bridge (on a 3ft 6in. gauge) and opened in January 1901, with cars 1–12, ERTCW open-toppers; a second route, north up Wigan Lane to the Boar's Head, opened on 7 June that year. More lines followed and the car fleet grew to keep pace with the addition, in 1901, of open-toppers 13–24 and, in 1902, of open-top bogie car 26, all from ERTCW again (No.25 was a works car).

In 1902 the Corporation bought out its independent steam rival (see above) and, on 29 May 1903, the reconstructed Platt Bridge line reopened, though no more narrow-gauge cars were bought for it as the decision had been taken to construct all future routes to standard gauge and re-gauge existing ones. The following year cars 1–12 were sold accordingly to Coventry Corporation.

The Pemberton line closed on 10 April 1904, reopening on 26 July with electric trams on the new gauge; these were bogie single-deckers 27–50 from HN. On 2 September that year the re-gauged Platt Bridge line reopened with the very last steam trams running on 26 September, to Hindley. (The steam services were worked on lease by the Wigan & District Tramways Co. Ltd.) As the system continued to enlarge, so did the car fleet. In 1904–05 ERTCW supplied bogie combination cars 51–80, which met the tramway's needs until 1914, when UEC top-covered bogie vehicles 1–6 were bought, followed, in 1920, by EE top-covered cars 7–12, whilst in 1921–22 the local firm of Massey Brothers constructed identical cars 81–92, using EE electrics, in Pemberton Depot. (No.80, with a unique cream livery, could be hired for weddings.)

It appears that the tramway, from the start, was not a financial success, and a thorough overhaul of working practices was attempted and economy measures introduced. By the time of the First World War the narrow-gauge track and cars were in an especially bad way, and on 15 July 1923 the north-easterly route to Aspull via New Springs was closed for re-gauging, with only the Wigan–New Springs section (inside the borough boundary) reopening in stages to 23 December. (The outlying section was replaced by a bus service.) On 7 May 1925 the north-westerly route to Maitland Mill – the last narrow-gauge line left – was closed with trolleybuses taking over the same day. On 22 August 1927 the Platt Bridge

Wigan Corporation's Central Depot, opened in 1904 to house its electric cars, and later used by buses (from 1919) and trolleybuses (from 1925). From the 1908 Ordnance Survey 25in. to 1 mile map.

service was reduced to just the morning and evening workmen's cars (the other services replaced by buses), followed, on 30 November 1930, by the closure of the Ashton route entirely. On 28 February 1931 the Platt Bridge line closed for good, as did the Hindley route, leaving just the routes north to Standish (the extended Boar's Head line) and west to Abbey Lakes (the extended Pemberton line) to last another four weeks.

In many respects, the story of Wigan's tramways was one of lost opportunities. Not only was the town saddled with operating two systems of different gauges, but it failed to take full advantage of the proximity of its southern neighbour, the SOUTH LANCASHIRE TRAMWAYS, with connections at Ashton and Hindley only being made in 1926 and 1927 respectively.

Wirral Tramway(s) *see* Birkenhead: Wirral Tramway (1) *and* (2)
Woollen District *see* Yorkshire (Woollen District)

City of York Tramways
Authority: York Tramways Order 1879
Gauge: 4ft
Traction: Steam, horse
Opened: 27 October 1880
Taken over: 27 February 1909
System: Branching
Length: 2.75 miles
Stock: 1 dd steam; 10 sd, 5 dd horse
Livery: Chocolate & white

Unidentified City of York
double-decker in The
Mount, on the western
edge of this small system,
on a 1906-franked postcard.
(Author's Collection)

The first serious proposals for tramways in York were made in the late 1870s and came rapidly to fruition with an 1879 Order authorising the construction of two lines on the south and east sides of the city. Only the first of these was eventually built, though, running northwards along the Fulford Road from the Plough Inn to Fishergate, just over the River Foss from the Castle. Services began with three single-deck Starbuck horse trams and a Perrett patent double-deck steam car. Complaints were received from residents about the latter vehicle and it was returned to its Nottingham makers, Manlove, Alliott & Fryer, in the December after the opening. (A similar car worked on the Dublin & Lucan tramway in Ireland – see Volume 2.)

On 29 July 1882 a westwards extension of the line was opened through the city centre via Tower Street, Clifford Street, Micklegate, Blossom Street and The Mount to Mount Vale, Knavesmire. A short branch of less than 3 furlongs, from the end of Bridge Street round into Station Road, to serve the NER's York station completed the tiny system (though this branch closed just four years later). Both lines were single-track, except for a short section in Clifford Street.

Following the opening of the extension and station branch, two more cars were ordered but were later disposed of, and five others – all single-deckers – were purchased, possibly from Starbuck again. In 1885 the line's owners, the York Tramways Co., was taken over by IMPERIAL TRAMWAYS and, from 1 January 1886, the system was operated by a subsidiary, the City of York Tramways Co.

In 1890 seven of the eight cars had stairs and upper-deck seating added, which made for a very real hazard for passengers when negotiating the Micklegate Bar archway through the city walls! In 1903 five second-hand cars, all double-deckers, were acquired to replace the same number from the ageing fleet.

The opening years of the twentieth century were marred by disputes between the Company and the Corporation over the state of the tramway's track; by now the Corporation was entitled to purchase the system and in 1909 exercised this right, the actual takeover day being 27 February. Thereafter, the Corporation operated the line until work on its expansion and electrification scheme necessitated full closure later that year (see below).

York Corporation Tramways

Authority: York Corporation Light Railways Order 1908
Gauge: 3ft 6in.
Traction: Horse/overhead electric
Took over: 27 February 1909
Closed: 16 November 1935
System: Radial
Length: 8.49 miles
Stock: 8 dd horse?; 5 sd, 45 dd electric
Livery: Royal blue & cream to 1931, then bright blue & white
Last Car: No.1 (official)

Work began on converting York's horse tramway (see above) on 1 September 1909, just before it closed (on 7 September), and the first route opened (on 20 January 1910) was the rebuilt 2-mile Fulford–Nessgate portion of the old line, with the (enlarged) depot at Fulford Cross housing Brush open-toppers 1–18, delivered in batches before and after the reopening.

The next line opened ran for 1¾ miles from Nessgate across the River Ouse and along the route of the horse line branch to the station, then on via Queen Street to Blossom Street to rejoin the old main line, which it followed south-west to Knavesmire, continuing on to Dringhouses on the Tadcaster Road. This extension opened on 17 March 1910 (with the whole line being worked as one route), together with a short spur west off Blossom Street to the railway bridge in Holgate Road. This line was then extended along Acomb Road to the district of that name on 9 June, using two cars based on a temporary depot at Acomb, passengers having to cross Holgate Bridge on foot until 1 August 1911 while it was being rebuilt. Also opened on 9 June 1910 was a northern line from the railway station – the natural hub of the system – across Lendal Bridge and out through Bootham Bar (½ mile) and Clarence Street to Haxby Road, which it followed for another mile to Rose Street (extended in January 1916 a couple of hundred yards to the Rowntree Cocoa Works). To cope with the increased traffic, Brush open-toppers 20–23 were added to the fleet, followed in 1911 by Nos 24–27, four more of the same.

On 30 July 1913 a southern route was opened, from the Queen Street/Blossom Street junction along Nunnery Lane, New York Street, Bishopthorpe Road, Balmoral Terrace and Queen Victoria Street, to South Bank. Four more Brush open-toppers (Nos 28–31) were purchased, but these were apparently not sufficient and the following year single-deck trailers 32–35 were also bought from that company (who had unsuccessfully offered the Corporation its ex-Canvey Island cars – see Volume 1) for use at peak periods; these were joined in 1916–17 by open-toppers 36–41 from the same firm.

On 14 June 1916 the mainly double-track system was completed with the opening of an eastern branch from Nessgate along Walmgate and Lawrence Street to the Bee's Wing Hotel on the Hull Road. In 1925, EE single-deck one-man car 37 entered service after a fleet renumbering: Nos 20–31 became 19–30, Nos 36–41 became 31–36 while the water car (No.19) and the trailers lost their numbers – the latter vehicles presumably being withdrawn.

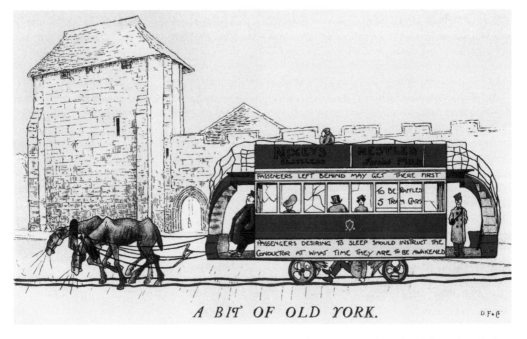

A BIT OF OLD YORK.

In the early twentieth century those horse tramways not converted to electric working found themselves the butt of satirical local press cartoons and postcards – such as this one. *(Author's Collection)*

In 1929 the Corporation built itself open-toppers 37 and 38 using two trailer car bodies, a spare truck and the truck from the water car (the former No.37 was cut down to serve as a salt/sand wagon) and these were joined the same year by Nos 39–41, three ex-Wolverhampton Corporation UEC open-toppers (possibly Wolverhampton 46, 50 and 56), and in 1930 by Nos 42–45, ex-Burton-upon-Trent Corporation UEC top-covered cars (Burton 21–24, which had their top covers removed before delivery). By now, though, the trams were running at a loss and the Corporation decided to replace them (and the feeder trolleybuses it had been operating since 1920) with motor buses, setting up on 1 April 1934 a Joint Committee with the West Yorkshire Road Car Co. to carry out this policy with their shared bus fleets. On 6 January 1935 the Dringhouses route was abandoned, and less than a year later the remainder of the system followed suit, the official Last Car ironically being the very one that had opened it a quarter of a century before.

Yorkshire (West Riding) Electric Tramways
Authority: The West Riding Tramways Act 1904
Gauge: 4ft 8½in.
Traction: Overhead electric
Opened: 15 August*
Closed: 25 July 1932*
System: Network + single line
Length: 24.69 miles*
Stock: 83 dd
Livery: Crimson lake & cream to 1924, then green & cream
Last Car: No.13*

The Yorkshire (West Riding) Electric Tramways Co. Ltd was registered on 4 April 1905 to acquire, construct and operate a network of some 50 route miles of tramways in the West Riding area; half this network, however, was never constructed and the final grand scheme comprised only the WAKEFIELD & DISTRICT system (which had opened in 1904) and a second separate line linking the towns of Normanton and Pontefract via Castleford. This latter tramway, a single-track, single-line route 7.18-miles long, opened on 29 October 1906 using six ex-W&D cars; by the time the route closed on 1 November 1925 a total of sixteen were housed at Castleford Depot (of which ten were left for later sale). The route was never a financial success – partly because its planned branches were never built, but primarily because neither were its planned connections with the Wakefield portion of the system – and the inevitable motor bus competition of the 1920s quickly killed it off. The last service car over this portion of the system was No.13, one of the ex-W&D vehicles.

As for the Wakefield network, this lasted until the 1930s before the buses won out. The main route from Leeds to Sandal (and the associated Rothwell branch) closed on 31 May 1932, whilst the Agbrigg–Ossett line followed suit just two months later.

The two parts of the system were worked by eighty-three passenger cars in all: the fifty-five ex-W&D vehicles, six UEC top-covered double-deckers of 1906 (Nos 56–61), six UEC open-toppers of the same date (Nos 62–67), eight top-covered double-deckers built by Brush in 1899 for LEEDS, covered in 1913, hired in 1913 and purchased in 1919 (Nos 68–75) and eight EE top-covered double-deckers of 1920, numbered 21–28 to replace eight cars destroyed in a 1917 fire in Castleford Depot. The system also employed, among its fleet of works cars, four unnumbered salt trailers rebuilt from ex-DEWSBURY, BATLEY & BIRSTAL steam trailers.

Yorkshire (Woollen District) Electric Tramways
Authority: Spen Valley Light Railways Order 1901
Gauge: 4ft 8½in.
Traction: Overhead electric
Opened: 18 February 1903?
Closed: 31 October 1934
System: Network

Length: 22.92 miles
Stock: 31 sd, 50 dd
Livery: Crimson lake & cream pre-1914, then maroon & primrose
Last Car: No.11

The Yorkshire (Woollen District) Electric Tramways Ltd, a BET subsidiary, was registered on 19 November 1901 to build and operate tramways in what was known (on account of the type of goods manufactured there) as the Heavy Woollen District of the West Riding of Yorkshire. The bulk of these lines had been authorised by a LRO of 1901, radiating from the towns of Thornhill in the south, Ravensthorpe in the south-west, Dewsbury in the centre and Cleckheaton and Birkenshaw in the north-west (to connect with the BRADFORD system, though the latter's gauge of 4ft prevented through-running).

Left: Local photographers were never slow to issue postcards recording tramway accidents and other disasters. Here Yorkshire (Woollen District) cars are held up by a flood at Batley Carr on 25 May 1925. *(Author's Collection)*

Below: Map of the Yorkshire (Woollen District) Electric Tramways in relation to its neighbours, from the 1904 *Manual of Electrical Undertakings.*

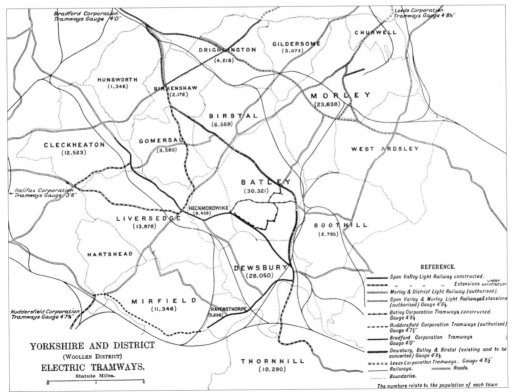

The first section to open was the 2½-mile southerly branch running northwards from Combs Hill through Thornhill to Dewsbury, followed, on 15 March, by the neighbouring Ravensthorpe to Dewsbury branch; an isolated section from a terminus in Moorend, down the Bradford Road, through Cleckheaton to Heckmondwike Market Place, opened on 24 April of the same year. The reason for opening separated sections was that the Company was in dispute with Batley Corporation over the use of part of the network north of Dewsbury intended to link them; with the resolution of the disagreement that same year, however, the rest of the system, with one exception, was open by 13 October. The only portion to be added to the network was the former DEWSBURY, BATLEY & BIRSTAL line (now electrified); this opened to the public on 23 November 1905, together with its short connection from the former terminus at Gomersal to the main route to Bradford.

Generally speaking, the lines started out from their termini as single tracks, doubling when they neared Dewsbury. Like its neighbours though – DEWSBURY, BATLEY and the YORKSHIRE (WEST RIDING) systems – the tramway was killed off by bus competition in the 1930s, the only difference being that the Company itself became a bus operator, closing routes in quick succession between 19 March 1932 (Liversedge–Hightown and Birstall–Birkenshaw) and 31 October 1934 (Dewsbury–Cleckheaton).

The tramway operated a fleet of eighty-one passenger cars in all, made up as follows:

Nos 1–6: Brush single-deckers of 1902
Nos 7–48: Brush open-toppers of 1902–03
Nos 49–56: BEC open-toppers of 1903 (BATLEY CORPORATION cars)
Nos 57, 58: Brush single-deckers of 1903
No.59: BEC single-decker of 1904
Nos 60–69: Brush single-deckers of 1904–05
Nos 70–73: Brush single-deckers of 1900 bought from SHEFFIELD CORPORATION in 1919
Nos 74–81: a mixed lot of ex-Sheffield single-deckers bought in 1920

Part 7

Tramways of Scotland

The development, history and location of tramways in Scotland were influenced by the same factors that applied south of the border. The three main concentrations of systems were centred on the three great firths of the Clyde, Forth and Tay – not surprisingly, for this was where, for historical and geographical reasons, the main centres of population and industry were to be found. Unlike in England, Wales and Ireland though, isolated systems outside these main concentrations were extremely rare and almost without exception found in towns along either the east or the west coast.

One feature of the Clyde network deserves special mention: the whole interconnected network of different systems used the unusual gauge of 4ft 7¾in. as it was envisaged from the start that railway goods wagons would be run over tramway lines in Glasgow and the surrounding conurbation. (See **Introduction**.) So it proved, with private industrial operators moving their own freight trains, hauled by their own steam and electric locomotives, over the street lines between railway sidings, factories and shipyards in this major area of heavy industry.

The last portion of the Clyde tramway network was abandoned in 1962, closing a chapter not only in Scottish transport history, but also in that of the whole British Isles, for it was the last tramway abandonment to take place, leaving just a handful of surviving lines to struggle on. None, alas, were in Scotland.

Aberdeen District Tramways
Authority: Aberdeen District Tramways Act 1872
Gauge: 4ft 8½in.
Traction: Horse
Opened: 31 August 1874
Taken over: 27 August 1898
System: Network
Length: 10.95 miles
Stock: 3 sd, 37 dd?
Livery: Route colour & cream

Aberdeen's first tramways were promoted and operated by the Aberdeen District Tramways Co., though not without some initial financial difficulties, which meant that the track-laying did not start until April 1874, three years after fundraising began. The first routes opened were an east–west line from North Church via Castle Street, Union Street and Albyn Place, to near the depot at Queens Cross (1¼ miles), and a north–south line from Causewayend, down George Street and St Nicholas Street, to meet the other route in Union Street (1 mile). Two single-deckers and four double-deckers were supplied for the opening, possibly by Starbuck, joined at the end of 1875 by another pair of double-deckers.

On 12 June 1876 the system's first extension opened: a stretch of about 200yd from the Causewayend terminus to the GNSR's station at Kittybrewster; at the same time, another double-decker was bought. On 1 September 1880 three further extensions opened. The first ran south-west from the Union Street/ Albyn Place junction ('Holborn Junction'), down Holborn Street and Great Western Road, to the district of Mannofield (1¼ miles), whilst the second was a short extension of the North Church route, up King Street to the Cattle Market; the third extended the line from Kittybrewster up the Great Northern Road to Woodside (again about 1¼ miles), where a small depot was constructed. (A second small depot was constructed in Love Lane off King Street.) The following year the Company began running horse buses as feeders to the tramway and, in 1882, added two more double-deckers to the car fleet, followed by another a year later (this last being built by R. & J. Shinnie of Union Row, Aberdeen). All routes were single-track originally, though several central sections were later doubled as the routes lengthened and traffic increased.

After a shocking financial start, it seemed that the enlarged system was a success (doubtless helped by the concurrent growth of the city) and further extensions and new routes were planned. During late December 1883 a length of just over ¼ mile continued the Holborn Street line down to Bloomfield Road, and on 30 November 1888 a circular route from Queens Cross, north and east through Rosemount, then south to Union Street, was opened, to work which a further four Shinnie double-deckers were purchased.

In 1889 three more Shinnie double-deckers were added to the fleet, plus a Company-built toastrack for summer workings, followed, two years later, by (probably) five more double-deckers from Shinnies. Some of these were intended to work the lengthened King Street route, which was extended in July 1892 to University Road and, on 24 August that year, as far as Bridge of Don, terminating just short of the bridge on the southern bank of the river. Three more Shinnie cars were bought after this line's opening.

The next new route ran in the opposite direction, south from Bloomfield Road to Bridge of Dee, where the line again terminated just short of the river crossing, this time on the northern bank. This opened on 24 August 1894, by which time another (probably) nine Shinnie double-deckers had been added to the stock, followed two years later by three more. The system's last extension, opened 22 August 1896, was a ½-mile branch west from Queens Cross, along Queens Road to Bayview. By now Aberdeen Corporation was expressing an interest in taking over the system (as a prelude to electrifying it) – as was the GNSR – and after obtaining the necessary authority, did so from midnight of 26 August 1898 (see below).

No mention has so far been made of the car fleet numbers. This is because, unusually, the trams carried route numbers only (which were interchangeable); they also, not so unusually, were painted in distinguishing colours to denote which route they worked. (One of the cars, converted to electric working by the Corporation and numbered 1, can now be seen at the Grampian Transport Museum, Alford.) Four of the Shinnie cars, numbered 1, 4, 5 and 6 were sold by the Corporation, in 1900, to the Strabathie, or Strabathie & Blackdog, Light Railway (also known as the Murcar Railway), just north of Bridge of Don, to the north of the city. This was a 3ft gauge industrial line serving the Blackdog Brickworks and the cars, converted into single-deck carriages, were loco-hauled for the workers and visitors (and later for members of the Murcar Golf Club). Nos 1, 4 and 5 are believed to have been of 1891 vintage, with No.6 dating from two or three years later.

Aberdeen District horse car No.1, later converted to electric working by the Corporation, now restored at the Grampian Transport Museum, Alford. *(Grampian Transport Museum)*

The Aberdeen District Tramways Co. was unique amongst British tramway operators in that, from December 1878 onwards, it ran a public sledge service over the tramway routes when the Scottish winters prevented the horse cars from running. Pulled by a team of four horses, each sledge seated twenty passengers on a wooden frame mounted on iron runners.

Aberdeen Corporation Tramways

Authority: Aberdeen Corporation Tramways Act 1898
Gauge: 4ft 8½in.
Traction: Horse, overhead electric
Took over: 27 August 1898
Closed: 3 May 1958
System: Network
Length: 15.78 miles
Stock: 39 sd & dd horse; 168 dd electric?
Livery: Route colour & cream horse; route colour, dark green & white electric
Last Car: No.20 (service) and No.36 (official)

Following its takeover of the ABERDEEN DISTRICT TRAMWAYS (see above), Aberdeen Corporation set about modernising the system, with the first refurbished route, St Nicholas Street to Woodside, reopening on 23 December 1899 and the remainder following within the next two years. Also built at this time was a new easterly branch from Castle Street to Sea Beach (opened 4 July 1901) and two south-easterly routes to Torry and Duthie Park via Ferry Hill, to complete the system for the present. The first cars were Nos 1–8 (originally Woodside 1–8), Brush open-toppers of 1899 followed two years later with similar cars 9–20 (again, originally in a route number series). In 1902–03 BEC supplied open-toppers Nos 21–56; at the same time, as well as having taken over its lines, the Corporation gained ownership of a total of thirty-nine of the District's horse cars and some of these – it is thought thirteen double-deckers – were rebuilt as open-top electric cars Nos 57–69 as they were needed. The old Queens Cross Depot was rebuilt as the main electric car shed and the two smaller depots at Mannofield and Woodside also converted.

In 1912 MV supplied balcony cars 68–71, in 1913 balcony cars 72–77 were supplied by J.T. Clark of Aberdeen (using Brill trucks and Brush motors) and these were joined the next year by similar Brush vehicles 78–83, and in 1918–19 by Nos 84–86, Corporation-built open-toppers. Another fourteen Corporation balcony cars, Nos 66–67 and 87–98, were added in 1920–21, followed by five more (Nos 57–61) a year later. Although Corporation bus services had begun by this time, the tramways were by no means neglected and during the period 1923–31 the Corporation constructed another twenty-eight cars, all enclosed vehicles (Nos 62, 63, 99–105 and 116–124); Nos 106–115 were 1925 enclosed Brush vehicles. On 16 July 1924 a 2-mile westerly branch to the residential area of Hazelhead (with a short branch off it to Woodend) was opened.

The system's first closure came in 1931 when, on 28 February, the Torry route closed, followed on 30 May by the Duthie Park line. This did not signal the end of the tramways, however, but was rather a way of making the system more efficient. Indeed, in 1937 a short new line – an out-and-back loop off the Bridge of Don route to serve the football ground at Pittodrie – was opened, followed by an extension of the Woodside line to Scatterburn, formerly part of the ABERDEEN SUBURBAN TRAMWAYS route.

Meanwhile, twelve Brush enclosed cars had been added in 1929 (Nos 126–137), whilst eighteen ex-NOTTINGHAM CORPORATION enclosed double-deckers had been bought in 1936 and numbered 1–18 to replace ageing original cars; four years later modern EE streamlined double-deckers, Nos 138–141, were added to the fleet. (The first two of these were bogie vehicles.)

After the Second World War, the Corporation retained its faith in tramways while many others in Britain were losing theirs, and continued to upgrade the system in all departments. In 1948 it purchased fourteen ex-MANCHESTER CORPORATION 'Pilcher' enclosed cars, Nos 39–52, and the next year bought twenty new streamlined bogie vehicles from Pickerings (Nos 19–38). It was a last, valiant gesture, for as older cars were withdrawn so were more of the services. On 3 March 1951 the Mannofield route

Above left: Aberdeen Corporation No.1 of 1899 in Union Street, captured on a 1904-franked postcard. *(Author's Collection)*

Above right: Two later balcony cars passing on Aberdeen's famous Union Bridge in the city centre – still at a time when any motor traffic was conspicuous by its absence. *(Author's Collection)*

Left: In the 1920s Aberdeen Corporation adopted a policy of buying fully enclosed cars, this example being No.132 of 1929 from Brush. *(Author's Collection)*

closed; on 2 October 1954 Rosemount circle and, on 26 November 1955, the Woodside line were closed. In 1956 the Hazelhead and Woodend lines went (7 October and 17 November respectively) and, on 13 March 1957, the Sea Beach line, leaving the main north–south Bridge of Don–Bridge of Dee to be the last to go.

Aberdeen Suburban Tramways

Authority: Aberdeen Tramways Order 1902
Gauge: 4ft 8½in.
Traction: Overhead electric
Opened: 23 June 1904
Closed: 9 June 1927?
System: Two single lines
Length: 4.59 miles
Stock: 11 dd
Livery: Red & white
Last Car: No.11

The Aberdeen Suburban Tramways Co. belonged to that small group of tramway owners who operated systems made up of two separate sections. The first of these ran for some 2½ miles, from the ABERDEEN CORPORATION terminus at Mannofield – being, in effect, a single-track continuation of that body's Great Western Road route – through Pitfodels and Cults to Bieldside church on northern Deeside; the second, the Donside route, opened 9 July 1904, was a single-track continuation of the Corporation's Great Northern Road line from Woodside out through Scatterburn and Bucksburn to Bankhead, terminating at Stoneywood church.

The system's first six cars were Brush double-deckers, of which Nos 1 and 5 were open and the others top-covered. These were joined in 1905 by Nos 7–9, UEC top-covered cars, in 1911 by No.10 and in 1914 by No.11, two similar cars from the same firm. Small depots were sited at Mannofield and Bankhead.

Through-running over the Corporation's lines had been agreed before the opening, with the Deeside trams starting from Castle Street and the Donside ones from St Nicholas Street. Each line was worked by three cars on regular services, with the extra cars (as they were acquired) providing extra cover as needed – usually on Sundays and Bank Holidays on the Deeside line, which was very popular with day-trippers.

In 1914 the Company began running three Tilling-Stevens petrol-electric buses as feeders to the tramways, but now the Corporation, unhappy about its arrangement with the Company, began exploring the possibility of taking the two lines over, only to baulk at the asking price. It seems the Company missed its chance for, by the end of the First World War, track and stock were in a bad way – and rapidly getting worse – and because of this, effective from 9 June 1926, the Corporation terminated through-running from both routes. It was then just a year before the Company went under, with the last Deeside 'Subbies' running on Saturday 2 June 1927, the Donside service ceasing a few days (possibly one week) later. The track was lifted the following year, though part of the Donside route was relaid ten years later by the Corporation (see above). The lower saloon of car No.11 survives, converted for use as a trailer on the nearby 2ft gauge Alford Valley Railway, next to the Grampian Transport Museum.

Airdrie & Coatbridge Tramways

Authority: Airdrie and Coatbridge Tramways Act 1900
Gauge: 4ft 7¾in.
Traction: Overhead electric
Opened: 8 February 1904
Taken over: 1 January 1922
System: Single line
Length: 3.63 miles
Stock: 15 dd
Livery: Maroon & cream

A dozen miles east of Glasgow, the Lanarkshire towns of Airdrie and Coatbridge prospered as iron-working centres in the nineteenth century but, although tramway links to Glasgow had been proposed since the 1870s, it was not until the next century that one was constructed. The line was built by the BET (who had succeeded the promoters, the Scottish House-to-House Electricity Supply Co.) and operated through a subsidiary, the Airdrie & Coatbridge Tramways Co.

A postcard view of Airdrie & Coatbridge Tramways No.8 of 1904 loading in Main Street, Coatbridge, looking eastwards. *(Author's Collection)*

The first section of the single-track line to be opened ran from Motherwell Street, in Airdrie, westwards along the main road, through Airdrie Cross and Coatdyke, to the burgh boundary at Kirkwood Street, Coatbridge, a distance of 3½ miles. Twelve open-top double-deck cars were supplied by Brush and a depot was erected for them on Main Street, midway between Coatbridge and Coatdyke. The following year three more Brush double-deckers were purchased (No.14, with a top cover, and Nos 13 and 15, so equipped soon after arrival) and, on 16 August 1905, an extension of 368yd took the western terminus to Woodside Street.

By the end of the First World War the track was in need of major repair work, if not outright replacement, and on 20 September 1920 the line was purchased jointly by Airdrie and Coatbridge town councils for £77,550 before being passed on for working, as from the first day of 1922, to GLASGOW CORPORATION. In May that year, a start was made on connecting the line to the Glasgow system via a short link from Coatbridge to Bailleston, and on 28 December this was completed (with a formal opening two days later).

Although through-running was now possible, this did not occur until the old track had been replaced (and doubled), the line being closed on 3 June 1924 to allow the work to be done; it reopened on 23 May following. The Company's trams were absorbed into the Glasgow fleet, taking the numbers 1073–1087, and withdrawn for scrapping in the early 1930s (though former Nos 1 and 4 became, briefly, a decorated car and an overhead inspection works vehicle respectively).

Ayr Corporation Tramways

Authority: Ayr Burgh Act 1899
Gauge: 4ft 8½in.
Traction: Overhead electric
Opened: 26 September 1901
Closed: 31 December 1931
System: Branching
Length: 6.46 miles
Stock: 4 sd, 25 dd
Livery: Dark chocolate & primrose
Last Car: No.9

Spurred into action by a private promotion, Ayr Town Council sought powers in 1898 for its own tramway operation, securing them the following year. It seems that electric traction was envisaged from the outset, the town becoming one of the first users of that mode of traction in Scotland.

Ayr Corporation No.8 of 1901 in the town's High Street, with its landmark Wallace Tower directly behind. *(Author's Collection)*

(Only GLASGOW and ABERDEEN had by then adopted it.) The Council was also one of the first to ask for permission to operate lines beyond its boundaries, an innovation later picked up by other local authorities.

The first 4 miles opened ran from Prestwick Cross, north of the town, southwards along the Ayr Road for 1¼ miles to the municipal boundary, then on past the depot at Newton Park, through the town centre (where the track was double for a mile) to a temporary terminus by St Leonard's church at the start of Monument Road. Services were operated by a fleet of HN open-top double-deckers (Nos 1–10), using electricity supplied by the Council's own generating station.

The line was an immediate success and the Council quickly pushed ahead with the remaining rural 1½ miles authorised down Monument Road to the village of Alloway for the benefit of visitors to the twin attractions of the Burns Cottage and the Monument to the poet at Brig o'Doon. This section (again single-track) opened on 29 May 1902 and necessitated the purchase of a further six open-toppers (Nos 11–16) from HN. Car No.18, which arrived from the same firm in 1904, was a luxurious open-top vehicle built for the 1902 Tramways Exhibition in London and was used on special occasions as well as working normal services, whilst Nos 19 and 20 were 1907 HN open-toppers. (No.17 was a works car.)

The only further section built (authorised in 1908) was the double-track Hawkhill branch, which ran due east from the town centre for a mile, along George Street and Whitletts Road, to serve the racecourse. This opened on 18 August 1913 and added two more HN open-toppers (Nos 21 and 22) to the car fleet. Nos 23 and 24 were HN top-covered vehicles of 1915, Nos 25–28 ex-MANCHESTER CORPORATION single-deckers built by Brush in 1899, bought in 1922 and converted to one-man operation for the Hawkhill branch, whilst Nos 29 and 30, bought six years later, were formerly DUMBARTON Nos 31 and 32, large EE top-covered cars of 1921 vintage. These last two survived the post-closure scrapping of the trams by being sold to SOUTH SHIELDS.

Although the tramway served well both residents and visitors to this popular holiday coast, it succumbed, inevitably, to the competition offered by the motor bus when the Council faced a choice between committing to serious expenditure on the track and rolling-stock or curtailing the routes and withdrawing many of the cars. In December 1931 the concern was sold to the Scottish Motor Traction Co. Ltd of Edinburgh, who promptly killed it off by the simple expedient of not reopening it the day after the takeover.

Bridge of Allan *see* Stirling & Bridge of Allan
Broughty Ferry *see* Dundee, Broughty Ferry & District

Carstairs House Tramway

Carstairs has been an important railway junction in the Scottish Lowlands since 1884 when the Caledonian Railway opened its lines from there to Glasgow, Edinburgh and Carlisle. During the 1880s Joseph Monteith, an amateur engineer, built a small water turbine and generator to light his residence, Carstairs House, south of the village. Then – probably in 1888 – work began on the construction of an electric 'tramway' to link the house with the railway station. The 2ft 6in. gauge line was 1,890yd long and was possibly inspired by a demonstration line at the 1886 Edinburgh International Exhibition. It was laid wholly on estate land and commenced by the East Lodge, just across the road from the station, and followed the main driveway, then a farm boundary, to (and through!) the estate sawmill before reaching the house. Several short branches came off the single-track line, including one at the station to interchange sidings (used mainly for coal for the house) and, at the other end, to the boiler house and to a small, rustic car shed.

As with all such early electric lines, the distinction between 'railway' and 'tramway' was a blurred one, with, in this case, current supplied and returned by means of raised conductor strips either side of the line (except at level crossings, which were coasted over).

Details of the stock are annoyingly sketchy. The principal car is thought to have been constructed locally and was a four-wheeled saloon seating six passengers. There were, in addition, at least two goods or luggage trucks – possibly conversions of the two North Metropolitan cars used at the Edinburgh International Exhibition rumoured to have passed to the line.

Electric working seems to have ceased *c.*1895 (possibly it came to be regarded as dangerous) and the line was then horse-operated, apparently for goods traffic only. In 1924 the house was purchased by the Diocese of Glasgow for use as a children's institution; extensive alterations were made to the property and the tramway was most likely abandoned then. What remained was sold for scrap *c.*1932, thus ending the life of Scotland's first permanent, if private, electric line.

Coatbridge *see* Airdrie & Coatbridge

Coatbridge: Summerlee Heritage Park

Opened in March 1988, east of Glasgow near Airdrie on the site of the former Summerlee Ironworks (opened 1832 and later levelled for a crane factory), Summerlee Heritage Museum was designed to showcase the industrial, engineering, transport and social history of central Scotland.

To help visitors around the 25-acre site, a 300yd-long standard-gauge overhead-electric tramway was installed for the opening to run from the entrance to other parts of the site (and has since been more than doubled in length to some 700yd). During the life of the tramway – currently the only working tramway in Scotland – operational duties have been shared between continental single-deckers Oporto 150 (now scrapped), Brussels 9062 (also scrapped), Graz 225 (sold) and Düsseldorf 392 (adapted for disabled visitors), together with restored open-topper LANARKSHIRE 53 of 1908 and GLASGOW CORPORATION single-decker 1017 (ex-PAISLEY 17) of 1904. A number of other Scottish cars are currently undergoing long-term restoration. Closed in October 2006 for a £10 million major redevelopment, the museum reopened in September 2008 under its new name.

Cruden Bay Hotel Tramway

Authority: -*
Gauge: 3ft 6in.
Traction: Horse/overhead electric
Opened: Mid-June 1899
Closed: 31 October 1932 (officially)*
System: Single line
Length: 0.66 miles
Stock: 2 sd
Livery: Light green & white with GNSR purple lake dashes, then LNER teak
Last Car: ?

Constructed by the GNSR to link its Cruden Bay Hotel (opened 1 March 1899) and golf course with Cruden Bay station on its Ellon–Boddam branch (opened 2 August 1897), this short line carried both passengers (to the front door of the hotel) and goods (via a short spur to the tradesmen's entrance). Perhaps more importantly, all the GNSR's laundry was done at the hotel and the tramway was built as much to carry this as to carry passengers.

Cruden Bay Hotel was constructed under the Great North of Scotland Railway (Various Powers) Act of 1893, though this document makes no mention of a tramway, which was built on land secured by local agreements. It opened three months after the hotel did, and commenced with a paved loop and two terminal stubs in the station forecourt, before skirting then crossing a public highway onto a rural reserved section, where the track was sleepered and ballasted; bullhead rails were used throughout. At the (paved) front of the hotel, a triangular junction denoted the point where the goods siding to the laundry and depot diverged. Two small combination cars were built for the tramway by the GNSR at its Kittybrewster Works in Aberdeen, each with a passenger saloon and an end platform for luggage and laundry baskets. All in all, they were rather sumptuous vehicles with ornate ironwork, etched and bevelled window glass, velvet curtains and upholstery of a gold colour. For the first few months, until the electrification of the line was completed, the cars were horse-drawn. In 1901 the hotel manager apparently proposed that they be used as staff sleeping quarters, thus freeing-up more rooms for guests, but it is not known if this ever came about. There was also a handful of goods vehicles.

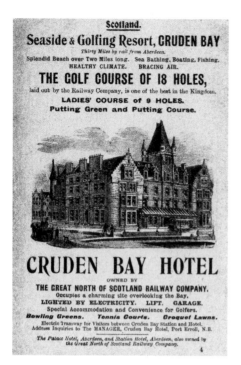

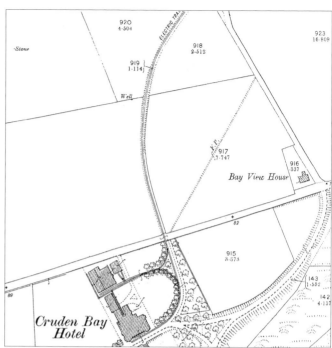

Above left: A typical guidebook advertisement for the Cruden Bay Hotel, mentioning the tramway as an added convenience for guests.

Above right: The Cruden Bay Tramways Depot, next to the laundry block, was completed shortly after the line opened in 1899, prior to which the two cars were stored in the open. Note the turntable access to the car shed, seen here on the 1901 Ordnance Survey 25in. to 1 mile map.

After the 1923 Grouping control of the tramway and hotel passed to the LNER, who repainted the cars in its own passenger stock livery and numbered them 1 and 2; it is thought that one was now reserved for passengers and the other – inevitably less well maintained – used for goods. When the railway branch closed to passengers from Monday 31 October (with the last train running the previous Saturday) the cars were withdrawn from passenger service – presumably 29 October as well – and the line then ran as a goods-only service. During its life, the passenger service had been free to hotel guests, though non-residents could use it for a fee.

In September 1939 the hotel was requisitioned by the army, and around March 1941 the tramway was closed and the cars sold locally for use as summer houses – a common fate for obsolete trams, though seldom, if ever, ones as luxurious as this pair. Happily, one was rescued in 1987 for preservation and can now be seen in static restored condition as car No.2 at the Grampian Transport Museum, Alford. The hotel was sold for demolition in 1950 and its site is now occupied by the golf course's new (1998) clubhouse.

It should be noted that a number of slightly different track gauges – including 3ft 6½in. – have been cited for this tramway in the past, but the recent discovery of original car drawings would appear to settle the matter at a nominal 3ft 6in.

Dumbarton Burgh & County Tramways
Authority: Dumbarton Tramways Order 1904
Gauge: 4ft 7¾in.
Traction: Overhead electric
Opened: 20 February 1907
Closed: 3 March 1928

System: Branching
Length: 13.1 miles
Stock: 4 sd*, 28 dd
Livery: Chocolate & cream to 1908, then green & cream
Last Car: ?

Although the envisaged through-running between the two systems never came about, the Dumbarton main line had an end-on connection with the Glasgow network and so provided a convenient escape route for the inhabitants of that city to the shores of Loch Lomond and its surrounding countryside.

The tramway was constructed by DK and was operated initially by the Electric Supply Corporation Ltd (as the sole tramway among its power generating interests), but shortly after the opening the undertaking was transferred, under the provisions of the Dumbarton Burgh and County Tramways Order 1907, to a subsidiary, the Dumbarton Burgh & County Tramways Co. Ltd (though power was still supplied by the ESC from its generating station).

The line, as opened, consisted of a main line running north-west from Dumbuck via Dumbarton High Street to Dalreoch Quarry (some 3 miles), plus a branch from the High Street northwards along Bonhill Road – past the depot and power station – to Barloan Toll (about ½ mile). In February 1908 construction recommenced and the main line was extended northwards, beyond the burgh boundary, to Alexandria. This section opened on 7 May the same year and was followed on 25 June by two further extensions: northwards again to Balloch, at the southern tip of Loch Lomond, and, at the other end of the line, along the northern bank of the River Clyde to Dalmuir West, where the aforementioned connection with the Glasgow system was made.

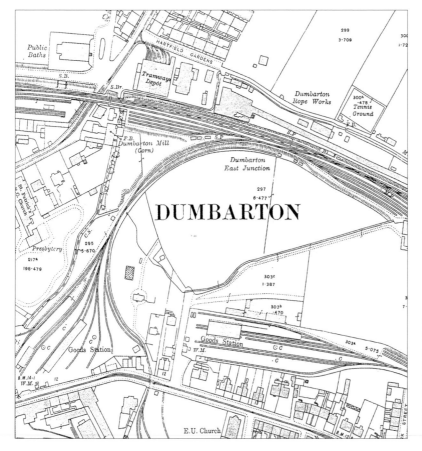

The Dumbarton Tramways' one depot, opened in 1907 in Bonhill Road, on the 1918 Ordnance Survey 25in. to 1 mile map. It closed in 1928 with the tramways.

The final route to open (on 24 January 1909) was a second short branch, this time from Alexandria, south-east to Bonhill, then north to Jamestown. All routes were single-track in what were then principally country roads.

The original car fleet was made up of Brush open-canopied double-deckers 1–6; these were augmented, in 1908, by UEC open-toppers 7–26 and in 1909 by four converted double-deck horse cars from GLASGOW CORPORATION (Nos 27–30). These latter vehicles were used on the Jamestown branch, with the upper seats and superstructure removed, and the stairs boarded up, on account of a low bridge in Bank Street, Alexandria. In 1920 the line's last two cars, EE open-toppers Nos 31 and 32, were purchased.

After its initial success, the tramway was soon hit by motor bus competition on this major route from Glasgow to the Highlands and no dividend was paid to shareholders after 1922; matters were not helped by the fact that local authority wrangling – notably with Clydebank Town Council immediately to the east – preventing through-running to Glasgow. After closure, all the cars were scrapped except the two youngest – Nos 31 and 32 – which went to AYR.

Dundee & District Tramway

Authority: Dundee Tramways Act 1872
Gauge: 4ft 8½in.
Traction: Horse, steam
Opened: 30 August 1877
Taken over: 1 June 1899
System: Radial network
Length: 7.25 miles
Stock: 2 sd, 20 dd horse; 13 locos, 11 dd steam
Livery: Polished mahogany to 1879, then dark red & yellow to 1894, then dark green & cream

Dundee's first tramway was a double-track affair just over 1¼ miles in length – the first part of a grander authorised scheme – running eastwards from Windsor Street off Perth Road, along Perth Road, Nethergate, the High Street and Reform Street to the main Post Office in Euclid Crescent. It was promoted by the Dundee Tramway & Omnibus Co. Ltd, constructed by the Police Commissioners (the local authority), then leased to the Dundee & District Tramway Co. Ltd (incorporated August 1877)! All in all, it seems to have been a rush job in order to prevent the powers of its Act from lapsing, so much so, in fact, that two cars from the EDINBURGH STREET TRAMWAYS and three from the GLASGOW TRAMWAY had to be hired for the opening. These were open-top double-deckers numbered 1A–5A respectively and were quickly joined by similar vehicles 6A and 7A purchased, rather than hired, from Glasgow (whereupon 4A and 5A were returned). In December, the line received its first new cars, three open-toppers built by the Glasgow Tramway & Omnibus Co. and numbered 3A–5A; the remaining hired cars were then returned.

In 1878 work began on expanding the system, and on 24 December 1879 a ½-mile single-track extension of the Perth Road route to West Park Road, and a 1¾-mile double-track branch from the other end of the line, northwards up Lochee Road to the village of that name (and the site of the tramway's permanent depot), were opened. Five more double-deckers were bought, these being constructed by the local firm of T. Swinton & Sons; mounted on Eades patent reversible trucks, these were numbered – bizarrely and uniquely on British tramways – in Roman fashion: CI, CVIII, CIX, CX and CXI.

Two further 'East End' branches were opened, on 19 June 1880, eastwards from the Post Office to Baxter Park and Morgan Hospital, both via Victoria Road. Two smaller, conventional cars (Nos CXII and CXIII) were built by Swinton to help work these lines with another, of unknown origin, No.2 (!) added two years later, followed in 1883 by two open-top single-deck summer cars (Nos 14 and 15).

In 1885 the Company began serious use of steam traction (a Dickinson combined car had been experimented with four years earlier) when tram locomotives 1 and 2 were supplied by Greens, and a covered double-deck bogie trailer (No.16) bought, probably from Lancaster, for use on the Lochee route. Two further locos (Nos 3 and 4) followed in 1885 and, with only the one purpose-built trailer available, towed pairs of horse cars behind them. After trials, public services with the new motive power began on 20 June 1885 and, from 8 July 1886, on the East End routes as well with two more Green locos. By the end of 1894 the loco stock numbered thirteen and, unusually, they carried names as well as numbers. Double-deck trailers were also purchased from a variety of builders, as well as being constructed from pairs of surplus horse cars.

The last new routes opened, on 17 July 1894, were a short single-track branch off Victoria Road, northwards through the aptly named Hilltown to the village of Fairmuir, and a short single-track line along Morgan Street to link the two East End routes. (The last horse cars, Nos 22 and 24, were added at this time.)

The tramway now seemed so attractive to Dundee Corporation that the authority decided to purchase it outright and pay the Company £2,100 a year until the lease ran out in 1907; consequently, from 1 June 1899 the Corporation became both owner and operator (see below). The Company was left with the bus side of the business (which it had maintained and expanded) and remained in existence until 1922, when it went into voluntary liquidation.

Dundee City Tramways
Authority: Dundee Corporation (Tramways) Act 1898
Gauge: 4ft 8½in.
Traction: Horse, steam, overhead electric
Took over: 1 June 1899
Closed: 20 October 1956
System: Radial network
Length: 16.57 miles
Stock: 10 dd horse; 13 locos, 10 dd steam; 6 sd, 103 dd electric
Livery: Indian red (dark red-brown) & white
Last Car: No.25

Work began on electrifying the Dundee system shortly after the Corporation takeover (see above), beginning with the Perth Road and Lochee lines. Public services with the new cars began over the first of these on 12 July 1900 (the horse cars stopping the same day) and over the second on 22 October. Thereafter, the remainder of the old system was electrified and extended (with some short central sections abandoned), with the last steam trams running on 14 May 1902 on the Fairmuir route. (The Baxter Park steam line was abandoned until reopened on 20 August 1906 with electric working.)

The first ten electric cars (Nos 1–10) were ERTCW open-top bogie double-deckers (later top-covered), based on the old Lochee Depot, and were followed between 1900 and 1901 by open-toppers Nos 11–40 (also later top-covered). In 1902 eight Milnes open-toppers (Nos 41–48, renumbered 11–18 in 1927), again later top-covered, were bought together with HN bogie combination cars 49–54, the tramway's only single-deckers. On 20 November that year a new route, off the Fairmuir line, was opened to Hilltown and, in 1901, a new depot was built at Maryfield. Further short extensions followed in 1907 and, on 12 November 1908, a short southern branch to Craig Pier on the River Tay was opened. By this time, more balcony cars had been purchased: Nos 55–60 (1907 Brush) and Nos 61–66 (1908 MV).

Three of Dundee City Tramways' new electric cars passing in the busy High Street – a common Edwardian postcard image – with No.16 of 1900 leading. *(Author's Collection)*

In 1912 the Corporation began trolleybus operations, but abandoned them two years later – the first such services to go in Britain. Instead, further short tramway extensions were opened; on 1 June 1919, however, the loss-making Craig Park branch closed.

In 1916 the Corporation acquired second-hand balcony cars Nos 69–74 from PAISLEY DISTRICT TRAMWAYS, and HN top-covered cars 75–78 were bought in 1916, followed by similar vehicles 67, 68 and 79–90 during the period 1920–21 (and which, like many of the Dundee cars, were later renumbered or even renumbered again). Corporation motor bus services commenced in 1922, and on 26 February 1928 the Constitution Road line was abandoned, though not before the Corporation had built nine enclosed cars (Nos 91–99 of 1923–25) and bought, in 1930, ten wide-bodied Brush enclosed cars (Nos 19–28) for the Lochee route. The next closure came on 16 May 1931, with the abandonment of the easterly route to Belsize Road, where it connected with the DUNDEE, BROUGHTY FERRY & DISTRICT line, after the Corporation had purchased that tramway and closed it (see below). On 2 October 1932 the Baxter Park route closed.

The tramway survived the Second World War comparatively unscathed with fifty-six serviceable cars and traffic heavy. Also heavy was general road traffic, though, and on 26 April 1952 the Moncur Crescent route was closed (except to football specials). The Blackness route followed on 26 November 1955, and the Downfield route in the early hours of the next morning. The last routes closed less than a year later, on 20 October 1956, with a special farewell procession from Maryfield Depot to Lochee in the early hours of the 21st.

Dundee, Broughty Ferry & District Tramways

Authority: Dundee Broughty Ferry and District Tramways Order 1904
Gauge: 4ft 8½in.
Traction: Overhead electric
Opened: 27 December 1905
Closed: 15 May 1931
System: Single line
Length: 5.1 miles
Stock: 16 dd
Livery: Lake & cream
Last Car: ?

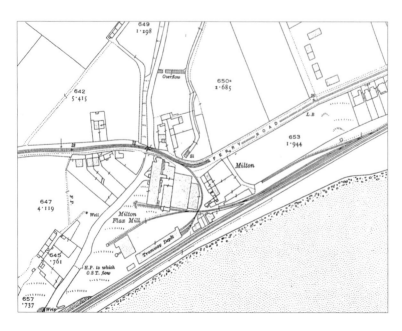

The Dundee, Broughty Ferry & District Tramways' Milton Depot, opened in 1905 off Ferry Road, on the 1922 Ordnance Survey 25in. to 1 mile map. After being abandoned by the trams, it was later used to house a carpet factory.

After several false starts, the idea of an electric tramway along the north shore of the Firth of Tay became a reality when George Balfour (see BALFOUR, BEATTY & CO. LTD in Part 6) successfully promoted its authorising Act. The line, almost all double-track, was laid quickly and ran eastwards for some 4 miles from Craigie Terrace in Dundee (where it made an end-on connection with the DUNDEE CITY line), on a mixture of road and reserved sections, all predominantly rural in character and roughly parallel to the Dundee & Arbroath Joint Railway line between those two places, through various settlements (the principal one being Broughty Ferry), to the village of Monifieth, where it terminated in the High Street. (It was extended in 1908 by some 300yd to Tay Street.)

Twelve Brush open-top double-deckers were bought for the opening and a depot constructed at Milton, nearly a mile from the eastern terminus. Two more Brush cars (Nos 13 and 14) followed in 1907, these being top-covered vehicles similar to those supplied to Dundee Corporation that same year – a similarity all the more confusing to the casual observer as through-running was operated.

A second increase in route mileage came in 1914 when the operator, the Dundee, Broughty Ferry & District Tramways Co. Ltd, bought from the Corporation nearly a mile of track and overhead from Craigie Terrace back to the burgh boundary at Belsize Road; at the same time, it purchased two of the Corporation's worn-out 1900 ERTCW cars (Nos 13 and 16), these becoming Nos 15 and 16 in its fleet. It appears that relations between the two operators later began to deteriorate – the Corporation ran a rival bus service during the period 1921–22, for example – but they united in 1930, against the threat from private bus operators, by inaugurating their own joint bus service. After that it became clear that the future lay with the buses and the last trams to Monifieth ran at the end of the following financial year, the line having been purchased for £25,000 by the Corporation, who immediately closed it.

Dunfermline & District Tramways

Authority: Dunfermline and District Tramways Order 1906
Gauge: 3ft 6in.
Traction: Overhead electric
Opened: 2 November 1909
Closed: 4 July 1937
System: Branching
Length: 18.36 miles
Stock: 2 sd, 45 dd
Livery: Bright green & cream
Last Car: ?

This, by far the largest of Fife's three tramway systems, was built and operated by the Dunfermline & District Tramways Co., a subsidiary of the Fife Electric Power Co. (itself a member of the BB group). The first 5¼ miles from Dunfermline High Street/East Port, eastwards along the Dunfermline Road and through Crossgates to Cowdenbeath, were followed on 3 November 1909 by a 1¼-mile branch northwards from Dunfermline to Main Street, Townhill; on 23 December of that year the Cowdenbeath line was extended another 2½ miles to Bank Street, Lochgelly.

On 17 November 1910 a branch northwards of some 2 miles was opened from Cowdenbeath, up the Perth Road to Main Street, Kelty, followed on 5 December 1912 by a 2½-mile extension of the main line from Lochgelly to Lochore; a mile-long branch from Dunfermline to Rumblingwell opened on 27 December 1913, with a 3½-mile branch south from Dunfermline to Rosyth Dockyard (17 May 1918) completing the system, although hopes were long entertained of extending even further east to link up with KIRKCALDY half a dozen miles away. All lines were single-track, and the Rosyth route was mainly reserved; the main depot was in Cowdenbeath, on the north side of Broad Street, with a second smaller one just south of Dunfermline at St Leonards, on the Rosyth branch.

The car fleet was built up over the years to keep pace with the expanding system and, by the time the last route opened, the Company operated UEC open-top double-deckers Nos 1–20 of 1909, 21–14 of 1910, 25–28 of 1912 and 29–43 of 1918, supplemented in 1919 by Nos 44 and 45, two similar ERTCW

Dunfermline open-topper No.16 of 1909 in Port Street, on a postcard perhaps purchased in the shop on the left. *(Author's Collection)*

vehicles of 1902 vintage, acquired from the Nottinghamshire & Derbyshire Tramways; these latter two cars were replaced in 1932 by two Brush single-deckers bought from WEMYSS & DISTRICT (and renumbered 44 and 45 from 19 and 18).

During the decade after the First World War a multiplicity of motor bus operators appeared on the scene in Fife, and in 1924 the Company joined the fray with a fleet of Tilling-Stevens petrol-electric buses – and a track-doubling programme to speed up its tram services. This was, at best, a stop-gap measure and, on 26 October 1931, the Kelty branch closed, leaving the remainder of the system to soldier on for another six years. All surviving cars were scrapped after closure, with the exception of two that were dismantled and shipped to the Giant's Causeway, Portrush & Bush Valley Tramway in Ireland.

Edinburgh Street Tramways

Authority: Edinburgh Tramways Act 1871
Gauge: 4ft 8½in.
Traction: Horse, steam
Opened: 6 November 1871
Taken over: 23 October 1904[*]
System: Network
Length: 18.53 miles
Stock: 160+ sd & dd horse; 2 locos steam
Livery: Red-brown & cream, later various

Scotland's first street tramway – and the forerunner of the country's second largest system after GLASGOW – was a short line running from Haymarket, west of the city centre, north-east to Bernard Street in Leith via West Maitland Street, West End and Princes Street as far as the Post Office, then Leith Walk and Leith Street. This was joined on 29 May 1872 by a line south from the Post Office via North Bridge, South Bridge, Nicholson Street and Clerk Street to Powburn, Newington. The lines were a mixture of single and double tracks and services were worked by (probably) twelve open-top double-deckers constructed by the British & Foreign Tramways Co. Ltd of Greenwich. These cars, however, were found to be too heavy for the job and, in 1872–73, were replaced by sixteen similar, but much lighter, vehicles built by John Croall & Sons and Drew & Burnett of Edinburgh, and R.J. Boyall of Grantham.

After 1873 the use of fleet numbers was discontinued in favour of route numbers and, as the system grew, so the car fleet was increased by the purchase, during 1876–77, of at least ten open toastracks and eleven double-deckers from Starbuck, Boyall and Stephenson of New York. Between 1879 and 1882 some fourteen double-deckers were built by the Edinburgh Street Tramways Co., the system's owner and operator, whilst BM supplied at least five double-deckers. After that, all new additions were constructed by the Company – including ten long single-deckers numbered 90–99 – up to 1893, when the fleet strength (after several withdrawals) stood at one hundred. On 9 December that year, though, Edinburgh Corporation exercised its powers to purchase the bulk of the system within its boundaries (see EDINBURGH & DISTRICT), leaving the Company to operate just thirty cars in Leith. This it did until October 1904, when the lines there were purchased by LEITH CORPORATION.

After trials in early 1881, the Company had introduced steam traction on 23 April that year, using a Kitson tram locomotive (No.1) on its route east to Portobello. This was joined in March 1882 by loco No.2, also from Kitsons, though their use (towing horse cars) was discontinued after 27 October that year, their licences not having been renewed in the face of local authority and public opposition.

Edinburgh Northern Tramways

Authority: Edinburgh Northern Tramways Act 1884
Gauge: 4ft 8½in.
Traction: Cable
Opened: 28 January 1888
Taken over: 1 January 1897*
System: Two single lines
Length: 2.61 miles
Stock: 2 sd, 16 dd
Livery: Blue & cream

The origins of Edinburgh's extensive cable tramway system – by far the largest and most complicated of its kind in the British Isles – lay with the Edinburgh Northern Tramways Co. who, in 1888, opened a line northwards along Hanover Street and Dundas Street in the New Town district of the city to Ferry Road, Goldenacre – a distance of some 1½ miles. The first cars (Nos 1–8) were Metropolitan open-top bogie double-deckers, which were housed in the depot in Henderson Row, off to the west of Dundas Street. This was also the site of the winding house for the cable, which was hauled continually through a conduit in the centre of each of the line's two tracks, and to which the cars could be attached (or released) by means of driver-operated grippers.

Edinburgh's first tramway depot was opened on 6 November 1871 by the Edinburgh Street Tramways Co., in Shrubhill on the west side of Leith Walk. It was rebuilt and enlarged several times over the next decades to become the large electric car depot shown here on the 1931 Ordnance Survey 25in. to 1 mile map.

A second, 1¼-mile route was opened on 17 February 1890 from George Street, just west of Hanover Street, northwards up Frederick Street and Howe Street, then north-west through Stockbridge to Comely Bank. Between 1890 and 1892 another eight bogie open-toppers (Nos 9–16) were bought to work the new route, this time from Falcon, and to enable them to reach the new line the spur to the depot was extended along Hamilton Place to meet it midway.

In 1894, in accordance with the new local authority licensing policy, the tramway's cars were renumbered 121–136, and were joined that year by No.137 and, in 1895, by No.138, long single-deckers of unknown origin that saw service for only a few years. Although further routes had been planned from the outset, no more had been constructed by the end of 1896, when the Company relinquished operation of the system to the EDINBURGH & DISTRICT TRAMWAYS (see below) before, on 1 July 1897, selling it for £110,000 to EDINBURGH CORPORATION for leasing to the EDT Co. (under the Edinburgh Corporation Act of that year) to become the nucleus of the municipally owned cable tramway network.

Edinburgh & District Tramways

Authority: Edinburgh Corporation Act 1893
Gauge: 4ft 8½in.
Traction: Horse, cable, overhead electric
Took over: 9 December 1893
Taken over: 1 July 1919
System: Radial network
Length: 18.65 miles
Stock: 2 sd, 96 dd horse; 2 sd, 227 dd cable; 4 dd electric
Livery: Various horse; madder & white cable and electric

By 1890 EDINBURGH CORPORATION had decided that it wished to see a unified tramway system within the city and, accordingly, with twenty-one years having passed, announced that it would take control of that part of the system within its boundaries. On 9 December 1893 it became the owner of the bulk of the EDINBURGH STREET TRAMWAYS, for the price of £185,000 including seventy cars; these were then resold to DK who had leased the tramways from the Corporation for another twenty-one years and who, on 6 March 1894, incorporated the Edinburgh & District Tramways Co. Ltd as its operating subsidiary. On 31 January 1896 the EST Co.'s line from Waterloo Place to Meadowbank was purchased by the Corporation for £13,615 upon expiry of its lease, the last stretch of the line to Portobello following suit two years later.

The decision was made, in 1895, to convert the tramways to cable traction in order to cope with the many hills an expanded system would encounter, and this work was carried out by DK, commencing the following year. Before operations could begin, the EDINBURGH NORTHERN TRAMWAYS' two lines had been taken over, from 1 January 1897, and it was, in fact, one of that company's cars, No.142, which was used on 1 June 1899 to officially open the new system with a trip from the winding house at Shrubhill to St Andrew Street and back. Public services began on 26 October between Pilrig, on the Leith boundary, and Braid Hills Road, with the rest of the system being converted over the next three years and new routes opened in the 1900s. The last horse cars ran on 24 August 1907, on the south-western route to Craiglockhart.

The horse car fleet inherited at the end of 1893 was made up of sixty-one cars (Nos 1–13, 16–19, 22, 24, 25, 27, 40–43, 48, 55–62, 64–78, 86, 88, 89, 91–94 and 96–100), all double-deckers with the exception of the last vehicle which was an open toastrack. This fleet was not large enough to work the system, but help was at hand for in July 1894 the Glasgow Tramways & Omnibus Co., the displaced operator of the GLASGOW TRAMWAY, had its own fleet to dispose of and the Company purchased thirteen double-deckers, numbering them 101–105 to continue its series and 25, 60, 61, 66, 73, 74, 76 and 94 to replace existing cars of those numbers. In 1895 Metropolitan supplied double-deckers 106–109 and that year the Company constructed double-decker 110, which was followed by similar cars 55, 71, 72, 75, 88, 89 and 111 a year later.

In 1896, with the purchase of the EST Co.'s line to Meadowbank, came cars 23, 44, 49, 52, 53 and 85, again all double-deckers, except the last which was another open toastrack. A year later double-deckers 113 and 114 were built by the Company and, in 1898, it acquired double-deckers 47, 50, 51 and 80 from the

Edinburgh & District Tramways double-deck cable cars 100 and 117 of 1898–99 in Portobello High Street. *(Author's Collection)*

EST Co. With the advent of cable traction the horse car fleet then began to shrink, with five cars being sold back to the EST Co. in 1900 and three more the next year; in 1900, six (including the two toastracks) were sold to the STIRLING & BRIDGE OF ALLAN TRAMWAYS as well. By 1903 the horse car fleet had been reduced by further sales and scrappings to just twenty, and by 1905 to seven – though two were then bought back from the EST Co. By the end of horse traction, only Nos 5, 47 and 72 were in service.

The Company's first cable car, No.112, was a prototype bogie open-top double-decker, longer than the ENT Co.'s double-deckers – which had been renumbered 121–138 (with single-deckers 137 and 138 being renumbered 7 and 13 later) – constructed in 1897 at its Shrubhill Works. This was joined that year by similar cars 139–144 from Milnes. By 1901 another twenty-five had been ordered from Milnes and 120 from BM. (Some of these took lower, horse car numbers whilst others extended the main series – with some gaps – up to 208.) By the time cable services began, twenty-four had been delivered. In 1903 ERTCW supplied twenty more (Nos 209–228) and in 1906 the Company constructed Nos 25 and 27, followed by Nos 37 and 48 a year later. These last two cars were roofed (37 enclosed and 48 top-covered), after which the earlier cars (except the four listed below converted to electric traction) were top-covered as well. By this time, former horse cars 15, 17, 19, 53 and 113 had been rebuilt as cable cars. The Company now constructed a further dozen cars (Nos 5, 13, 35, 47, 49–52, 54, 59, 66 and 72) between 1908 and 1911 to complete the cable car fleet, which was housed in depots at Shrubhill, Tollcross, Henderson Row and Portobello.

Although the myriad mechanical problems of using cable traction were ingeniously overcome, the system was not a total success and before the advent of the First World War the Corporation was already considering other methods of propulsion for the future. The neighbouring burghs of MUSSELBURGH (1904) and LEITH (1905) had already put electric trams onto their streets and, on 8 June 1910, Edinburgh followed suit with the Corporation opening a branch off the south-western cable route to Georgie, from Ardmillan Terrace, in a roughly parallel direction, to Slateford. This was leased to the Company, who worked it with open-top cable cars 28, 38, 64 and 74 converted to electric traction for that purpose. The war years put a temporary halt to the modernisation programme, though, and when the Company's lease of the cable lines expired on the last day of June 1919, the Corporation assumed operating responsibility (see below).

Edinburgh Corporation Tramways
Authority: Edinburgh Corporation Tramways Order 1919
Gauge: 4ft 8½in.
Traction: Cable, overhead electric
Took over: 1 July 1919
Closed: 16 November 1956
System: Network
Length: 47.25 miles
Stock: 205 dd cable; 597 dd electric
Livery: Madder & white
Last Car: No.217

With the Corporation's takeover, in 1919, of the EDINBURGH & DISTRICT TRAMWAYS (see above), it became the owner of 205 cable cars and four electric conversions; when it acquired the LEITH CORPORATION system the following year it added a further thirty-seven electric double-deckers to its fleet, numbering them 231–267 to fill the gap created by the renumbering of the ex-EDT electric cars, which had become 229, 230, 268 and 269 (EDT 28, 30, 64 and 74 respectively).

In 1921 work began on preparing the conversion of the cable lines to electric working and by 23 June 1923, when the eastern route to Portobello reopened, the task had been completed; extensions and new routes eventually produced an extensive network focussed on Edinburgh in the centre (and, to a lesser degree, Leith) stretching out to Costorphine in the west, Colinton, Fairmilehead and Liberton to the south, and Levenhall in the east, after the Corporation's 1928 takeover of the surviving portion of the MUSSELBURGH & DISTRICT line. (No connections were ever made to other systems, the only near neighbour being unreachable across the Firth of Forth at DUNFERMLINE.)

With the conversion of the cable system came a corresponding conversion of the cable cars, a total of 184 being so treated during the early 1920s. At the same time, a batch of top-covered cars was supplied by McHardy & Elliott of Edinburgh (sixteen cars), Leeds Forge (fourteen) and the Corporation itself (another fourteen) which, with some renumbering, completed the Nos 1–269 fleet series. These were then joined, during 1923–29, by similar vehicles 270–311 (Leeds Forge), 312–331 (EE) and 332–366 (the Corporation again), plus another forty from the Corporation, which took on numbers of withdrawn older cars.

Between 1930 and 1934 the Corporation built another fifty-three double-deckers, fully enclosed ones this time, to take the number series to 371 (and again replace some older vehicles), while Pickerings supplied Nos 250–259 and Metro-Cammell Nos 260 and 265 – all similar-type vehicles. The last new cars of this period, all varieties of double-deckers built 1934–35, were Nos 11–18, 231, 239 and 240 from HN, Nos 25–30, 241, 242, 244–246 and 249 from Metro-Cammell and Nos 19–24, 262, 263 and 267 from EE.

The last extension to the system, to Maybury on the Costorphine route, was opened on 14 February 1937 with the Second World War putting paid to any further expansion plans. The car-building programme continued, however, with eighty-four replacement enclosed double-deckers constructed between 1934 and 1950, after which the only additions to the fleet resulted from the purchase, between 1947 and 1949, of Nos 401–411, enclosed double-deckers of early 1930s vintage, from MANCHESTER CORPORATION. In 1950, though, Edinburgh decided to partially abandon its tramways, with buses replacing the first route (Waverley to Comely Bank) on 1 June 1952 – the same year that the decision was taken to abandon the trams altogether.

The last route to go, Granton Road Station–Morningside, went on 16 November 1956, after which the remaining trams were quickly scrapped, there being virtually no second-hand market left for them. Only one complete car survives in preserved form at present: Corporation-built No.35 of 1948, currently on loan to the National Tramway Museum at Crich after running for several years at BLACKPOOL.

By way of contrast, Edinburgh Corporation's enclosed double-deckers 364 of 1929 and 402 (ex-Manchester 676 of 1932) in suburban service provide a study in changing tramcar design over nearly three decades. *(Author's Collection)*

Edinburgh Tramway*

Authority: Edinburgh Tramway (Line Two) Act 2006; Edinburgh Tramway (Line One Act) 2006
Gauge: 1.435m
Traction: Overhead electric
Opening: 2012*
System: Single line*
Length: 20km*
Stock: 27 sd
Livery: ?

Although this tramway – the newest in the British Isles and as yet not official titled – is not open, it has been accorded a main entry as it is very much a work in progress and the opportunity has consequently been taken to include here as much information as possible, correct at the time of going to press. The project is being overseen by Transport Initiative Edinburgh (TIE), an arms-length company backed by the Council, with a total cost estimated in 2007 of some £592 million. In 2004 it was announced that the French giant Transdev (operator of Nottingham Express Transit) had been awarded the contract to run the tramway, with a new company being formed with the Council-owned Lothian Buses in order to integrate public transport across the city.

It was hoped to have at least part of the system open in 2008; lengthy scrutiny, however, by the Scottish Parliament has put this date well into the future. The first section to be opened, known as Phase 1a, will run for some 20km, from the Waterfront in the developing business and social centre of Newhaven to the north-east of the city, through Leith (by the new Scottish Parliament building) and then via Princes Street, Haymarket, Murrayfield Stadium and Ingliston, on to Edinburgh Airport. Phase 1b will be a branch from between Haymarket and Murrayfield to Granton via Roseburn and Craigleith; Phase 2 will be a link from Granton along the Forth coast to Newhaven to complete the loop, whilst Phase 3 will be a branch from Ingliston to Newbridge – though currently all except Phase 1a (mainly off-road and linking the airport, Parliament and the city centre) are on hold for financial reasons.

Political and financing problems have made for an on-off-on progress, and it was not until July 2007 that a start was made on physically relocating utilities (by Alfred McAlpine, at a cost of £40 million). Early that year, some 300 landowners were informed that their properties would be purchased by the Council. In September 2007 it was announced that Spain's main tram and railway rolling-stock constructors, CAF, were to build twenty-seven cars, these to be articulated low-floor units each 42.8m in length and capable of carrying 250 passengers. The first unit was completed in August 2009. It was also announced, in October 2007, that the tramway would be designed, built and maintained by a consortium of Siemens and Bilfinger Berger UK, to be known as BBS, with the Phase 1a contract valued at £220 million. Track-laying began in 2009.

Errol Tramway

In 1847 the Dundee & Perth Railway (later part of the Caledonian Railway) opened its main line between those two places along the northern bank of the Firth of Tay. In order to serve the district immediately inland its successor, the Dundee & Perth & Aberdeen Railway Junction Co., constructed two short branches to INCHTURE and North Inchmichael; the second of these ran from the village of Errol north-west for some 2 miles and was to have been worked (for passengers at least) as a horse tramway. Earthworks were constructed and some track laid but, in 1850, it was decided that the branches were costing too much and would not both be profitable, so the Errol project was abandoned in favour of the other and the rails were lifted.

Falkirk & District Tramways

Authority: Falkirk and District Tramways Order 1901
Gauge: 4ft
Traction: Overhead electric
Opened: 21 October 1905

Closed: 21 July 1936
System: Branching circle
Length: 7.8 miles
Stock: 19 sd, 18 dd
Livery: Prussian blue & cream to 1929, then red & white
Last Car: ?

This modest Stirlingshire system began life as a circular route linking the town of Falkirk with (in clockwise order) the villages of Camelon, Larbert, Stenhousemuir, Carron and Bainsford and, having added then lost a branch, ended up as a circle once more. Originally to have been built by the Falkirk & District Tramways Co., nothing happened until 24 October 1904, when BP set up the Falkirk Electric Construction Syndicate Ltd to take over the FDT Co., after which construction began.

At first, the line was worked in two halves, owing to problems with the two bridges over the Forth & Clyde Canal, which bisected the tramway's circle, but round working began on 12 March 1906 using the original fleet of open-top double-deckers Nos 1–15 from the Compagnie Générale de Construction of St Denis in France, plus three of a similar type but different design (Nos 16–18) from Brush. (These last three ran top-covered between 1908 and 1913.)

On 3 September 1909 a 1½-mile branch from Falkirk (at the bottom of the circle), running due east to Mary Square, Laurieston, was opened to complete the system (the only one of 4ft gauge in Scotland); like the main line, this was primarily single-track. In 1913 the Company began motor bus operations (a turn of events ignored in its 1914 change of name to the Falkirk & District Tramways Co. Ltd) and, in 1920, was taken over by the BB company, the Fife Tramway, Light & Power Co. (see DUNFERMLINE & DISTRICT). By now the track and stock were in bad shape but the new owner set to, tackling these problems with a relaying and partial-doubling of the circle route, the closing on 20 July 1924 of the Laurieston branch and, in 1929–30, the purchase of ten modern Brush single-deckers (Nos 1–10), after which the double-deckers were gradually scrapped. Four similar cars were added in 1931 (Nos 13–16), followed in 1934 by five single-deckers (number 11, 12 and 17–19) acquired from the DEARNE DISTRICT system in Yorkshire.

Despite the fortunes of the Company being now much improved, in 1935 the Scottish Motor Traction Co. Ltd succeeded in buying up enough of the Company's shares to close the system down the following year, and so clear the way for its own bus services.

 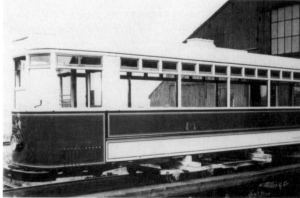

Above left: French-built Falkirk & District No.14 of 1905 negotiating the swing bridge over the Forth & Clyde Canal at Camelon. *(Author's Collection)*

Above right: Works photograph of Falkirk's other No.14, a single-decker supplied by Brush in 1931; its body – seen here resting on temporary trucks prior to final assembly – is now the subject of a long-term restoration project. *(Author's Collection)*

Glasgow Tramway

Authority: Glasgow Street Tramways Act 1870
Gauge: 4ft 7¾in.
Traction: Horse*
Opened: 19 August 1872
Taken over: 1 July 1894*
System: Radial network
Length: 30.21 miles
Stock: c.300 sd & dd
Livery: Menzies tartan & white/cream, later route colour

Glasgow's electric tramway system – the largest in Scotland – began with horse tramways, leased from Glasgow Corporation, operated by the Glasgow Tramway & Omnibus Co. The first route ran from St George's Cross to Eglinton Toll, through the city centre via Cambridge Street, Sauchiehall Street and Renfield Street, and was followed by a succession of other radial routes over the next two decades. It was the second street tramway in Scotland, opening less than a year after the EDINBURGH STREET TRAMWAYS, but from the outset used a gauge slightly narrower than the standard gauge adopted by its rival, thereby setting the gauge for later tramways in the area. (See beginning of this Part.) Glasgow also pioneered the practice of painting its cars in different colours to denote which routes they worked, an idea taken up elsewhere (and retained in Glasgow into the electric era).

Many details of the car fleet are lacking. The first trams, Nos 201–314, were open-top double-deckers built by the Tramway Car & Works of Greenwich and Glasgow during the first four years of the tramway's life. After that (1875–76), Stephenson supplied two single-deckers and fifty-four double-deckers (numbers unknown); following which, many of the earlier cars were rebuilt or replaced by new cars (given vacated numbers) built by the Company at its Crownpoint Works. All these were double-deckers (including some for mule-haulage), except for two single-deck vehicles. Twenty more double-deckers were bought in 1884 and a similar number two years later, from Metropolitan.

In 1893 westward expansion was aided by the leasing of the GLASGOW & IBROX and VALE OF CLYDE tramways from Govan (the latter having been worked during 1873–74 by the Company), but this arrangement was not to last very long. The Company's original lease from Glasgow Corporation had been for twenty-one years, from July 1871, and in 1891 the Corporation obtained authority to modernise its lines and began negotiating with the Company over terms. The latter body was reluctant to let go of the business and the dispute dragged on until the Company relinquished control of its lines in the city on the last day of June 1894 (it continued to operate the Govan lines until 10 November 1896), after which it sold or scrapped its cars rather than sell them to the Corporation, such was the ill-feeling between them.

Glasgow Corporation Tramways

Authority: Glasgow Street Tramways Act 1870
Gauge: 4ft 7¾in.
Traction: Horse, overhead electric
Took over: 1 July 1894
Closed: 4 September 1962
System: Network
Length: 141.37 miles
Stock: 384 dd horse; 22 sd, 1,205 dd electric
Livery: Crimson lake & cream + route colour horse; cadmium yellow & cream + route colour, later orange, green & cream electric
Last Car: No.1174

Following its takeover of the GLASGOW TRAMWAY tracks (see above), the Corporation inaugurated its own service the same day with its own fleet of horse cars, starting with Nos 302–541, double-deckers built by Metropolitan, BM and Midland (1894) and Nos 542–545, specimen double-deckers ordered from the

Above left: Glasgow Corporation horse car No.543 being moved out of the former Museum of Transport premises in Albert Drive at the start of its journey to its new home in Kelvin Hall. *(Glasgow Museums & Art Galleries: Museum of Transport)*

Above right: Glasgow Corporation's unique car 92, a former horse car converted to a motorised single-decker for one-man operation. *(Author's Collection)*

Left: Corporation No.914 of 1900, later to be fully enclosed as the Glasgow fleet was modernised. *(Author's Collection)*

Below left: Preserved Glasgow 'Coronation' 1173 of 1938, representing a new, streamlined design for British pre- and post-Second World War tramcars. *(Glasgow Museums & Art Galleries: Museum of Transport)*

Below right: Glasgow cars in their more natural habitat: a 1907-franked postcard of four double-deckers on the Jamaica Street Bridge. *(Author's Collection)*

North Metropolitan Tramways of London (two cars), Milnes and Falcon. There was also a driver training car (possibly No.301) thought to have come from the VALE OF CLYDE TRAMWAYS. These were joined, between 1894 and 1897, by Nos 546–664 from Metropolitan, BM, Midland and the Corporation's works at Coplawhill. The only other additions to the horse car fleet, in 1896, were Nos 280–300, ex-Glasgow Tramway & Omnibus Co. cars taken over with the Govan lines on 11 November that year.

Electric services began on 13 October 1898 from Mitchell Street, just off Argyle Street in the city centre, northwards up West Nile Street and Parliamentary Road to Springburn Road; the first electric cars, Nos 665–685, were Corporation-built bogie single-deckers nicknamed 'Room and Kitchen' cars on account of their two (smoking and non-smoking) compartments. These were followed by a batch of open-top double-deckers (fitted with top covers after 1904 and later fully enclosed) numbered 686–1000, all constructed between 1898 and 1900 by the Corporation, with the exception of Nos 901–980 which were from Gloucester.

During 1900–01 the Corporation converted a third of its horse cars to electric traction (and given the new fleet numbers 1–120) as they became redundant, in which guise most of them saw service for another twenty years. (No.92 was cut down to a single deck in 1906, four were sold to DUMBARTON in 1909 and one to Luton in 1923.) These were followed, in 1901–02, by more open-toppers (Nos 440–664), again built by the Corporation (and later treated similarly to the first batch).

Meanwhile, the system was continuing to expand – hence the demand for new cars – across the Clyde and beyond the burgh boundaries. After the GTO Co.'s lease of the Govan lines to the west had expired in 1896, these were taken over by the Corporation and electrified; Rutherglen, to the south-east, was reached in 1902, and in 1923 both the PAISLEY and AIDRIE & COATBRIDGE systems were bought to form the western and eastern extremities of the network. To the north-west a connection was made with DUMBARTON, and to the south-east one was made with LANARKSHIRE TRAMWAYS, though in both these cases through-running did not operate.

With the 1923 purchases came sixty-eight Paisley double-deckers, which the Corporation numbered 1001–1038, 1041–1049 and 1052–1072 and fitted with top covers where needed, and fifteen A&C double-deckers, which were renumbered 1073–1087 (all open-toppers except for the last three in the sequence). Additions to the car fleet after that were as follows:

No.1089: Corporation bogie single-decker of 1926
Nos 1090–1140: enclosed double-deckers of 1927–29 by the Corporation, HN, Pickerings and Brush
Nos 1141–1292: Corporation streamlined bogie double-deckers of 1936–40
Nos 6, 1001–1004: Corporation streamlined double-deckers of 1940–43
Nos 1005, 1293–1398: Corporation streamlined bogie double-deckers of 1947–54
Nos 1006–1016, 1018–1038, 1041–1049, 1052–1056: streamlined bogie double-deckers of 1936–37 bought from LIVERPOOL 1953–54

There was also, as would be expected in a system of this size, an extensive fleet of works vehicles, many of which were conversions of former passenger cars.

The Corporation inaugurated its own bus services towards the end of 1924 but, as can be gathered from the above stock list, they posed no threat to the trams for three decades, with only two routes closing in the 1930s: the western portion of the Paisley line through Johnstone to Kilbarchan on 30 April 1932 and, on 25 March 1933, the short branch north from Paisley to Abbotsinch.

New routes continued to be opened, with the system reaching its greatest extent in 1948 when 1,208 cars were in service on a sprawling network of lines – less than 1 mile of which was single-track and over half of which was outside the city boundaries. However, that year saw the closures start again when the south-eastern line to Uddingston was cut back to Broomhouse on 29 August, after which buses and trolleybuses began nibbling away at the other outlying routes. It was not until early 1956, however, that the Corporation decided to abandon those routes left outside its boundaries. The last tram (No.1277) ran in Paisley in the early hours of 12 May 1957 and on 6 February of the following year the Corporation voted to close the system altogether, the last route to go being that from Dalmuir West, eastwards to Auchenshuggle in September 1962.

As might be expected from the size of its car fleet and the late date of its closing, several of Glasgow's trams have been preserved. Horse car 543 is in the city's transport museum, as are electric cars 672 of 1898, 779 of 1900 and Nos 1088, 1089, 1173 and 1392, whilst No.585 of 1901 is in the London Science Museum. Nos 22 of 1922, 812 of 1900 and 1100, 1115, 1282, 1297, plus a works car, are at the National Tramway Museum, Crich and No.1245 is at the East Anglia Transport Museum, Carlton Colville.

Glasgow Garden Festival

The Glasgow Garden Festival of 1988 was held in Govan, on the south bank of the Clyde, on a 120-acre site that had previously been disused dockland. (See **Introduction**.) A single 4ft 8½in. gauge track ran for about ½ mile along the former quayside, linked at each end to a parallel return track a short distance away, so completing an out-and-back-circuit. Four Scottish tramcars were used throughout the duration of the festival (from 28 April to 26 September 1988): GLASGOW CORPORATION 22 and 1297, EDINBURGH CORPORATION 35 and PAISLEY DISTRICT 68, all supplied by the National Tramway Museum at Crich, plus BLACKPOOL 'Boat' open car No.606. (Glasgow 1115 was repainted and kept in readiness as a reserve car at Crich, but was never called upon to go.) Two years later, the track and overhead installation were used for a similar purpose at the GATESHEAD GARDEN FESTIVAL.

Glasgow & Ibrox Tramway

Authority: Glasgow and Ibrox Tramway Act 1877
Gauge: 4ft 7¾in.
Traction: Horse
Opened: 18 July 1879
Closed: 25 May 1891
System: Single line
Length: 1.55 miles
Stock: 1 sd, 3 dd?
Livery: Blue & cream?
Last Car: ?

This short, single-track line, owned by the Glasgow & Ibrox Tramway Co., ran from Whitefield Road in Ibrox, eastwards along Paisley Road to the Paisley Road Toll on the Govan boundary with Glasgow (thus traversing the whole of the burgh of Govan), where it connected with the eastern end of the VALE OF CLYDE line coming in from Fairfield to the north-west. The tramway is thought to have been worked by just four Ashbury reversible cars: double-deckers 1 and 2 of 1879, 3 of 1880 and single-decker 4 (probably constructed between 1880 and 1884), which shared the VoC's depot in Greenhaugh Street.

One of the Scottish tramcars employed at the 1988 Glasgow Garden Festival was Glasgow Corporation No.22 of 1922, seen here at its usual home, the National Tramway Museum at Crich in Derbyshire. *(Author)*

Greenock & Port Glasgow Tramways No.18
of 1901 skirting the mouth of the River
Clyde on its way to the Ashton terminus.
(Author's Collection)

The line was not a commercial success and closed after just twelve years' operation, with the Company going bankrupt. It was not quite dead though because, in 1893, under the Govan Burgh (Tramways) Act of that year, it was purchased by the Govan Commissioners of Police – the local authority of the time – and, along with the VoC line, leased to the GLASGOW TRAMWAY's operating company.

Greenock & Port Glasgow Tramways

Authority: Greenock Street Tramways Act 1871; Vale of Clyde Tramways Act 1871
Gauge: 4ft 7¾in.
Traction: Horse, overhead electric
Opened: 7 July 1873
Closed: 15 July 1929
System: Branching
Length: 7.42 miles
Stock: 25 dd horse?; 7 sd, 39 dd electric
Livery: Red & cream horse?; dark red & white electric
Last Car: No.10

Built on the south bank of the mouth of the Clyde to serve an ancient area of fishing, shipbuilding and allied industries, this line had a somewhat complicated history for so simple a system. The western half of the original single-track horse tramway from Ashton, up Albert Street and through Gourock via Shore Street, Chapel Street and Cardwell Street to the Gourock/Greenock boundary (about 2 miles), was built and owned by the VALE OF CLYDE TRAMWAYS Co., whilst the rest of the line, through Greenock via Eldon Street, Brougham Street, Grey Place, West Blackhall Street, Hamilton Street and Cathcart Street to Rue-End Street (another 2 miles), was promoted and owned by the then local authority, the Greenock Police Board, and leased to the VoCT Co.

Services began over the Greenock section on 7 July 1873, with open-top double-deckers Nos 1–10 supplied by the Tramway Car & Works Co. Ltd of Greenwich and Glasgow, housed off Chapel Street in Gourock. Half the Gourock section opened on 18 July that year (to Princes Pier, served by a short spur), and the final Albert Street stretch along the seafront on 1 November. Another two open-toppers were purchased in 1875 and, during 1878–79, the Company conducted steam locomotive trials on the line, though these were not followed up.

In 1886 an eastwards continuation of the tramway was promoted by what became the Greenock & Port Glasgow Tramways Co., who secured the Greenock & Port Glasgow Tramways Act in 1887 to construct about 2½ miles of line along Main Street and East Hamilton Street, through the district of Ladyburn and so into Port Glasgow by way of the Port Glasgow Road, Ardgowan Street, Shore Street, Scarlow Street and Fore Street. Opened on 29 November 1889, the double-track line was worked by Milnes open-toppers Nos 1–11 as a separate service until 15 May 1893, when the GPGT Co. took over the VoCT Co.'s lease and began operating through to the Gourock boundary. The following year the Gourock Police Commissioners bought out the VoCT Co. and, from 12 February, leased that portion of the line to the GPGT Co. who then operated the whole tramway using its own cars and (probably) six of the former VoC cars (renumbered 12–17). The last three trams acquired, Nos 18–20, were added in 1900 and were presumably double-deckers again.

In 1900 the line was double-tracked throughout (except for the Albert Street section) and electrified by the BET (see Part 6), who had taken control of the Company; the western half reopened on 3 October 1901, with ten Brush double-deckers. (The Princes Pier spur was abandoned.) On 7 November that year the electric cars took over from the horse cars on the Rue-End Street to Port Glasgow half of the tramway and by the end of the year the initial order of thirty Brush bogie open-toppers (Nos 1–30) had arrived; in July 1902 a new depot was opened for them at Ladyburn.

In 1904 six Brush single-deck combination cars (Nos 31–36) were purchased (and rebuilt two years later as open-top double-deckers); in 1906 another three Brush open-toppers were bought (Nos 37–39), followed, in 1908, by UEC No.40, a single-deck demi-car. The last new cars purchased were also from Brush, these being Nos 41–43 in 1911 (top-covered double-deckers) and 44–46 in 1916 (open-top double-deckers). That year also saw the arrival, on loan, of ROTHESAY single-deckers 11 and 12 (renumbered 47 and 48), to which system No.40 was sent three years later when these two cars were returned.

By the end of the 1920s the tramway was running at a steady loss and, with Greenock Corporation refusing to take it over, in 1928 the Company obtained the necessary Act to abandon it and replace the trams with motor buses, which it did the following year.

Hamilton, Motherwell & Wishaw Tramways *see* Lanarkshire Tramways
Ibrox *see* Glasgow & Ibrox

Inchture Tramway

This was a 2-mile branch of the Caledonian Railway built in 1849, like its ill-fated ERROL counterpart immediately to the west, to serve a village on the northern side of the Firth of Tay. The junction with the main Perth–Dundee line was at Inchture station in Perthshire and from there it ran north-west in a straight line beside the road to the village of Inchture itself, where it terminated at the crossroads, known as Crossgates, on the edge of the village. (Later mineral branches from here served a clay pit and brickworks, and carried wagons of horse manure from Dundee for local farmers.)

The line was a single track, with one passing loop, very lightly laid with wrought-iron rails, and was originally constructed by the Dundee & Perth & Aberdeen Railway Junction Co. (from 1863 the Scottish Central Railway and from 1865 part of the CR); its closest relative in the British Isles was the Fintona Branch in Ireland (see Volume 2). Goods trains were steam-hauled, but passenger services were provided by an old horse-drawn four-wheeled coach, replaced in 1895 by a CR-built closed single-deck four-wheeled tramcar numbered 1 and painted CR crimson lake and white. The car shed was what would otherwise have been the end cottage in a short terrace.

The line was closed as a wartime measure in 1916 (possibly 31 December) and the rails lifted for use in France (though the ship carrying them is reputed to have been sunk). The car shed was converted into a cottage to match its neighbours; the fate of its former occupant is unknown.

The Inchture Tramway's second and splendid last passenger car, No.1 of 1895, built especially for the line by the Caledonian Railway. It is standing here outside its tiny depot, now the end house in the terrace. *(Author's Collection)*

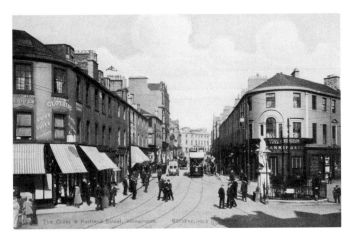

Kilmarnock Corporation No.10 in Portland Street, seen from the Cross, the focal point of the system where the Hurlford branch (off to the right) met the main line. *(Author's Collection)*

Kilmarnock Corporation Tramways

Authority: Kilmarnock Corporation Act 1904
Gauge: 4ft 8½in.
Traction: Overhead electric
Opened: 10 December 1904
Closed: 3 May 1926
System: Branching
Length: 4.24 miles
Stock: 14 dd
Livery: Olive green & cream
Last Car: ?

Hard on the heels of Kilmarnock Town Council setting up its own electricity and gas supply undertakings, came its proposals to operate its own trams; these were to be electrically powered from the start, there being no existing horse tramways to take over and modernise.

As built, in plan form the system resembled a letter T laid on its side with a north–south main line from the burgh boundary at Beansburn, running straight down through the town, to its southern boundary at Riccarton. The line was single-track throughout, except for a ½-mile section from the railway station southwards, through the town centre, to the Kings Street church near Fowlds Street. (This double track was extended another ¼ mile, in 1905, as far as the depot in Greenholm Street.) The one single-track branch ran for 1¾ miles, from the Cross in the town centre (close to the Tramways Office), eastwards along the London Road and through the village of Crookedholm to Hurlford Cross.

Original stock comprised HN open-toppers Nos 1–11, which were joined in 1905 by one similar car (No.12) and two top-covered cars (Nos 13 and 14), all from HN again.

Despite a promising start, very soon after the system's opening it became apparent that it was not going to be a roaring financial success, probably due to a combination of poor management, Council policies and a fluctuating employment situation in this industrial northern Ayrshire town (and hence erratic revenues); the situation was not improved by constant permanent way problems and the general neglect occasioned by the First World War. After the war, an easy solution to the tramway's problems was offered by the increasingly reliable motor bus and, in 1923, the Council decided to replace the Hurlford route (the part of the system in worst shape) with a bus service and the last cars ran on 15 December of the following year, the replacement buses introduced that same afternoon, establishing Kilmarnock as the first Scottish local authority to replace its own electric trams with such vehicles.

The remaining line's end came by default when the tramway staff joined the 1926 General Strike and services were brought to an abrupt halt. The Council decided not to resume them and so one of Britain's later-built electric tramways of the period became one of its earlier closures.

Kirkcaldy No.7 of 1902 in the narrow, eastern end of the town's High Street. *(Author's Collection)*

Kirkaldy Corporation Tramways

Authority: Kirkcaldy Corporation and Tramways Act 1899
Gauge: 3ft 6in.
Traction: Overhead electric
Opened: 28 February 1903
Closed: 15 May 1931
System: Branching circle
Length: 6.11 miles
Stock: 26 dd
Livery: Dark olive/bronze-green & cream
Last Car: ?

The first section of the municipally owned tramways in Kirkcaldy, on the northern shore of the Firth of Forth, was the single-track 'Lower Route' from the Turret Tavern in Gallatown along Rosslyn Street, St Clair Street, Nether Street, the Path, the High Street and Links Street to the latter's junction with Pratt Street in West Bridge. This was followed on 28 September 1903 by the double-track 'Upper Route': this branched off St Clair Road westwards up Junction Road by the railway station, to loop through the back of the town before eventually rejoining the Lower Route where Whytescauseway met the High Street (with a short branch south to the Beveridge Park Gates just before this). To cope with the increased traffic the new lines generated, another twelve Milnes open-top double-deckers (Nos 11–22) were bought in 1903–04 to add to the original fleet of ten similar cars. The depot was in Oswald Road, just off Rosslyn Street by the Gallatown terminus. From 27 September 1906 through cars began running to the railway station via the Upper Route from Leven, at the far end of the WEMYSS line (though when the Kirkcaldy cars were used as opposed to the Wemyss single-deckers, passengers were not permitted to ride on the upper decks in order to lower the cars' centre of gravity as a safety precaution on the Wemyss tramway's more exposed, reserved track).

On 26 February 1911 a 1-mile branch north-east to the parish church in Dysart – a separate burgh until 1930 – was opened to complete the system; this left the Lower Route at the junction of St Clair Street and Nether Street, following the Dysart Road. Four HN open-toppers were added to the fleet in 1914 and given the numbers 23–26; these were the last to be bought, for burgeoning bus competition after the First World War effectively killed the tramway. When the end came, eight of the cars (including Nos 23–26) were acquired by Wemyss, but only lasted there a matter of months before that system too closed down.

Lanarkshire Tramways

Authority: Hamilton Motherwell and Wishaw Tramways Act 1900
Gauge: 4ft 7¾in.
Traction: Overhead electric
Opened: 22 July 1903
Closed: 14 February 1931

System: Branching circle
Length: 28.43 miles
Stock: 92 dd
Livery: Briefly light blue & cream, then green & cream
Last Car: No.86

Situated immediately to the south-east of Glasgow, the Lanarkshire system was built up over the years before the First World War to serve the towns of this industrial area and link them to the GLASGOW network. The first stretch to be opened ran from Low Blantyre eastwards through Hamilton and Motherwell, to Wishaw, and was promoted by the Hamilton, Motherwell & Wishaw Tramways Co., which, in 1903, changed its name to the more succinct Lanarkshire Tramways Co. On 15 July 1905 a 1-mile branch from Hamilton Old Cross was opened to Ferniegair station on the Caledonian Railway; this was extended on 23 July a further 3 miles to Larkhill.

On 20 January 1907 a westwards extension from Blantyre to Cambuslang was opened, providing the envisaged physical connection with the Glasgow tramways, though through-running never took place. The next addition to the system came on 7 August 1908, when a short line was opened from Motherwell Cross to the burgh boundary at Coursington Bridge; at the same time, a short branch was opened from Hamilton to the burgh boundary at Bothwell Road, by the racecourse. This latter line was extended to Uddington Cross in June 1909, the same time as the original line was extended another two miles to Newmains. In August 1911 the Coursington Bridge line was extended a further 1½ miles to New Stevenston. (All lines were single-track, though a limited track-doubling programme in the Motherwell and Hamilton areas had been embarked upon.)

Above: Lanarkshire Tramways No.28 of 1904 in Cadzow Street, Hamilton, one of the focal points of the system. *(Author's Collection)*

Above right: Restored Lanarkshire Tramways No.53 of 1908 at the Summerlee Heritage Park, Coatbridge. *(David Peace, Summerlee Heritage Museum)*

Right: Lanarkshire was also home to the firm of Hurst, Nelson & Co. Ltd (1880–1960). Although its principal business was the manufacture of railway wagons, the company established itself as an important British tramcar builder.

THE MANUAL OF ELECTRICAL UNDERTAKINGS

Electric Bogie Car with Top Cover.

HURST, NELSON, & CO. Ltd.,
.. BUILDERS OF ..

RAILWAY CARRIAGES, WAGONS, ELECTRIC CARS,
OMNIBUS BODIES, and LIGHT RAILWAY ROLLING
STOCK OF EVERY DESCRIPTION.

Makers of WHEELS AND AXLES, RAILWAY PLANT, PRESSED STEEL AND SMITHWORK,
IRON AND BRASS CASTINGS, also ALL CLASSES OF TRAMCAR TRUCKS.

The Glasgow Rolling Stock & Plant Works,
MOTHERWELL.

BRANCH WORKS-
CHATSWORTH WAGON WORKS, near CHESTERFIELD.
BRIDGEND WAGON WORKS, BRIDGEND, GLAMORGANSHIRE.

Glasgow Office: *Manchester Office:* *London Office:*
46 WEST NILE STREET. NORTHERN ASSURANCE BDGS., 14 LEADENHALL STREET,
ALBERT SQUARE. E.C.

"Standard" Solid Forged Frame Truck.

As some 7 miles of the various authorised lines had still not been constructed, Lanark County Council decided to intervene, and in 1912 obtained powers to link New Stevenston via Mossend and Bellshill (opened September 1913) with Uddingston (opened 11 February 1914); a 1½-mile branch from Mossend, doubling back to Holytown (opened 24 October 1913), completed the system. These lines (6.11 miles in total) were leased to the LT Co., which could now operate a grand circular route linking Motherwell, Hamilton, Bellshill, Uddingston and Bothwell, in addition to the main Cambuslang–Newmains line and the Larkhill and Holytown branches.

In May 1921 the leased County Council lines were purchased for £60,981 by the Company, but by now the writing was on the wall for the tramway as regards the growing bus competition – not least from the Company's own fleet. The first parts of the system to close were the Hamilton–Larkhill and Hamilton–Uddingston lines (both officially closed on 14 September 1928, though the latter section remained in use for race-day traffic), followed on 6 October 1930 by the whole of the Newmains–Motherwell–Hamilton–Cambuslang main line, leaving the last remnants to close the following year, replaced by Company buses. (On 1 October 1930 the Company had changed its name to the Lanarkshire Traction Co.)

As would be expected, the Lanarkshire fleet grew to keep pace with the expanding system, the first seventy-six cars all being open-top double-deckers numbered as follows: Nos 1–25 (BEC 1903), 26–35 (Brush 1904), 36–40 (Brush 1905), 41–46 (Brush 1906), 47–53 (UEC 1908), 54–60 (Brush 1909), 61–64 (Brush 1911) and 65–76 (Brush 1913). In 1923 the Company built a prototype low-level, top-covered car (No.77) and two years later HN supplied twelve similar vehicles (Nos 78–89); these were joined that same year by three more built by the Company, these taking the numbers 45, 56 and 88 from withdrawn vehicles. By the time of closure, only sixteen cars survived (or were considered fit enough) to be put up for sale – but there were no takers for them. One tram has been saved for preservation: No.53 of 1908, which can be seen operating at the Summerlee Heritage Park at COATBRIDGE.

Leith Corporation Tramways

Authority: Leith Corporation Tramways Order 1904
Gauge: 4ft 8½in.
Traction: Horse, overhead electric
Took over: 23 October 1904
Taken over: 20 November 1920
System: Network
Length: 9.09 miles
Stock: 29 horse; 37 dd electric
Livery: ? horse; Munich lake & white electric

After taking over part of the EDINBURGH STREET TRAMWAYS in 1904, Leith Corporation set about reconstructing and extending the tramways for electric working. Track-laying began early in 1905, on a new route from Pilrig, along Pilrig Street (and the burgh boundary) to Bonnington, followed by the conversion of the rest of the system. The first electric services began on 18 August that year, on the Pilrig–Foot of Leith Walk–Stanley Road route, with the bulk of the system reopening on 16 September. The official inauguration took place on 3 November, the day after the Seafield Place horse services ended; this was the last route to be worked by the last surviving horse cars (which had operated services as well as possible during the reconstruction of each route). Electric services to Seafield Place began on 21 November, the new system comprising the old horse routes (now double-tracked), plus the Pilrig Street line (also double).

Thirty-six open-top cars were bought for the opening of the electric tramways: Nos 1–15 and 31–33 were from BTH and Nos 16–30 and 34–36 from Brush. (Many of these were later top-covered.) The only other passenger car added to the fleet was No.37, which had started life as BTH single-decker 61, used for driver training before the opening then fitted with an open upper deck in 1906 (and renumbered) for passenger use. The shed for the new cars was constructed on the site of the former horse depot.

Leith Corporation No.25 of 1904 in Main Street, Leith, probably soon after the system's electrification – when the trams had almost sole possession of the roads at many times of the day. *(Author's Collection)*

The system's only extensions came in 1909 when, under the provisions of the Leith Burgh Act of 1908, another 1.9 miles of double-track were laid. The first section opened (11 May) ran westwards from Newhaven, along the coastal St Arbank Road and Lower Granton Road, to Granton; the second section (opened 2 July) ran south from here to Goldenacre via Granton Road, whilst the third (opened 3 August) ran eastwards along Ferry Road (and past the EDINBURGH & DISTRICT's terminus in Inverleith Row) to Bonnington Terrace, thus completing a large circular route.

Following the 1920 local government absorption of Leith by its larger neighbour, control of the system passed to EDINBURGH CORPORATION TRAMWAYS and the cars were renumbered 231–267 (Leith 1–37 respectively) in that fleet.

Musselburgh & District Tramway

Authority: Portobello and Musselburgh Tramways Order 1900
Gauge: 4ft 8½in.
Traction: Overhead electric
Opened: 12 December 1904
Closed: 25 February 1928*
System: Single line
Length: 6.53 miles
Stock: 6 sd, 16 dd
Livery: Red & ivory to 1923, then dark & light green
Last Car: ?

Six miles east of Edinburgh, on the southern shore of the Firth of Forth, lies the town of Musselburgh. Here, at the end of the nineteenth century, the idea of a tramway link to the Scottish capital was promoted, but it was not until 1903 (and after at least one false start) that any physical progress was made. The tramway was built by the NEC and, when opened, was a double-track line from the EDINBURGH system's easterly terminus at Joppa, just beyond Portobello, to Bridge Street (roughly halfway), then single-track along the High Street, past the Town Hall and depot, to the terminus at Levenhall, a distance of some 3 miles in all.

In August 1905 another company was formed to operate the line, the Musselburgh & District Electric Light & Traction Co. Ltd, and extensions were planned: on 5 August 1909 the single-track line was extended eastwards to Tranent Road in Cockenzie, and on 31 December to Port Seton, its final terminus.

The original car fleet was made up of ten open-top double-deckers from BEC (Nos 1–10), with four closed-top cars (Nos 11–14) added in 1905 from Brush. Two similar cars (Nos 15 and 16) were purchased in 1909 to meet the demands of the Port Seton extension.

During the First World War the stock suffered badly from lack of maintenance – and accidents – and in 1918 three single-deckers (Nos 17–19) were acquired from SHEFFIELD.

On 24 June 1923 through-running from Edinburgh commenced, that corporation's Portobello route having been electrified from cable operation, and a further three single-deckers (Nos 20–22) were purchased from Sheffield. The line was not a financial success, though, and it closed to the general public

Two Musselburgh & District
double-deckers in the High Street
passing loop, with No.6 of 1904 closest
to the camera on this 1906-franked
card. *(Author's Collection)*

in February 1928, although it is believed that miners' specials continued to run through to Prestongrange Colliery, midway along the line, for another month or so; thereafter, operation of the Joppa–Levenhall section was taken over by Edinburgh Corporation from 1 March. However, the line itself was not acquired until 1932, when ownership was assumed under the Edinburgh Corporation Act of that year.

Paisley Tramways

Authority: Paisley Tramways Order 1885
Gauge: 4ft 7¾in.
Traction: Horse
Opened: 30 December 1885
Taken over: 21 November 1903
System: Single line
Length: 2.44 miles
Stock: 4 sd. 7 dd
Livery: Red & white

Some 7 miles west of Glasgow, on the south bank of the River Clyde, the Renfrewshire town of Paisley grew greatly during the nineteenth century, notably because of the weaving industry centred there, and during the 1870s proposals were made for a local tramway. None were successful, however, until 1885, when the Paisley Tramways Co. Ltd (incorporated 24 December 1884) was empowered to build a short line through the town. Construction began in December 1885, with the first mile of route, from Garthland Place in the east to Broomlands in the west, via the High Street and Paisley Cross, opening later that month.

On 20 April 1886 extensions were opened at both ends of the line: east to Greenlaw Road at the end of Garthland Street, and west to Thomas Street, with the final extension, from Greenlaw Road along Williamburgh to Hawkhead Road (East Toll), opening on 29 October 1888 to complete the single-track line.

Services began with three open-top double-deckers licensed by Paisley Town Council as Nos 35–37, joined shortly after by two more (probably Nos 38 and 39), maker unknown. They were followed, in 1887, by Nos 47 and 48, a pair of single-deckers built by the Glasgow Tramway & Omnibus Co. Ltd; that same year one of the double-deckers was rebuilt as an experimental battery car by a local mill owner, James Gibson, but the experiment was discontinued some five months later (though the vehicle was never apparently returned to the horse car fleet). The depot was in Incle Street by the original Garthland Place terminus.

Initially successful, the line soon began to make a loss as the novelty of the (short and slow) trips wore off – hence the purchase of the lighter single-deckers, two more of which (probably numbered 36 and 37) were bought in 1890; four years later, two of the double-deckers were hired to GLASGOW CORPORATION for driver training on its new system and then sold to it, leaving just two double-deckers (which had been rebuilt in 1893, presumably to make them lighter) at Paisley. The only other cars added to the fleet were ex-GC double-deckers 360 and 630, bought in 1901, probably as replacements for older cars.

At the end of the 1890s the BET tried to acquire the line, but no agreement could be reached, and on 17 September 1903 the tramway was bought for £15,797 by William M. Murphy, an Irish contractor with numerous tramway interests, including chairmanship of the Dublin United Tramways, with the Company being wound up two months later. Murphy had already obtained the necessary powers to electrify the tramway (see below) and began reconstruction work at the eastern end of the line, the horse car service being cut back accordingly over the next two months.

Paisley District Tramways

Authority: Paisley District Tramways Act 1901
Gauge: 4ft 7¾in.
Traction: Overhead electric
Opened: 13 June 1904
Taken over: 1 August 1923
System: Radial
Length: 18.25 miles
Stock: 1 sd*, 76 dd
Livery: Scarlet & cream

Although Paisley's horse car service ceased in November 1903 (see above), electric services over the rebuilt system did not begin for another six months, though on 26 November 1903 GLASGOW CORPORATION began operating electric cars over its new route from Crookston to Hawkhead Road, the last ½ mile of which was actually inside the town boundary. Murphy's first route was from Paisley Cross to Hawkhead Road, where an end-on connection was made with the GC line, both being double-track. After that expansion was rapid, with a double-track line over the rest of the old horse route extended westwards through Fergulie Mills, past Elderslie Depot and on to Houston Square at the end of Johnstone High Street opening on 12 July, a single-track branch south from the Cross to Potterhill following on 29 July, and a double-track line north-east to Renfrew on 22 September, terminating at Renfrew Ferry on the Clyde. A second depot was built midway along this 3-mile route, at Newmains Road off the Paisley Road. The last of these early routes, opened on 9 November, was a mirror image of the Potterhill line, running north for 1½ miles up Love Street and Inchinnan Road to Abbotsinch.

The tramway's first cars, Nos 1–39, were open-toppers from the BEC works in Manchester – another of Murphy's financial interests – and were followed in 1905 by Nos 40–49, ten similar vehicles. That same year saw the through-running of GC cars to the Cross (from 20 March), a service which reached its apogee that spring holiday (24 April), when the Glasgow public houses were forced to remain closed and so cars were run at the rate of one a minute to its 'wet' neighbour!

On 4 July 1906 a 1-mile extension westwards from Johnstone to the beauty spot village of Kilbarchan was opened, together with a 2-mile southwards extension from Potterhill, through the residential areas of Glenfield and Cross Stobs, to Barrhead; both lines were single-track. The latter route was extended eastwards on 31 December 1910 through Parkhouse and from there, on reserved sleepered track,

Paisley District No.40 of 1905 in Houston Square at the end of Johnstone High Street, apparently before the line was extended (in 1906) left of picture to Kilbarchan. (*Author's Collection*)

to Spiersbridge, where it met (but did not connect with) Glasgow's Rouken Glen route. This last, double-track line completed the Paisley system (apart from a 300yd extension at Kilbarchan on 25 June 1913 to take the tramway into the village).

In 1907 a HN open-topper was bought and numbered 52 (Nos 50 and 51 being works cars) and was followed in 1911 by Nos 53–58, top-covered cars from the same firm. These did not prove satisfactory, however, and were sold to DUNDEE CITY TRAMWAYS just three years later. In 1912 Brush supplied open-toppers 59–62, and 53–58 in 1915; the last double-deckers acquired were HN 63–67 of 1916 and 68–72 of 1920 (again top-covered vehicles). The tramway's only single-decker was ex-SHEFFIELD CORPORATION 202, which was purchased, re-gauged and sent to Paisley in 1920, though it is not certain if it ever actually saw service there. At least two Paisley cars are currently undergoing restoration, though the only survivor so far brought back to operational condition is No.68 of 1920, now running (after re-gauging to standard gauge) at the National Tramway Museum, Crich.

In 1921 Glasgow Corporation began to negotiate the purchase of the system, the two sides agreeing on 21 June 1922 to a price of £25,000 to take effect the year following.

Perth & District Tramways
Authority: Perth and District Tramways Order 1892
Gauge: 3ft 6in.
Traction: Horse*
Opened: 17 September 1895
Taken over: 7 October 1903
System: Branching
Length: 4.26 miles
Stock: 1 sd, 8 dd
Livery: Dark crimson & cream to 1898, then dark red-brown & yellow

The purpose of this tramway system was to link the town of Perth, on the west bank of the River Tay, with the dormitory village of Scone some 3 miles to the north-east. It was promoted by the Perth & District Tramways Co. Ltd which, on 8 May 1894, bought out the Scone & Perth Omnibus Co. before starting work on the tramway. Construction was by Alex Brunton & Sons of Inverkeithing, the result being a single-track line, commencing in Glasgow Road near Rose Crescent, running eastwards through Perth via York Place (near the Caledonian Railway's Perth General station), County Place, the High Street and George Street before crossing the river on the Perth Bridge to the district of Bridgend. From here it followed Strathmore Street and the Perth Road to Scone, terminating at the depot there. The first cars were open-top double-deckers 1–4 and single-decker 5, all from BM.

In 1897 authority was obtained for extending the line, first with a ½-mile branch south from County Place down King Street, Kings Place and St Leonard's Bank to terminate in Priory Place, Craigie. (This line crossed the railway at the other end of the station to the first route.) The second extension was

Two Perth & District double-deckers – believed to be Nos 8 and 9 – in Perth High Street, on the last day of Corporation horse car services. *(Author's Collection)*

down Glasgow Road from the former terminus for another ½ mile to Cherrybank. The new lines opened in April and December 1898 respectively and the car fleet increased to cope by the addition of new double-deckers Nos 6–9 (possibly the last two were second-hand vehicles). It is believed that, for a short time, mules were used on the line, a rare event on a British tramway. (See also the GLASGOW TRAMWAY.)

Proposals for the electrification of the system came at the end of the century, but before the Company could put these into effect it sold the line to the Town Council for £21,800 and the cars ran under their new ownership from 7 October 1903 as Perth Corporation Tramways (see below).

Perth Corporation Tramways

Authority: Perth Corporation (Tramways) Order 1903
Gauge: 3ft 6in.
Traction: Horse/overhead electric
Took over: 7 October 1903
Closed: 19 January 1929
System: Branching
Length: 5.02 miles
Stock: 1 sd, 8 dd horse; 12 dd electric
Livery: Lake & cream and olive green & cream*
Last Car: ?

The Perth horse line was electrified under the Corporation's Order of 1904 – the same year that saw (unsuccessful) trials with a petrol tram, a converted double-deck horse car from the Stirling Motor Construction Co. Ltd of Granton, Edinburgh. The electric trams took over during the afternoon of 31 October 1905, covering the whole system (which now included a ½-mile branch from the High Street north along Dunkeld Road), all routes still being largely single-track.

Twelve open-top double-deckers were supplied by HN: Nos 1–9 were painted lake and cream, whilst Nos 10–12 were olive green and cream – presumably for identification purposes as they were 3in. lower to enable them to work under a railway bridge on the Craigie route. (When this King Street bridge was raised in 1907 all cars could work the line and the green livery disappeared.) Horse car No.5 was converted into a water car and the others scrapped or used as passenger shelters, whilst the old depot was rebuilt for the new trams.

As elsewhere, the First World War saw neglect of the track and other maintenance and during the following decade the Corporation took the decision to replace the trams with buses. When, in 1927, the Perth General Omnibus Co. began running buses over the main tram route the Corporation's hand was forced and, in an ironic reversal of the events of the 1890s, on 3 April 1928 it bought out the PGO Co. in order to operate the buses itself. By September that year only two trams were fit to run and they staggered on – often empty – until early the following year.

Port Glasgow *see* Greenock & Port Glasgow

Rothesay Tramways (1)

Authority: Rothesay Tramways Order 1880
Gauge: 4ft/3ft 6in.
Traction: Horse
Opened: 1 June 1882*
Closed: 19 August 1902?
System: Single line
Length: 2.37 miles
Stock: 19 sd
Livery: Maroon & cream
Last Car: ?

The only island tramway in Scotland, the single-line Rothesay tramway, on the popular holiday resort island of Bute in the Firth of Clyde, served the town's residents and visitors alike for some seventy years. It began life as a horse tramway, promoted and operated by the Rothesay Tramways Co. Ltd (registered in Edinburgh on 25 November 1879), running from Guildford Square, close to the pier in Rothesay, the island's principal settlement, northwards beside Rothesay Bay and then westwards along Ardbeg Road, past Pointhouse Depot to Port Bannatyne, a total distance of a little over 2 miles, of which the first half was double-tracked.

Construction began in early 1882 and the line was ready by June; the public opening preceded the obligatory BoT inspection, resulting in its closure until 10 June. The original eight toastracks with canvas roofs (Nos 1–8) and four closed single-deck saloons (Nos 9–12) were all built by the Saville Street Foundry & Engineering Co. Ltd of Sheffield and were augmented, at the end of July, by two roofed toastracks (Nos 13 and 14) constructed by a local joiner, James McBride. In 1891 two more toastracks (Nos 15 and 16) were supplied by William Lauder of Rothesay and the same builder probably produced the tramway's final three similar cars: Nos 17 and 18 in 1894, and No.19 three years later. By then thoughts of electrification were in the air and, following repeated overtures, the Company sold out to the BET in 1901, after obtaining an Order for the reconstruction; on 2 March 1902 the tramway was closed in preparation for this, the work being carried out by DK. Ten of the cars were, however, re-gauged and put back into service on the relaid, narrower gauge line on 17 May and it is thought a horse service was operated until the electric cars began running (see below).

Rothesay Tramways (2)

Authority: Rothesay Tramways Order 1900
Gauge: 3ft 6in.
Traction: Overhead electric
Opened: 19 August 1902
Closed: 30 September 1936
System: Single line
Length: 4.87 miles
Stock: 24 sd
Livery: Maroon & cream to 1932, then blue & white
Last Car: No.14 (service) and No.9 (official)

With the horse tramway closed (see above), the rails were lifted and sold prior to new track being laid to the more common electric tramway gauge of 3ft 6in.; this work was done by early June 1902 and the whole line was ready for reopening that August. The official inauguration was on 13 August, again before the BoT inspection, the consequence of which was that public services could not commence for another week.

In 1905 a 2½-mile extension on a reserved right of way across the island, from the old tramway terminus at Port Bannatyne to Ettrick Bay on the west coast, was constructed, opening on 13 July that year to complete the system. On 1 January 1914 control of the line passed to the Scottish General Transport Co. (incorporated 24 September 1913), a subsidiary of the BET. The beginning of the end came in the 1920s when motor bus operators began to compete with the tramway; in 1925 the Company began operating its own three charabancs between Port Bannatyne and Port Ettrick; consequently, as they proved profitable, the writing was on the wall for the trams. On 6 November 1931 the line was acquired by the Scottish Motor Traction Group, a concern moving into bus operation in a big way, and on 1 June 1932 the Company name was changed to the Western Scottish Motor Traction Co. Ltd. Four years later the tramway closed for good.

The tramway's first cars were roofed toastracks 1–10 and single-deck combination saloons 11–15, all from ERTCW. One of these – usually No.14 – worked as an illuminated car during the late summer Rothesay illuminations season. Five roofed toastracks (Nos 16–20) were bought from Brush in 1903 to complete the original fleet. In 1916 the bodies of Nos 11 and 12 were sent to GREENOCK & PORT GLASGOW to help cope with the increased traffic generated by the war effort there, and three years later the Company equipped the freed trucks with two locally-built open toastrack bodies (which took

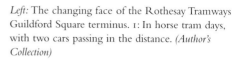

Left: The changing face of the Rothesay Tramways Guildford Square terminus. 1: In horse tram days, with two cars passing in the distance. *(Author's Collection)*

Below left: 2: With cross-bench electric car No.16, one of the 1903 Brush purchases, loading for its next journey across the island. *(Author's Collection)*

Below right: An unidentified Stirling & Bridge of Allan Tramways toastrack, with the road virtually to itself, on a 1907-franked postcard. *(Author's Collection)*

the old car numbers). In return, Greenock sent Rothesay a 1908 UEC demi-car which, with its truck re-gauged, ran as No.21 until 1920, when it was re-bodied as an open toastrack numbered 22 – the seaside nature of the line being reflected in the predominance of open cars. Whilst the official Last Car was No.9, the final service was worked by No.14, illuminated and decorated for the last time.

Stirling & Bridge of Allan Tramways

Authority: Stirling and Bridge of Allan Tramways Order 1872
Gauge: 4ft 8½in.
Traction: Horse, petrol
Opened: 27 July 1874
Closed: 20 May 1920
System: Single line
Length: 4.35 miles
Stock: 8 sd, 11 dd horse?; 1 dd petrol
Livery: Various, finally red-brown & cream
Last Car: No.22

The purpose behind the construction of this tramway, as indicated by its name, was to link the town of Stirling, on the River Forth, with the village of Bridge of Allan, some 3 miles to the north, which had developed during the first half of the nineteenth century as a spa. Although the Caledonian Railway already linked the two places, at least two groups of promoters believed the potential traffic for a tramway was there and in 1872 an Order was obtained for a simple single-track line.

Construction, by the Stirling & Bridge of Allan Tramways Co. Ltd, began in May 1874 and was completed in time for the annual Strathallan Games held every August in Bridge of Allan. The 3¼-mile line ran south-east from that village for 1½ miles until it approached the hamlet of Causewayhead, where it swung south-westwards to pass the NBR's station on the Alloa line and the tramway depot. It then paralleled the railway until it reached the Forth, which it crossed after passing under the aforementioned CR line, to run south through the centre of Stirling to terminate on Port Street at the junction with Melville Terrace (though the last 100yd or so, from the junction of King Street with Port Street, were only used when specials were run in connection with Public Hall functions).

Precise details of the tramway's car fleet (and their numbers) are tantalisingly sketchy. Originally there were two double-deckers (possibly Nos 1 and 2) and a single-deck saloon (possibly No.3), all supplied by the Tramway Car & Works Co. Ltd of Glasgow. Later, during 1874, the single-decker was rebuilt as a double-decker and all three cars ran until 1877, when the depot caught fire and one was destroyed, along with the Company's horse bus. Replacements for both were bought, the new double-decker (possibly No.1) coming from an unknown source in Glasgow. The following year a Dickinson double-deck steam car was tested on the line, but permission was granted for one day of public service trial only (during the Strathallan Games).

In 1885 three open toastracks (Nos 4–6) were purchased cheaply from somewhere in England – they were possibly an unfinished order for the aborted Ramsgate & Margate tramway (see Volume 1) – and two years later a reversible-body double-decker was acquired, possibly ex-EDINBURGH & DISTRICT, followed over the next eighteen years by a succession of second-hand vehicles from other Scottish systems (including GLASGOW and LEITH) as they abandoned horse-haulage.

In 1897 authority was obtained for a southwards extension of just over a mile to Weaver Row in the village of St Ninians; this opened on 29 January 1898 and was normally worked from King Street as a separate route. As elsewhere, by this time prospects of electrification were in the air, but the three main interested parties – the BET, the NEC and Stirling Council – all backed out at the last minute.

Modernisation, when it came, took the form of double-deck car No.22, an ex-Edinburgh & District double-decker acquired in 1902 and rebuilt in 1913, with a 25hp petrol engine and mechanical drive, by the Lanarkshire Motor Co. Ltd of Glasgow. It began regular duty on 9 December that year and gave sterling service – mainly on the St Ninians route – until the very last day of the tramway. By the end of the First World War there were only three cars (No.22 and ex-Leith double-deckers Nos 47 and 48) in everyday use. In November 1919 the Company put a pair of motor buses into service, and that was the end of the tramway. The last horse car ran on 5 February 1920, with the petrol car soldiering on for another three months until it too was displaced by the buses (and, more importantly, larger competing operators).

Strabathie & Blackdog Light Railway *see* Aberdeen District Tramways
Summerlee Heritage Park *see* Coatbridge: Summerlee Heritage Park

Vale of Clyde Tramways
Authority: Vale of Clyde Tramways Act 1871
Gauge: 4ft 7¾in.
Traction: Horse/steam
Opened: 1 January 1873
Taken over: 10 July 1893
System: Single line
Length: 2.48 miles
Stock: 14 dd horse*; 20 locos, 22 dd steam
Livery: Brown & cream?

The Vale of Clyde Tramways Co. operated two widely separated systems in the region west of Glasgow. Both were opened in 1873, the first being in Govan, midway between Glasgow and Paisley, and the second at Gourock on the Firth of Clyde (see GREENOCK & PORT GLASGOW TRAMWAYS). The first line was a horse-worked single-track tramway that ran for nearly 2½ miles from the Park

The Last Car to Govan

Another 'Cynicus' last car of the day postcard (see p.10), this time overprinted for Govan. *(Author's Collection)*

House Toll House on Paisley Road at the Glasgow/Govan boundary, north-west along the Govan Road beside the Clyde dockyards to Linthouse Ship Yard in Fairfield. This was worked by open-top cars from a batch Nos 1–12 built by Starbuck and the Tramway Car & Works Co. Ltd of Greenwich and Glasgow, with the operation of the line leased until 1 January 1874 to the Glasgow Tramway & Omnibus Co. (and through-working to St Vincent Place in the centre of that city). The depot was in Greenhaugh Street, off the Govan Road immediately south of Govan Cross. Most likely not all the Company's cars worked the Govan tramway, some of them being used on the GPG line as well.

In 1874 two more cars (Nos 13 and 14) were bought to complete the horse car fleet for in 1876, under the provisions of the Vale of Clyde Tramways Act of that year, mechanical traction was authorised to facilitate the working of railway wagons (hitherto horse-hauled) from Govan railway sidings to the Farfield Shipbuilding & Engineering Co. Ltd's dockside premises. Between 1877 and 1880 Hughes tramway locomotives Nos 1–10 were bought to pull open-top double-deck trailers Nos 1–12. After the arrival of the first of these, three of the horse cars were sold and the remainder were transferred to Gourock. Half of the original steam trailers were, in turn, sold in 1881 and eight Metropolitan double-deck bogie cars bought and numbered 1–8, followed by similar vehicles 9 and 10 two years later. During that same period a new batch of locos (Nos 1–9) were bought from Kitsons, to be joined in 1892 by another Kitson, No.10, purchased from the Cavehill & Whitewell Tramway in Ireland.

In 1893 the line was bought for £60,000 by the Govan local authority, the Commissioners of Police, under the Govan Burgh (Tramways) Act of that year and leased to the Glasgow Tramway & Omnibus Co. (see GLASGOW TRAMWAY).

Wemyss & District Tramways
Authority: Wemyss Tramways Order 1905
Gauge: 3ft 6in.
Traction: Overhead electric
Opened: 25 August 1906
Closed: 30 January 1932
System: Single line
Length: 7.45 miles
Stock: 29 sd
Livery: Wemyss yellow (mustard) to 1913, then maroon & cream
Last Car: ?

The Wemyss tramway came into being as a direct result of the early success of the KIRKCALDY system. It was promoted and built by Randolph G.E. Wemyss, the local laird, and ran, for the most part, across his own estates from Gallatown in Kirkcaldy, eastwards and roughly parallel to the coast, through

[5 EDW. 7.]   *Wemyss Tramways Order Confirmation*   [Ch. cxci.]
Act, 1905.

CHAPTER cxci.

An Act to confirm a Provisional Order under the Private   A.D. 1905.
Legislation Procedure (Scotland) Act 1899 relating to
Wemyss Tramways.   [11th August 1905.]

WHEREAS His Majesty's Secretary for Scotland has after
inquiry held before Commissioners made the Provisional
Order set forth in the schedule hereunto annexed under the provisions of the Private Legislation Procedure (Scotland) Act 1899   62 & 63 Vict.
and it is requisite that the said Order should be confirmed by   c. 47.
Parliament:

    Be it therefore enacted by the King's most Excellent Majesty
by and with the advice and consent of the Lords Spiritual and
Temporal and Commons in this present Parliament assembled
and by the authority of the same as follows :—

    1. The Provisional Order contained in the schedule hereunto   Confirmation
annexed shall be and the same is hereby confirmed.   of Order in
                                            schedule.

    2. This Act may be cited as the Wemyss Tramways Order   Short title.
Confirmation Act 1905.

Usually, several Tramway Orders would be confirmed in the one Act; occasionally, as with this Wemyss Tramway Order, one would have an Act to itself if no others were awaiting confirmation at the time.

the villages of West and East Wemyss, and Buckhaven, then along Wellesley Road, through Methil to Leven, where it terminated in Durie Street. This was a coalmining area and the single-track line was financed by the laird's Wemyss Coal Co. Ltd (and operated by the Wemyss & District Tramways Co. Ltd). Where the line served the villages, it did so as a street tramway, but on the frequent rural stretches it was more akin to a light railway, running on sleepered track on a fenced-off right of way.

    Construction began in July 1905 and the line opened the following year with Brush single-deckers Nos 1–9; services were soon extended, from 27 September 1906, when agreement was reached for running powers over the 2½ miles of Kirkcaldy's Upper Route metals from Gallatown to Whytecauseway in the town centre. (This arrangement lasted until 15 January 1917.) Four more identical cars (Nos 10–13) were added to the fleet in order to meet the increased traffic demands followed, in 1907, by four MV long bogie cars (Nos 14–17) to serve specifically as miners' transport. (The line was restricted to using single-deck vehicles on account of its narrow gauge and railway-type sections.) The depot was at Aberhill in Innerleven, near the eastern end of the tramway.

    The inevitable bus competition appeared on the scene shortly before the First World War and expanded dramatically in the 1920s. The 'poaching' of waiting passengers by the motor buses led the Company – in the hands of the BB group since 1912 – to invest in three petrol-electric buses in 1922; four years later it bought up its principal rival, the General Motor Carrying Co. Ltd, a year after it had added bogie cars 18 and 19 to its fleet, this time from Brush. (These were sold to DUNFERMLINE in January 1932, just before the tramway closed.)

    In 1928 two bogie cars from the Potteries Electric Tramways were bought and numbered 20 and 21 and, following the closure of the Kirkcaldy system in 1931, eight of its double-deckers were purchased and numbered 22–29 (and the top decks and stairs removed) to briefly augment the remaining fleet. The last trams ran on 30 January 1932, with their bus replacements taking over the following day, a Sunday.

Part 8

Tramways of the Isle of Man

The Isle of Man has long been a railway and tramway enthusiast's paradise. In just 221 square miles it has managed to accommodate – at more or less the same time – a narrow-gauge steam railway system (a section of which still operates), a narrow-gauge steam pleasure railway (rebuilt and reopened), a narrow-gauge horse tramway (still working), a narrow-gauge cable tramway, a narrow-gauge electric tramway (still working), a narrow-gauge electric mountain railway (still working), a standard-gauge electric tramway, five funicular railways (at four locations), a pier tramway and a former mine railway, rebuilt as a passenger-carrying pleasure line – not to mention sundry contractors', miniature, mine and other industrial lines!

Whilst the gauges of the above lines ranged from a few inches (miniature railways) to 7ft ¼in (Port Erin breakwater), thus adding further to their astonishing variety, the 'standard' gauge for the island was 3ft, a figure arrived at by a combination of traffic and other financial considerations, chance, Irish narrow-gauge influence and the relatively short route mileages involved. As the Isle of Man was self-governed and Crown-dependent, authority for the construction of tramways had normally to be obtained from the island's ancient legislature, the Tynwald.

Although many of the island's lines have closed, victims of much the same pressures felt on the mainland, the tramways have, in terms of mileage, fared far better than their railway companions. Of an original five tramways, two have survived – and these two are probably the most important ones.

Given its position as the island's modern capital, largest town, principal port and resort, it is not surprising that the Isle of Man's tramways were centred on Douglas. Two of the five served Douglas only: the cable, the town and the horse tramway the long succession of seafront promenades. Another two were scenic lines running south (the Douglas Southern) and north (the Manx Electric Railway) from the capital whilst the fifth, the Ramsey Pier Tramway, was sited at the other end of the MER. (There were also two harbour tramways, serving the quaysides at Peel and Ramsey, built as adjuncts to the steam railway network; of these, only that at Peel is known to have carried passengers – see below.)

This concentration of tramways on the island's east coast was the result of the occupation by the earlier narrow-gauge railway system (also naturally centred on Douglas) of the southern region beyond Port Soderick to Castletown and Port Erin, the central region across through St Johns to Peel, and the west coast northwards from there to Ramsey. Thus, by the time the electric tramways arrived, all but one of the major settlements outside Douglas were already served by rail. The one exception was Laxey – and so to Laxey the tramway went, and from there visitors could travel by mountain railway to the top of Snaefell, the island's highest point. Much to the delight of countless thousands of visitors each year, they still can.

Douglas Bay Tramway
Authority: Douglas Bay Tramway Act 1876
Gauge: 3ft
Traction: Horse
Opened: 7 August 1876
System: Single line
Length: 1.76 miles
Stock: 38 sd, 13 dd
Livery: Nos 1–8 dark blue & cream, others brown & red pre-1894, then red or teak & ivory or white, saloons cream for a while

The driving force behind the Douglas Bay Tramway was Thomas Lightfoot, a retired civil engineering contractor, who promoted the idea of a horse tramway along the grand sweep of the bay, with its fast-growing villa and hotel development and associated promenade construction. As opened in 1876, the single-track line operated with three cars running from Burnt Mill Hill (later renamed Summer Hill) in the north to the Iron Pier (demolished 1894) in the south, where the Promenade proper began;

The western end of the Douglas Bay Tramway, looking towards its Victoria Pier terminus. The modern-day terminus is roughly where the nearest tram is, on Loch Promenade. *(Author's Collection)*

An early postcard of holiday crowds on Victoria Pier, Douglas, where the steamers berthed – and the trams did a roaring trade taking visitors (and their luggage) to their seafront hotels and boarding houses. *(Author's Collection)*

the stretch from here to the Victoria Pier – where the steamers arrived – opened on 31 January of the following year. The stable block, built in 1877, was at Tramway Terrace, by the northern terminus.

On 6 January 1882 Lightfoot sold the tramway to what became the Isle of Man Tramways Ltd, who added further stock; four years later a new northern terminus and depot was opened at Derby Castle, at the far end of the bay, just on from Burnt Mill Hill, and a track-doubling programme (completed in 1897) was put in hand.

In 1894 the line was sold to the Douglas & Laxey Coast Electric Tramway Co. Ltd (see MANX ELECTRIC RAILWAY) who took over on 1 May, but requests by that Company to electrify the line were turned down by Douglas Corporation, who, in turn, took control of the line in 1901 after the Isle of Man Tramways & Electric Power Co. Ltd (the renamed DLCET Co. Ltd) had gone into liquidation, its offer of £50,000 being accepted on 25 September for the horse tramway and the UPPER DOUGLAS TRAMWAY (see below). Since then the line has managed to survive – but sometimes only just – in spite of fluctuations in the numbers of day-trippers and holiday visitors to the island, and the two world wars, which have all had their effect on the tramway. In 1927 it closed for the winter, reopening the next year as a summer-only service, as it has since remained. Its survival as the only horse tramway in the British Isles is perhaps best explained by recognising that it is very much a pleasure line now and, as such, is ideally situated (though it does provide a genuine and very useful public transport link to the MER's terminus). But often, especially in the 1950s and 1960s, it has been a very close-run thing. At the time of writing, concern over the fact that receipts fall far short of running costs has led to repeated calls for it to join the steam railway and the MER under governmental control.

Horse cars 26 of 1891 and 40 of 1902 pass near the western end of the line, the long sweep of the promenade to Derby Castle visible in the background. *(Author's Collection)*

At Derby Castle, with cars 24 of 1891 and one of the double-deckers to the fore. Note the line of MER cars awaiting their passengers. *(Author's Collection)*

Services began with three Starbuck cars: single-decker No.1 and double-deckers Nos 2 and 3; No.1 was converted to a double-decker in 1885 and disappeared at the end of the 1890s, whilst the other two lasted until the winter of 1948–49 when they were scrapped. These three were joined, in 1882, by No.4, in 1883 by Nos 5 and 6, and in 1884 by Nos 7 and 8, all Starbuck double-deck cars. Of this group, No.7 was scrapped in 1924 and the others in 1948–49 again. All subsequent orders were for single-deckers, these being Starbuck open toastracks 9 (scrapped 1952) and 10 of 1884, Starbuck/Milnes open toastrack 11 of 1886, Milnes open toastrack 12 of 1888, ditto 19 and 20 of 1889 (both withdrawn 1949 and scrapped 1952), ditto 21 and 22 of 1890, and 23–26 of 1891 (of which Nos 23–25 were scrapped in 1952 as well, while No.22 has been converted to a mobile shop). Milnes supplied closed saloons 27–29 in 1892, open toastracks 30 (scrapped 1952) and 31 in 1894, roofed toastracks 32–37 in 1896 and open toastracks 38–40 in 1902, these being followed in 1905 by Nos 41 and 42, a pair of MN open toastracks. Nos 43 and 44 were 1907 UEC roofed toastracks, 45 and 46 MV roofed toastracks of 1908 and 1909, and 47 a similar vehicle of 1911; in 1913 the latter firm supplied a new No.1, a closed winter saloon. (No.46 is, fittingly, currently preserved at the Pacific Road Museum in Birkenhead.) The last new cars for the line were purchased in 1935 from the Vulcan Motor & Engineering Co Ltd: numbered 48–50, these were roofed toastracks with folding wooden side-screens for protection against the weather.

The numbers 13–18, missing from the above listing, were allotted to six second-hand double-deckers from SOUTH SHIELDS, purchased in 1887; in 1903 Nos 17 and 18 were converted into single-deckers (though No.17 was withdrawn soon after). No.14 was scrapped in 1908, whereupon No.13 took its number (for superstitious reasons?) and survives to this day, being preserved in the Manx Museum at Douglas. No.16 was scrapped in 1915 and, in 1949, No.15 was likewise scrapped. During the summer season operational cars are normally available for inspection at Derby Castle, though some are often away for servicing or in store elsewhere (including No.49, the property of the Isle of Man Railway & Tramway Preservation Society). Also, at Derby Castle, there are a few cars reserved for running on special occasions only, and a display of Douglas tramway relics.

Upper Douglas Tramway

Authority: Upper Douglas Tramway Act 1895
Gauge: 3ft
Traction: Cable
Opened: 15 August 1896
Closed: 19 August 1929
System: Single line
Length: 1.56 miles
Stock: 16 sd
Livery: Red or teak & ivory or white
Last Car: ?

Following the success of the horse tramway (see above), the idea naturally arose for a line to serve at least some of the houses, hotels and shops of the town behind the seafront at Douglas. Because of the steepness of the streets rising up from the shore, it became clear that a mechanically-assisted form of traction would be called for and, accordingly, the promoters – the Isle of Man Tramways & Electric Power Co. Ltd (see DOUGLAS BAY TRAMWAY) – decided upon cable haulage. The route taken, as authorised by the enabling Act, was up Victoria Street from a terminus at the bottom, close to the southern end of the horse tramway (with a physical link between the two), then up Prospect Hill, along Buck's Road and Woodbourne Road, down into Ballaquayle Road (where the depot and winding house were built) and Broadway to meet the horse tramway again. (The authorised link between the two lines at this end of the tramway was never laid.)

The mainly double-track line had a steepest gradient of 1 in 10.6 and was worked in true cable fashion, i.e. the cable was wound continuously in a central conduit between the rails and the cars attached or detached by means of driver-controlled grippers. The original car fleet was made up of eight cross-bench cars, Nos 71–78, and four saloons, Nos 79–82, all bogie single-deckers from Milnes. (Car numbers 1–70 were initially reserved for the horse tramway.)

In 1900 the IOMTEP Co. Ltd collapsed and the line, together with the horse tramway, was purchased the following year by Douglas Corporation (see above). Although the steep and narrow depot–Broadway section was abandoned at the start of 1901 and the track lifted, plans were made to electrify the remainder of the line, but these came to nothing. In 1907 a pair of cross-bench cars (Nos 69 and 70) were bought from UEC, followed by a similar Milnes car (No.68) in 1909 and another (No.67) two years later, again all bogie vehicles.

Above left: The western terminus of the Upper Douglas cable tramway was by the clock on Loch Promenade, where it connected with the horse line. The waiting car has had its fleet number 82 highlighted by the postcard publisher. *(Author's Collection)*

Above right: Looking up Victoria Street from Loch Promenade, the start of the cable tramway's long northwards sweep around the town and down to the seafront. *(Author's Collection)*

By the 1920s the accumulated effects of wear and tear to virtually every part of the tramway meant the Corporation had to make a choice: either incur heavy expenditure on the line or abandon it in favour of its growing fleet of buses. For a while (from 1921 onwards) a compromise was effected whereby the buses replaced the trams in the winter months, but by the end of the decade even this solution no longer made financial sense. After the last, four-week season of the 1920s, the line closed for the final time. The cars were sold to become holiday bungalows, with Nos 72 and 73 surviving in this form until 1968 when they were rescued and painstakingly restored as a single car, numbered 72 at one end and 73 at the other, which can be seen on display at Derby Castle – and which, using battery power, is operated over the horse tramway on special occasions.

Douglas Southern Electric Tramways

Authority: -
Gauge: 4ft 8½in.
Traction: Overhead electric
Opened: 7 August 1896
Closed: 15 September 1939
System: Single line
Length: 3.25 miles
Stock: 16 dd
Livery: Crimson & white
Last Car: No.7?

The stretch of coast immediately south of Douglas is one of the most dramatic on the whole island and it is not surprising that, during the late nineteenth century, many schemes were suggested to improve tourists' access to view its rugged grandeur. In 1890 work began on the construction of a coastal toll road southwards from Douglas Head, at the southern limit of Douglas Bay; by November 1893 the builders – the Douglas Head Marine Drive Co. Ltd – had reached Keristal, nearly 3 miles away.

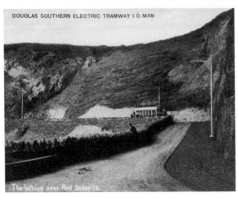

Above left: A multi-view postcard of the Douglas Southern Electric Tramways, once bought as a souvenir of their visit by holidaymakers who thereby obtained four scenes for the price of one. *(Author's Collection)*

Above right: The Douglas Southern had surely the most dramatic setting of any British tramway. This is the massive cliff-top archway that graced the Douglas end of the line – and still standing today. *(Author's Collection)*

Left: An unidentified DSET car on the Marine Drive at the Whing – a scene little altered today apart from the absence of the tramway. *(Author's Collection)*

It had already been agreed that an electric tramway should be built along the Marine Drive and, in 1894, two of the construction company's major shareholders secured the concession for such a line. This passed quickly through a number of hands before ending up, in February 1896, in those of the Douglas Southern Electric Tramways Ltd (incorporated 21 October 1895).

The first 2 miles of line, from Douglas Head to the Whing, were opened in August 1896, the next ¾ mile to Keristal not having been passed by the BoT. During the winter (the line having closed on 26 September at the end of the summer season) the final ¾-mile section from Keristal to the southern terminus at Port Soderick was completed, the whole line opening on 1 April 1897 in its final form.

As built, the single-track tramway was an undulating, winding affair with gradients steeper than 1 in 11 and curves as tight as 45ft radius, laid for the most part on the landward side of the Drive. The adoption of mainland standard gauge for a Manx line was somewhat surprising, though it was probably chosen for increased tramcar stability in view of the tramway's exposed position. The line commenced on Douglas Head itself, more than 180ft above sea level, and followed the Drive all the way to Port Soderick, the terminus above the beach there being at a similar altitude. A notable feature, which added greatly to the thrill of the ride, was the use of several girder bridges thrown across deep gullies and clefts in the cliffs; another was that for virtually the whole of the tramway's life each terminus was served from a lower level by a cliff railway. Current was supplied from the tramway's own power station at Pigeon Stream, ½ mile from Douglas Head.

Original stock comprised six motor cars (Nos 1–6) and six trailers (Nos 7–12), all open-top, open-sided Brush vehicles; these were followed in 1897 by four similar but lighter trailers (Nos 13–16), whereupon Nos 7 and 8 were converted to powered cars. The depot was at Little Ness, midway along the tramway, where there was a suitable patch of flat land, on the seaward side of the line, perched on an outcrop of the cliff.

In 1926, at the expiration of the tramway's operating concession, the Company merged with the DHMD Co. Ltd, cars 1–12 being re-lettered 'DOUGLAS HEAD MARINE DRIVE LTD' accordingly (Nos 13–16 simply had the old title painted out). Thirteen years later, the line closed for the duration of the Second World War, as it had for the 1914–18 conflict, though this time it was never to reopen. Track lifting and overhead removal took place in 1946 and 1947, with all cars (with the exception of No.1, now preserved in England at the National Tramway Museum, Crich) being broken up five years later. (The depot track fan was rescued in 1960 for re-use at Crich.) A particularly severe rockfall and the effects of coastal erosion closed most of the Drive to vehicular traffic in 1966 – it had only belated been reopened three years before after its wartime closure – though it remains open for pedestrians to savour the atmosphere of this unique British tramway route. (Consideration is given, periodically, to reopening the Drive to motor cars, but the scope of the engineering work involved – and hence the cost – has so far meant the idea has progressed no further.)

Laxey Browside Tramway

Not a tramway, but a little-known funicular railway, also known as the Laxey Wheel Incline Railway, which ran from c.1890 to shortly before the First World War to help visitors ascend a rise to view the famous Great Wheel in Laxey (the *Lady Isabella*). It was a two-track, water-balance line, but other than that few operational details relating to it are known: gauge was c.5ft, length c.100yd and its gradient 1 in 4, or thereabouts.

Manx Electric Railway

Authority: Howstrake Estate Act
Gauge: 3ft
Traction: Overhead electric
Opened: 7 September 1893
System: Single line
Length: 17.75 miles
Stock: 64 sd
Livery: Red, cream & teak, except for green & white 1957–58 and some recent individual applications

Above left: The Derby Castle terminus of the Manx Electric Railway on a pre-First World War postcard, with 1898 car No.15 to the fore. Sadly, the ornate canopy over the tracks was demolished in 1980. *(Author's Collection)*

Above right: A very early photograph of MER saloon No.3 and trailer 16 of 1893 outside Douglas. The troublesome Hopkinson bow collectors originally used by the tramway were replaced in 1898 by more conventional trolley poles. *(Author's Collection)*

Left: Postcard of the Groudle Glen Hotel (opened 1893), the MER's first northern terminus, with winter saloon No.9 of 1894 still with its original current collectors. *(Author's Collection)*

Above left: The MER's Laxey terminus, opened in 1894, on an Edwardian postcard, with winter saloon No.20 to the fore. *(Author's Collection)*

Above right: In 1993 the MER celebrated its centenary in a variety of ways. Seen here in Derby Castle Depot is winter saloon No.9 again, suitably decorated and illuminated in traditional tramway fashion. *(M. Donnison)*

Left: A typical guidebook advertisement of the pre-Second World War era for the MER. (Frank Edmondson, Engineer and General Manager, retired in 1936.)

The Manx Electric Railway

Station—**DERBY CASTLE** (Terminus of Horse Tramway).

The Royal Mail and Direct Route to Ramsey.

A Continuous Panorama of **Mountain, Glen, and Marine Scenery,** the Finest in the Island.

The Open Electric Cars offer unique facilities for enjoying the purest Sea and Mountain Air under ideal conditions.

No Holiday in the Island is considered complete unless **SNAEFELL SUMMIT** and the Charming **Tholt-y-Will** (**Sulby Glen**) have been visited by this popular Route.

ares :—Douglas to Ramsey 1/6 Single, Return 2/6 ;   Douglas to Snaefell Summit & Sulby Glen, 3/- Return ;   Douglas to Snaefell Summit and Ramsey, 3/6 Return.

General Offices, Douglas.   F. EDMONDSON, General Manager.

Linking Douglas and the northern town of Ramsey with a double-track roadside line along the more sheltered eastern side of the island, the MER began life as part of an 1880s development scheme centred on the Howstrake Estate, just north of Douglas. This first section was promoted by Douglas Bay Estates Ltd as a single-track electric line from Derby Castle in Douglas (the northern terminus of the DOUGLAS BAY TRAMWAY and the site of the MER's principal depot and works, rebuilt and extended over the years) to Groudle Glen, a noted beauty spot some 2 miles away. (Smaller depots were built later at Laxey and Ramsey.) Before it could open, though, a new concern appeared on the scene with greater plans (as evinced by its title): the Douglas & Laxey Coast Electric Tramway Co. Ltd, registered on 7 March 1893 and empowered by the Douglas & Laxey Electric Tramway Act of that year to take over the Howstrake tramway when completed and extend it to Laxey, 7 miles from Douglas. The extended line opened to the public on 28 July 1894, by which time the Company had purchased the Douglas Bay tramway and had renamed itself the Isle of Man Tramways & Electric Power Co. Ltd. (In 1896 it purchased the SNAEFELL MOUNTAIN RAILWAY as well.)

Authority to extend the line further up the coast to Ramsey was obtained in 1897 and this northern section opened on 24 July 1899; hard on the heels of the tramway's completion, however, came a succession of financial scandals – and trials – in which the Company was involved, the upshot being that it went into liquidation and was purchased, in 1902, by a new consortium, the Manx Electric Railway Co. Ltd. A more prosperous existence lasted until after the Second World War when, in the 1950s, the holiday trade upon which the now double-tracked line was reliant began to decline, and in 1957 the concern was nationalised by the Manx government, in whose ownership it has remained – occasional abandonment scares aside – safely ever since. Today, as a much-publicised (and much-loved) tourist attraction, its closure would be unthinkable, especially after the immense success of its 1993 'Year of Railways' centenary celebrations in bringing visitors to the island, though its winter service is always under threat – and has indeed been suspended on occasion.

All the MER's passenger cars (with one exception) have been single-deck bogie vehicles, beginning with Milnes saloons 1–3 and open (later roofed) toastrack trailers 49–54, followed in 1894 by similar powered cars 4–9 and roofed trailers 34–39, and in 1895 by powered cars 10–13 of a slightly different design, again all from Milnes. Car 60 of 1896 was another roofed trailer. In 1898 Milnes supplied open-sided cross-bench cars 14–18 and in 1899 saloon cars 19–22 and open-sided trailers 44–48, all for use on the Ramsey extension.

Large mail van No.16 of 1908, one of several vehicles used on the MER for the mail service referred to in the advertisement opposite. It is seen here in 1975 – the year the service ceased – after losing its end platforms but before its 1977 conversion to a works vehicle. *(Author)*

In 1899 Milnes supplied four sister cars to Nos 14–18, which ran without motors as Nos 40–43 until 1903, when they were motorised as Nos 24–27 upon the arrival of trailers 40–43; a year later the Company bought ERTCW open-sided powered cars 28–31 and trailers 55–58 (the last two of these being saloons). The final powered cars bought were UEC 32 and 33 in 1906 (vehicles similar to Nos 28–31) together with open-sided trailers 61 and 62; no further cars were purchased until 1930, when EE supplied open-sided trailers 40, 41 and 44 to partly replace eleven cars destroyed in a fire at Laxey on 5 April that year. As is only to be expected, given their age, many of the trams have been rebuilt during their lifetime and have had components exchanged between them – one example being the conversion in 1994–95 of cross-bench trailer No.56 into a disabled-access saloon trailer.

The line's only four-wheeled passenger car (though fitted with bogies five years later) was directors' saloon 59, built in 1895 by Milnes and which still sees occasional service, especially for private parties. Indeed, at the time of writing, nearly fifty powered cars (including Nos 1 and 2, thought to be the world's oldest working electric cars) and trailers are rotated in passenger service, living proof of the standard of care and attention they regularly receive. Over the years, the tramway has also operated a sizeable fleet of freight vehicles, including a bogie electric locomotive (No.23 of 1900, named *Dr R. Preston Hendry* in 1993), now preserved and occasionally operated by the Isle of Man Railway & Tramway Preservation Society. (See p.7.)

By no means are all the tramway's cars available for service on a day-to-day basis, with a good number 'mothballed' at any one time. It is quite possible that several cars will be disposed of in the near future, but exactly how this will be accomplished has not yet been decided. On a slightly bizarre note, in 2000 the body of ex-Lisbon No.360 of 1906 was placed at Derby Castle to serve as a waiting room, the idea of converting it into a wheelchair-friendly vehicle having come to nothing.

The age, stock, location, history and sheer survival of the MER have long made it a favourite amongst tramway enthusiasts and it has a body dedicated to its study and support, the Manx Electric Railway Society.

Peel Harbour Tramway

Not a passenger tramway in the usual sense, as it never carried paying members of the public – only non-paying passengers of a very specific kind. It was a purpose-built extension of the 3ft gauge Isle of Man Railway, which continued on from that company's Peel terminus (opened 1873), across the end of Station Road and along the Quay on the east side of the harbour. Length was some 200yd. It was laid in 1915 on the landward side of the quay (with a number of sidings extending across to its edge) for the express purpose of assisting in the transfer of troops, supplies and detainees from ships, during the First World War, to the Knockaloe Alien Detention Camp, set up just outside Peel. The camp was served by its own purpose-built branch off the main line, just out of Peel station; this closed in 1920 and was lifted 1923–24 along with the quayside tramway.

A superb view of Peel railway station – probably in the 1940s – with the route of the (lifted) quayside tramway across the harbour to the left. (*Author's Collection*)

Above left: Ramsey Pier's 'Planet' locomotive and trailer at the shore terminus, 1975. Note the trailer's side shutters lowered against the wind. *(Author)*

Above right: The siding at the shore end of the pier, again in 1975, with a large and a small luggage truck parked up in the unlikely event that one day they might be called into service again. *(Author)*

Ramsey Pier Tramway

Authority: –
Gauge: 3ft
Traction: Manual/ic
Opened: August 1899
Closed: 9 September 1981
System: Single line
Length: 0.39 miles
Stock: 1 sd manual; 1 loco, 1 railcar, 1 sd ic
Livery: Various
Last Car: 'Planet' loco + trailer

Like many such tramways, the line at Ramsey was built originally for the contractor's use during construction of the 2,160ft-long Queen's Pier (formally opened 22 July 1886). For the next three decades the line, with grooved rails running 2,080ft down the centre of the decking, was used to convey passengers' luggage on small hand-propelled trolleys from the various pleasure steamers and ferries that called there.

In 1899, at the same time as a new landing stage was opened at the pier head, an enclosed passenger van was added to the tramway's stock; this remained in service until 1937, when the owners of the pier and tramway, the Isle of Man Harbour Board, purchased a small 'Planet' petrol locomotive and a roofed bogie toastrack trailer from Hibberd, adding a tiny Wickham petrol railcar thirteen years later.

From the 1974 summer season onwards, the tramway was operated by the Manx Electric Railway Society on behalf of the IoM Harbour Board – previously it had been run by the pier concessionaire – using the Hibberd set, but the line failed to reopen after the 1981 season when it was discovered that extensive (and expensive) replacement of the wooden track beams would be necessary. The loco and trailer were given by the Harbour Board to the Ramsey Commissioners, who were considering constructing a pleasure line in the town's Mooragh Park, but this idea came to nothing and they are now owned by the Isle of Man Railway & Tramway Preservation Society and stored at Ramsey. They are operated on the MER in Ramsey on special occasions. The railcar was acquired by the Isle of Man Railway and used (with the 'Planet' loco) in the dismantling of its St Johns–Ramsey line in 1975; after the completion of this task, its engine was found to be life-expired and the car was broken up, presumably as a source of spare parts for the railway's small fleet of similar works vehicles.

The pier, now in the ownership of the harbours division of the Department of Transport, remains closed and slowly decaying – despite the structure being registered in 1995 – but the bulk of the tramway remains intact and it is well within the bounds of possibility that it will one day operate again if those lobbying for the restoration of the pier achieve their goal.

Snaefell Mountain Railway

Although often described as a tramway – and possessing several tramway features – this is actually an electric mountain railway of a type unique in the British Isles. Hard on the heels of the initial success of the MANX ELECTRIC RAILWAY came the proposal by the Isle of Man Tramways & Electric Power Co. Ltd to construct a similar line from Laxey to the summit of Snaefell, the highest point of the island at 2,034ft above sea level. It was built on land acquired without the need for compulsory purchase and so avoided delays occasioned by seeking the necessary authority from Tynwald, and it was finished in just seven months. (The line was built by the Snaefell Mountain Railway Association with the intention of selling it to the IOMTEP Co. Ltd, which it did in 1896.)

The railway opened on 21 August 1895 with six Milnes single-deck saloon cars, similar to those in use on the MER, and has always operated in summer only. A small fleet of goods and service vehicles has also been operated over the years – principally for maintenance work and for taking supplies up to the café at the top station – as well as a handful of Wickham railcars used formerly by the Air Ministry (and now by National Air Traffic Services, successor to the Civil Aviation Authority) for servicing a radar installation on the summit of the mountain.

Because of the more or less constant gradient of 1 in 12 on its 4½-mile spiral round the mountain, the railway was designed on the Fell system, employing a raised centre rail that can be engaged by grippers on the cars for braking purposes on the descent (the ascent being effected by adhesion only). The wider car bogies needed to accommodate these grippers meant adopting a wider gauge (3ft 6in.) than the MER, so ruling out through-running. The Fell rail is not installed on the level ground at Laxey, where the tracks parallel those of the MER, thus giving the line there the appearance of a tramway, but once the SMR begins the long climb on its own reserved sleepered track the resemblance quickly vanishes. A mixed-gauge siding in Laxey station, installed in the railway's closed winter season 1931-32, enables Snaefell cars to be jacked off their bogies and set on MER ones so that they can be towed to the MER's Derby Castle works for servicing.

Above left: The modern-day terminus of the SMR, with car No.3 of 1895 (left) and MER No.45 of 1899 (right), in the shared Laxey station. Note the absence of the Fell centre rail, not used on the more level sections of the railway. *(Author)*

Above right: A 1909-franked postcard of the SMR's halfway station, Bungalow, with the eponymous but now demolished hotel in the foreground and the Summit Hotel (and railway terminus) on the skyline. *(Author's Collection)*

Chronology

Major Landmarks in British Passenger Tramway History

1807	World's first railed passenger service inaugurated on the Oystermouth Tramroad in Wales
1859	William Curtis runs his patent omnibuses on a line in Liverpool Docks
1860	George Train opens the first genuine street railway in the British Isles (Birkenhead)
	Tramways Act (Ireland)
1863	First Act of Parliament for a street tramway (Portsmouth)
1864	First trials of steam traction (Ryde Pier)
1870	Tramways Act
1876	First regular use of steam traction on a British tramway (Wantage)
1877	First regular use of steam traction on a British street tramway (Vale of Clyde)
1879	Use of Mechanical Power on Tramways Act
1883	Giant's Causeway, Portrush & Bush Valley Tramway pioneers the use of electricity (third rail)
	Huddersfield becomes the first municipal operator
	Tramways and Public Companies (Ireland) Act
1884	Highgate Hill Cable Tramway pioneers the use of cable traction (London)
1885	First (conduit) electric tramway opens (Blackpool)
1889	Light Railways (Ireland) Act
1891	First overhead electric tramway opens (Leeds)
1896	Light Railways Act
1909	Last regular use of steam traction on a street tramway (Rossendale Valley)
1917	First abandonment of an electric system (Sheerness)
1924	Last new system for forty-six years opens (Dearne District)
1927	Last steam passenger service in England ceases (Wisbech & Upwell)
1928	Last use of horse traction outside the Isle of Man (Pwllheli & Llanbedrog)
1933	Last steam passenger service outside Ireland ceases (Glyn Valley)
1934	Channel Islands' only tramway closes (Guernsey)
1952	Largest system closes (London)
1959	Last steam passenger service (Arigna)
	Ireland's last tramway closes (Hill of Howth)
1960	Swansea & Mumbles Railway closes, leaving the Great Orme as Wales' sole surviving tramway
1961	Grimsby & Immingham Electric Railway closes, leaving Blackpool as England's sole surviving tramway
1962	Scotland's last tramway closes (Glasgow)
1963	National Tramway Museum opens at Crich, England
1970	First tramway to be built since 1924 opens (Seaton)
1992	Manchester Metrolink ushers in a new era of urban tramways

Appendix 1

English Passenger Tramway Locations by Former County

Bedfordshire
Luton

Berkshire
Reading; Wantage

Buckinghamshire
Wolverton & Stony Stratford

Cambridgeshire
Cambridge; Wisbech & Upwell (part)

Cheshire
Birkenhead; Chester; Manchester and district (part); Stalybridge and district (part); Stockport (part); Wallasey; Warrington (part)

Cornwall
Camborne & Redruth

Cumberland
Carlisle

Derbyshire
Burton & Ashby (part); Chesterfield; Derby; Glossop; Ilkeston; Matlock; Nottinghamshire & Derbyshire (part); South Yorkshire Supertram (part)

Devon
Exeter; Plymouth; Seaton; Torquay and district

Dorset
Poole

Durham
Darlington; Gateshead; The Hartlepools; Jarrow; South Shields; Stockton & Thornaby (part); Sunderland and district

Essex

Barking; Canvey Island; Colchester; East Ham; Ilford; Leyton; London (part); Southend-on-Sea;
Walthamstow; West Ham

Gloucestershire

Bristol (part); Cheltenham; Gloucester

Hampshire & Isle of Wight

Aldershot & Farnborough; Bournemouth; Gosport & Farnham; Portsmouth and district; Ryde; Southampton

Hertfordshire

London (part)

Huntingdonshire

Peterborough

Kent

Bexley (part); Chatham; Dartford; Dover; Erith; Folkestone, Hythe & Sandgate; Gravesend & Northfleet;
Herne Bay; Isle of Thanet; Maidstone; Sheerness; South Metropolitan (part)

Lancashire

Accrington & District; Ashton-under-Lyne; Barrow-in-Furness; Blackburn; Blackpool and district; Bolton;
Burnley; Bury; Colne & Trawden; Darwen; Farnworth; Heywood; Lancaster and district; Liverpool and
district; Lytham St Annes and district; Manchester; Middleton; Morecambe; Nelson; Oldham; Preston;
Rawtenstall and district; Rochdale; St Helens; Salford; South Lancashire; Southport; Stalybridge and
district (part); Stockport (part); Warrington (part); Waterloo & Great Crosby; Wigan

Leicestershire

Burton & Ashby (part); Leicester

Lincolnshire

Alford & Sutton; Grimsby and district; Lincoln; Skegness

London

Bexley (part); London (part)

Middlesex

London (part)

Norfolk

Norwich; Wisbech & Upwell (part); Great Yarmouth

Northamptonshire

Northampton

Northumberland

Newcastle; Tynemouth; Tyneside

Nottinghamshire

Mansfield; Nottingham; Nottinghamshire & Derbyshire (part)

Oxfordshire

Oxford

Somerset

Bath; Bristol (part); Taunton; Weston-super-Mare

Staffordshire

Birmingham (part); Black Country (part); Burton and district (part); Kinver (part); Potteries; Walsall;
    Wolverhampton

Suffolk

Ipswich; Lowestoft

Surrey

Croydon; South Metropolitan (part)

Sussex

Brighton and district; Hastings; Shoreham and district

Warwickshire

Birmingham (part); Coventry; Leamington & Warwick; Stratford & Moreton

Wiltshire

Swindon

Worcestershire

Black Country (part); Kidderminster & Stourport; Worcester

Yorkshire

Barnsley; Batley; Bradford; Dearne District; Doncaster; Halifax; Huddersfield; Hull and district; Keighley;
    Leeds; Mexborough & Swinton; Middlesbrough; Rotherham; Scarborough; Sheffield; Shipley; Stockton
    & Thornaby (part); Wakefield and district; York; Yorkshire (West Riding); Yorkshire (Woollen District)

Herefordshire, Rutland, Shropshire and Westmoreland have had no regular passenger tramways.

Appendix 2

Welsh Passenger Tramway Locations by Former County

(Including Monmouthshire)

Caernarvonshire
Llandudno and district (part); Pwllheli and district

Carmarthenshire
Llanelli

Denbighshire
Colwyn Bay and district (part); Glyn Valley; Wrexham

Glamorgan
Aberdare; Cardiff; Merthyr Tydfil; Neath; Pontypridd; Rhondda; Swansea and district

Merionethshire
Barmouth Junction & Arthog; Fairbourne; Harlech

Monmouthshire
Newport

Anglesey, Brecknockshire, Cardiganshire, Flintshire, Montgomeryshire, Pembrokeshire and Radnorshire have had no regular passenger tramways.

Appendix 3

Scottish Passenger Tramway Locations by Former County

Aberdeenshire
Aberdeen; Cruden Bay

Angus
Dundee and district

Ayrshire
Ayr; Kilmarnock

Buteshire
Rothesay

Dunbartonshire
Dumbarton

Fife
Dunfermline; Kirkcaldy; Wemyss

Lanarkshire
Airdrie & Coatbridge; Glasgow and district; Lanarkshire

Midlothian
Edinburgh; Leith; Musselburgh

Perthshire
Perth

Renfrewshire
Greenock & Port Glasgow; Paisley

Stirlingshire
Falkirk; Stirling & Bridge of Allan

Argyllshire, Banffshire, Berwickshire, Caithness, Clackmannanshire, Dumfries-shire, East Lothian, Inverness-shire, Kincardineshire, Kinross-shire, Kircudbrightshire, Morayshire, Nairn, Orkney, Peebleshire, Ross & Cromarty, Roxburghshire, Selkirkshire, Sutherland, West Lothian, Wigtownshire and Zetland have had no regular passenger tramways.

Appendix 4

Irish Passenger Tramway Locations by County

Antrim
Belfast (part)

Armagh
Glenanne & Loughgilly

Cork
Cork

Down
Belfast (part); Warrenpoint & Rostrevor

Dublin
Dublin and district (part); Hill of Howth

Fermanagh
Clogher Valley (part)

Galway
Galway & Salthill

Leitrim
Arigna (part)

Londonderry
Derry; Portstewart

Roscommon
Arigna (part)

Tyrone
Clogher Valley (part); Castlederg & Victoria Bridge

Wicklow
Dublin and district (part)

Carlow, Cavan, Clare, Donegal, Kerry, Kildare, Kilkenny, Laois, Limerick, Longford, Louth, Mayo, Meath, Monaghan, Offaly, Sligo, Tipperary, Waterford, Westmeath and Wexford have had no regular passenger tramways.

Appendix 5

Horse-only Tramways

Although the normal course of events for early British tramways was to start with horse traction and then modernise with electrification around the end of the nineteenth century (sometimes experimenting with steam traction along the way), a significant number of lines remained faithful to horse traction until the end, without it being replaced (or the tramway being rebuilt in some other form). The reason was usually financial, with low traffic receipts not justifying the cost of conversion. These horse-only systems are listed below, with their dates of operation and location.

BARMOUTH JUNCTION & ARTHOG	1899–1903	Wales
CAMBRIDGE	1880–1914	England
DERRY	1897–1919	Ireland
DOUGLAS BAY	1876–	Isle of Man
FAIRBOURNE	c.1896–c.1915	Wales
FOLKESTONE, HYTHE & SANDGATE	1891–1921	England
GALWAY & SALTHILL	1879–1918	Ireland
GLENANNE & LOUGHGILLY	1897–1918?	Ireland
HARLECH	1878–1880s	Wales
LANCASTER & DISTRICT	1890–1921	England
MORECAMBE CORPORATION	1898–1926	England
OXFORD	1881–1914	England
PWLLHELI CORPORATION	1899–1919	Wales
PWLLHELI & LLANBEDROG	1894–1928	Wales
SKEGNESS	c.1880–c.1882	England
WARRENPOINT & ROSTREVOR	1877–1915	Ireland

Appendix 6

Steam-only Tramways

Tramways that employed steam traction were of two broad types: urban street systems and isolated rural roadside lines. The type of locomotives used corresponded generally with the type of line: box-like, purpose-built tramway engines for the street systems and adapted railway engines for the others. In the towns, steam traction lasted little more than twenty years, from c.1880 to c.1900; in rural areas its use survived well into the twentieth century – and sometimes right up to a line's closure (though often with internal-combustion traction as well). The following list is of those tramways which used steam traction exclusively, with their dates of operation and location.

ALFORD & SUTTON	1884–1889	England
ARIGNA	1887–1959	Ireland
HULL: Drypool & Marfleet	1889–1901	England
PORTSTEWART	1882–1926	Ireland
WISBECH & UPWELL	1883–1927[*]	England
WOLVERTON & STONY STRATFORD	1887–1926	England

[*] retained steam (later diesel) traction for goods trains

Appendix 7

Cable Tramways

Cable traction on tramways, because of the complicated mechanical arrangements needed if more than one route was involved, was almost exclusively limited to short, single-line systems where steep gradients had to be conquered. (The one exception was Edinburgh.) Listed below are all British cable lines with their dates of cable operation and location.

BIRMINGHAM: Hockley Hill	1888–1911[*]	England
DOUGLAS: Upper Douglas	1896–1929	Isle of Man
EDINBURGH	1888–1922[*]	Scotland
LONDON: Brixton Hill	1892–1904[*]	England
LONDON: Highgate Hill	1884–1909[*]	England
LLANDUDNO: Great Orme	1902–	Wales
MATLOCK	1893–1927	England
SWANSEA: Constitution Hill	1898–1902?	Wales

[*] converted to electric traction

Appendix 8

Pier Tramways

Many of Britain's piers, quays and jetties have had, at one time or another, rails laid on them. In many cases these were simple extensions of the national railway system and used for the loading and unloading of passengers and goods from ferry boats and pleasure steamers; occasionally railway vehicles themselves would be transhipped. A few piers, though, possessed their own self-contained lines to carry passengers and their luggage between pier head and shore and, when there were no boats to service, to give rides to holidaymakers. Most of these lines were railways, fenced-off from the rest of the pier – a necessary precaution, as many were electrified on the third-rail system – but a handful were true tramways, laid flush with the decking. Those lines that carried passengers are listed below, with their dates of operation and location.

BLACKPOOL: North Pier	1991–1994	England
HERNE BAY (1)	1833?–1864	England
HERNE BAY (2)	1899–1939	England
RAMSEY	1899–1981	Isle of Man
RYDE	1864–1886	England
SOUTHEND-ON-SEA	1875?–1881?	England
SOUTHPORT	1863–1863?	England

A number of other piers are known to have had simple 'luggage lines' with hand-propelled trucks; that on the Old or Birnbeck Pier at Weston-super-Mare is known to have also carried passengers at some time, though further details are lacking.

Appendix 9

Railway-owned Tramways

A small number of British tramways were owned and/or operated by railway companies, for reasons almost as numerous as the lines themselves. The following list includes all such lines, with their original operating railway and location.

ARIGNA	Cavan & Leitrim	Ireland
BURTON & ASHBY	Midland	England
CRUDEN BAY	Great North of Scotland	Scotland
FOLKESTONE, HYTHE & SANDGATE	South Eastern	England
GRIMSBY & IMMINGHAM	Great Central	England
HILL OF HOWTH	Great Northern (I)	Ireland
HOYLAKE & BIRKENHEAD	Hoylake	England
PORTSTEWART	Belfast & Northern Counties	Ireland
WATERLOO & GREAT CROSBY	Liverpool Overhead	England
WISBECH & UPWELL	Great Eastern	England
WOLVERTON & STONY STRATFORD	London & North Western	England

Appendix 10

Tramway-owned Railways

Three British railways were owned and/or operated by tramway concerns for at least part of their lives. The following list gives the owner and location of each.

BABBACOMBE CLIFF RAILWAY	Torquay Tramways Co. Ltd	England
CLIFTON ROCKS RAILWAY	Bristol Tramways & Carriage Co. Ltd	England
CORRIS RAILWAY	Bristol Tramways & Carriage Co. Ltd	England

The two cliff railways were acquired as they were seen as useful adjuncts to the tramway system; the narrow-gauge Corris Railway was an investment asset to the Imperial Tramways Co. Ltd, owned by its Bristol subsidiary.

Bibliography

The Tramways of Lytham St Annes (Locomotion Papers No.189) P.H. Abell, J.A. Garnham & I. McLoughlin (The Oakwood Press, 1995) 0 85361 475 X

Double Century, Stan Basnett & Keith Pearson (Adam Gordon, Chetwode, 1996) 1 874422 18 4

The Isle of Man Railway Volume II (The British Narrow Gauge Railway No.2B) James I.C. Boyd (The Oakwood Press, 1994) 0 85361 469 5

The Tramways of Ayr, Ronald W. Brash (NB Traction, Dundee, 1983) 0 905069 19 6

Huddersfield Corporation Tramways, Roy Brook (Author, Accrington, 1983) 0 95058 91 9

The Dunfermline & District Tramways Company (Tramways of Fife and the Fourth Valley Part 5) Alan W. Brotchie (NB Traction Group, Dundee, 1978) 0 905069 09 9

Fife's Trams and Buses, A.W. Brotchie (NB Traction, Dundee, 1990) 0 905069 27 7

Lanarkshire's Trams, A.W. Brotchie (ed.) (NB Traction, Dundee, 1993) 0 905069 29 3

Stirling's Trams and Buses, A.W. Brotchie (NB Traction, Dundee, 1991) 0 905069 28 5

The Tramways of Falkirk (Tramways of Fife and the Forth Valley Part 1) Alan W. Brotchie (NB Traction Group, Dundee, 1975)

The Tramways of Kirkcaldy (Tramways of Fife and the Forth Valley Part 4) Alan W. Brotchie (NB Traction Group, Dundee, 1978) 0 905069 00 9

Tramways of the Tay Valley, Alan W. Brotchie (Dundee Museum and Art Gallery, 1965)

The Wemyss and District Tramways Company Ltd (Tramways of Fife and the Forth Valley Part 3) Alan W. Brotchie (The NB Traction Group, Dundee, 1976)

Dumbarton's Trams and Buses, A.W. Brotchie & R.L. Grieves (NB Traction, Dundee, 1985) 0 905069 24 2

Paisley's Trams and Buses: 'Eighties to 'Twenties, A.W. Brotchie & R.L. Grieves (NB Traction, Dundee, 1986) 0 905069 25 0

Paisley's Trams and Buses: 'Twenties to 'Eighties, A.W. Brotchie & R.L. Grieves (NB Traction, Dundee, 1988) 0 905069 26 9

Trams and Buses of the City of Chester, W.D. Clark & H.G. Dibdin (Manchester Transport Museum Society, 1979) 0 900857 16 1

Bradford City Tramways 1882-1950, D.M. Coates (Wyvern Publications, Skipton, 1984)

The Rothesay Tramways Company 1879–1949, Ian L. Cormack (Scottish Tramway and Transport Society, 1986) 0 900648 23 6

Tramways of Greenock, Gourock and Port Glasgow, Ian L. Cormack (The Scottish Tramway Museum Society, 1975)

Green Cars to Hurlford, Brian T. Deans (The Scottish Tramway Museum Society, 1986) 0 900648 22 8

D.D.L.R.: The Story of the Dearne District Light Railways and Competitors, A.S. Denton (The Omnibus Society, Bromley Common, 1980) 0 901307 35 1

The Story of Doncaster Corporation Transport (Doncaster Corporation, 1962)

The First in the Kingdom: a history of the buses and trams in Blackburn and Darwen, R.P. Ferguson, G. Holden & C. Reilly (Darwen Transport Group, 1981)

Tram to Supertram, Peter Fox, Paul Jackson & Roger Benton (Platform 5 Publishing, Sheffield, 1995) 1 872524 61 3

Sheffield Corporation Tramways, Kenneth Gandy (Sheffield City Libraries, 1985) 0 86321 032 5

Manx Electric, Mike Goodwyn (Platform 5 Publishing, Sheffield, 1993) 1 872524 52 4

The Manchester Carriage and Tramways Company, Edward Gray (Manchester Transport Museum Society, 1977)

Salford's Tramways Part One, Edward Gray (Foxline Publishing, Stockport, 1997) 1 870119 47

— Part Two (Foxline Publishing, Stockport, 1999) 1 870119 55 X

Trafford Park Tramways: 1897–1946, Ted Gray (Northern Publishing Services, Manchester, rev. Centenary ed. 1996) 1 899181 34 2

Rotherham & District Transport Vol.1: To 1914, Charles C. Hall (Rotherwood Press, Rotherham Central Library, 1996) 0 903666 89 8

—Vol.2: To 1939, Charles C. Hall (Rotherwood Press, Rotherham Central Library, 1998) 0 903666 92 8

—Vol.3: 1939 to 1974, Charles C. Hall (Rotherwood Press, Rotherham Central Library, 1999) 0 903666 93 6

Sheffield Transport, Chas C. Hall (The Transport Publishing Co., 1977) 0 903839 04 0

Tramways of the City of Carlisle, George S. Hearse (Author, Corbridge, 1962)

The Tramways of Gateshead, George S. Hearse (Author, Corbridge, 1965)

The Tramways of Jarrow and South Shields, George S. Hearse (Author, Corbridge, 1971)

The Tramways of Northumberland, George S. Hearse (Author, Blanchard, 1961)

Trams in the North West, Peter Hesketh (Ian Allan, 1995) 0 7110 2349 2

Halifax Passenger Transport: From 1897 to 1963 Trams, Buses, Trolleybuses (Series X84) Geoffrey Hilditch
      (The Oakwood Press, 2006) 978 085361 647 4

Manchester Metrolink (UK Light Rail Systems No.1) David Holt (Platform 5 Publishing, Sheffield, 1992) 1 872524 36 2

Liverpool Transport Vol.1: 1830–1900, J.B. Horne & T.B. Maund (The Light Railway Transport League, 2nd ed. 1995)
      0 86317 200 8

—*Vol.2: 1900–1930* (The Transport Publishing Co./The Light Rail Transit Association, 1982) 0 903839 50 4

—*Vol.3: 1931–1939* (The Transport Publishing Co./The Light Rail Transit Association, 1987) 0 86317 141 9

—*Vol.4: 1939–1957* (The Transport Publishing Co., 1989) 0 86317 148 6

Darlington Municipal Transport: Trams, Trolleys & Buses, Ron Howe (Darlington Corporation, 1972)

Edinburgh's Transport Vol.1: the early years, D.L.G. Hunter (Mercat Press, Edinburgh, 1992) 1 873644 02 7

—*Vol.2: The Corporation Years 1919–1975*, D.L.G. Hunter (Adam Gordon, Chetwode, 1999) 1 874422 23 0

A History of Public Transport in Ashton-under-Lyne, W.G.S. Hyde (Manchester Museum Transport Society, 1980)

The Manchester Bury Rochdale and Oldham Steam Tramway, W.G.S. Hyde (The Transport Publishing Co., 1979)
      0 903839 37 7

The Cruden Bay Hotel and its Tramway, Keith Jones (Grampian Transport Museum/Great North of Scotland
      Railway Association, revised reprint 2004) 0 902343 12 2

Bradford Corporation Tramways, J.S. King (Venture Publications, Glossop, 1998) 1 898432 80 5

Keighley Corporation Transport, J.S. King (The Advertiser Press, Huddersfield, 1964)

Middleton Tramways, A.K. Kirby (Manchester Transport Museum Society, 1976)

Oldham Corporation Tramways, Arthur Kirby (Triangle Publishing, Leigh, 1998) 0 95293333 14

100 Years at Shipley Glen: The Story of the Shipley Glen Cable Tramway, Michael J. Leak (S.G.T. Publications, Shipley
      2003)

Hull Trams: The Early Days (Lockington Publishing Co. Ltd, North Ferriby, 1977) 0 905490 01 0

Stockport Corporation Tramways, Maurice Marshall (Manchester Transport Museum Society, 1975)

The Aberdeen District Tramways (Public Transport in Aberdeen Vol.1) M.J. Mitchell & I.A. Souter (NB Traction,
      Dundee, 1983) 0 905069 20 X

The Aberdeen Suburban Tramways, M.J. Mitchell & I.A. Souter (NB Traction, Dundee, 1980) 0 905069 14 5

City of York Tramways, Joe Murphy (Author, York, 2003) No ISBN

The Horse Tramways of York, Hugh Murray (The Light Rail Transit Association, 1980) 0 900433 81 7

The Last Tram, C.A. Oakley (City of Glasgow Transport Department, 1962)

Blackpool by Tram, G.S. Palmer & B.R. Turner (The Transport Publishing Co., rev. ed. 1981) 0 903839 55 5

Next Tram to the Tower, Steve Palmer (Tramroad House, Fleetwood, 2008) 0 9536386 4 2

The Douglas Horse Tramway: A Millennium Year History, Keith Pearson (Adam Gordon, Chetwode, 1999) 1 874422 25 7

One Hundred Years of the Manx Electric Railway, Keith Pearson (Leading Edge Press & Publishing Ltd, Hawes, 1992)
      0 948135 38 7

The Tramways of Dewsbury and Wakefield, W. Pickles (The Light Rail Transit Association, 1980) 0 900433 73 6

The Glasgow Horse Tramways, Struan Jno. T. Robertson (Scottish Tramway and Transport Society, Glasgow, 2000)
      0 900648 25 2

The Tramways of Accrington 1886–1932, Robert W. Rush (The Light Railway Transport League, 1961)

Metrolink, John Senior & Eric Ogden (The Transport Publishing Co., 1992) 0 86317 155 9

The Lancaster and Morecambe Tramways (Locomotion Papers No.95) S. Shuttleworth (The Oakwood Press, 1976)

Leeds Transport Vol.1: 1830 to 1902, J. Soper (The Leeds Transport Historical Society, 1985) 0 951028 00 6

—*Vol.2: 1902–1931*, J. Soper (The Leeds Transport Historical Society, 1996) 0 9510280 1 4

—*Vol.3: 1932–1953*, J. Soper (The Leeds Transport Historical Society, 2003) 0 9510280 2 2

—*Vol.4: 1953–1974*, J. Soper (The Leeds Transport Historical Society, 2007) 978 0 9510280 2 5

The Tramways of Sunderland, S.A. Staddon (The Sunderland Echo, 2nd ed. 1991)

St Helens Tramways, E.K. Stretch (St Helens Town Council, 1968)

The South Lancashire Tramways Company 1900–1958, E.K. Stretch, revised and updated by Gray, Ted (Triangle
      Publishing, Leigh, 2006) 0 955003 0 24

The Tramways of Wigan, E.K. Stretch (Manchester Transport Museum Society, 1978)

Rochdale's Tramways, Clifford Taylor (The Manchester Transport Museum Society, 1987) 0 900857 26 9

Halifax Corporation Tramways, Eric Thornton & Stanley King (Light Rail Transit Association, 2008) 0 94810 631 x

Doncaster's Electric Transport 1902–1963, Peter Tuffrey (Author, Doncaster) 0 9508691 1 2

Cliff Railways of the British Isles (Locomotion Papers 223) Keith Turner (The Oakwood Press, 2002) 0 85361 594 2

Pier Railways & Tramways of the British Isles (Locomotion Papers 60) Keith Turner (The Oakwood Press, 2nd rev.
      ed 1999) 0 85361 541 1

75 Years of Municipal Transport in Warrington, Warrington Transport Dept (Warrington Borough Council, 1977)

The Manchester Tramways, Ian Yearsley & Philip Groves (The Transport Publishing Co., 1988) 0 86317 144 3

Tramways in Rochdale: Steam, Electric and Metrolink, Toby Young (Light Rail Transit Association, 2008) 978 0 948106 34 7

Index

This index to Parts 6, 7 and 8 of the Directory covers tramway promoters and operators not referenced or cross-referenced in the main alphabetical listings, other bus operators and tramways outside the geographical scope of this volume.

A

Atherton, Jacob and James 121

B

Balfour, George 23, 169
Beatty, Andrew H. 23
Birmingham 45
Birmingham Central 63
Birmingham & Midland 45
Blackpool, St Anne's & Lytham Tramway
    Co. 84
Brighton & Shoreham 45, 147
Bristol 70, 137
British Gas Traction Co. Ltd 84, 136, 137
British Railways see Grimsby &
    Immingham
Budapest 44
Burton-upon-Trent 68, 152
Burton & Ashby 140
Bury, Rochdale & Oldham Tramway Co.
    Ltd 92
Busby, Daniel and William 79

C

Caledonian Railway 182
Cambridge 45
Canvey Island 151
Carlton Colville: East Anglia Transport
    Museum 180
Castle, Charles 28
Cavehill & Whitewell 45, 195
Chatham 45
Cheltenham 23
Chesterfield 116
City of London Contract Corporation 91
Continental & General Tramway Co. Ltd 67
Cork 45
Coventy 148
Crich: National Tramway Museum 40, 43,
    61, 78, 83, 89, 101, 115–117, 135, 174, 180,
    190, 203
Curtis, William 79

D

Dartford 23
Devonport & District 45
Dick, Kerr & Co. Ltd 172
Douglas Bay Estates Ltd 205
Douglas & Laxey Coast Electric Tramway
    Co. Ltd 199, 205
Dover 53, 64
Dublin Southern District 70
Dublin United 189
Dudley & Stourbridge 45
Dundee & Perth & Aberdeen Railway
    Junction Co. 175, 182
Düsseldorf 163

E

East Anglia Transport Museum see Carlton
    Colville: East Anglia Transport Museum
East Yorkshire Motor Services Ltd 69
Edmundson's Electricity Corporation Ltd
    113
Electric Construction Co. Ltd 63
Electric Supply Corporation Ltd 165
Electric Tramways Construction &
    Maintenance Co. Ltd 84
Erith 69
Evans, Thomas 28
Exeter 62

F

Fife Electric Power Co. 169
Fife Tramway, Light & Power Co. 176
First Leisure Corporation 39

G

General Electric Tramways Co. Ltd 63
General Motor Carrying Co. Ltd 196
Giant's Causeway, Portrush & Bush Valley
    170
Gloucester 70
Gravesend & Northfleet 45, 71
Graz 163

Great Yarmouth see Yarmouth, Great
Greenwood, John 110, 111
Grimsby 126, 135
Grimsby & Immingham 61, 101

H
Harding, W. & Co. Ltd 103, 104
Haworth, John 85, 110, 111
Holden, Edmund & Co. Ltd 40, 58
Hong Kong 32

I
Ilford 134
Ilkeston 23, 48
Isle of Man Harbour Board 207
Isle of Man Railway & Tramway
    Preservation Society 206, 207
Isle of Man Tramways Ltd 199
Isle of Man Tramways & Electric Power Co.
    Ltd 199, 201, 205, 208
Isle of Thanet 45

J
Jones, Maurice 119

K
Kidderminster & Stourport 45

L
Lancashire Light Railways Co. Ltd 83
Lancashire United Tramways Ltd 84, 122
Leamington & Warwick 23, 45
Lightfoot, Thomas 198
Lincoln 105
Lisbon 206
Liverpool Overhead Railway 145
Llandudno & Colwyn Bay 21, 23, 54
Llanelly 23
Lloyd, T. 49
London 87
London County Council 108, 117
London United 36, 70
London Transport 78, 134
Lothian Buses 175
Luton 23, 179

M
Mansfield & District 23, 134
Manx Electric Railway Society 206,
    207
Merthyr Tydfil 45, 140
Metropolitan Electric 45

Mousehold Light Railway 43
Murphy, William M. 189

N
National Tramway Museum see Crich:
    National Tramway Museum
Neath 84
North Staffordshire 24, 35, 42, 44, 132
Norwich 43
Nottingham 175
Nottinghamshire & Derbyshire 23, 170

O
O'Dowd, C.J. 52
Oporto 26, 163
Oxford 98
Oystermouth 27

P
Percival's Motor Bus Service 48
Perth General Omnibus Co. 191
Peterborough 45
Poole & District 45, 140
Portsmouth 134
Potteries Electric 25, 97, 196

R
Ramsgate & Margate 123, 194
Reading 70
Rhondda 98

S
Scone & Perth Omnibus Co. 190
Scottish Central Railway 182
Scottish General Transport Co. 192
Scottish House-to-House Electricity Supply
    Co. 160
Scottish Motor Traction Co. Ltd 162, 176,
    192
Seaton 54
Serco Metrolink Ltd 90
Sheerness & District 45, 53
South Metropolitan 45
South Staffordshire 45, 63
Southampton 78
Southend-on-Sea 21
Speight, Joseph 119
Stagecoach 91, 119
Stratford & Moreton 27
Swansea 45, 96
Swansea & Mumbles 45

T
Taunton 45
Thomson–Houston International Co, 76
Torquay 98
Townson, W.W. 30
Train, George Francis 27, 28, 52, 78, 79, 110
Transdev 175

U
United Automobile Services Ltd 113
United Kingdom Tramways, Light Railways
    & Electrical Syndicate Ltd 135

W
Wantage 55
Wemyss, Randolph G.E. 195

West Metropolitan 70
West Yorkshire Road Car Co. 152
Western Scottish Motor Traction Co. Ltd
    192
Weston-Super-Mare 45
Wilson, Sam 120
Wolverhampton 45, 152
Worcester 45
Wrexham 45

Y
Yarmouth, Great 45
Yorkshire Electric Tramways Construction
    Syndicate Ltd 142
Yorkshire Traction Co. Ltd 55

Visit our website and discover thousands of other History Press books.

www.thehistorypress.co.uk